T0329957

Corporatism since the Great Recession

Corporatism since the Great Recession

Challenges to Tripartite Relations in Denmark, the Netherlands and Austria

Mikkel Mailand

Associate Professor and Research Director, Employment Relations Research Centre (FAOS), Department of Sociology, University of Copenhagen, Denmark

Edward Elgar
PUBLISHING

Cheltenham, UK • Northampton, MA, USA

Published by
Edward Elgar Publishing Limited
The Lypiatts
15 Lansdown Road
Cheltenham
Glos GL50 2JA
UK

Edward Elgar Publishing, Inc.
William Pratt House
9 Dewey Court
Northampton
Massachusetts 01060
USA

A catalogue record for this book
is available from the British Library

Library of Congress Control Number: 2020942857

This book is available electronically in the **Elgar**online
Social and Political Science subject collection
http://dx.doi.org/10.4337/9781788114561

ISBN 978 1 78811 455 4 (cased)
ISBN 978 1 78811 456 1 (eBook)

Printed by CPI Group (UK) Ltd, Croydon CR0 4YY

Contents

Acknowledgements

I would like to thank a number of people for their help and assistance in relation to the project behind the book and the book itself:

My colleagues at FAOS, University of Copenhagen, for persuading me to develop a mainly Danish-focused project on corporatism and tripartite cooperation into a genuinely comparative project; my colleague Christian Lyhne Ibsen for commenting on various chapters of the book and my colleague Søren Kaj Andersen for commenting on the chapter on Denmark; Maarten Keune, AIAS-HSI, University of Amsterdam, for suggesting Dutch interviewees and letting me stay twice at AIAS-HSI during the interview periods; Marc van der Meer, SBB/University of Tilburg, for suggesting Dutch interviewees and for commenting on drafts of various chapters of the book; Günter Hefler, Danube University Krems, Susanne Pernicka, Johannes Kepler University Linz and Adi Buxbaum, Arbeiterkammer Wien, for suggesting texts and commenting on a draft of the chapter on Austria; Bernd Brandl, Durham University and Georg Adam, FORBA, for suggesting Austrian interviewees; and Michael Mesch, Arbeiterkammer Wien, for facilitating multiple interviews at Arbeiterkammer Wien.

I would also like to thank the interviewees listed in the Appendix for taking the time to do the interviews, which enhanced my knowledge on tripartite cooperation, and for sending me written comments on drafts of various chapters.

Finally, I would like to thank the funding organizations – The Danish Ministry of Employment and various Danish employers' organizations and trade unions – for funding FAOS's research programmes of 2014–18 and 2019–23, of which this book forms part.

1. Introduction

1.1 CONTEXT AND MOTIVATION

Since the 1980s, the general perception in both social science and of the wider public has been that organized labour – due to the internationalization of production, technological development, spread of individualized norms, and other drivers – has been weakened across Europe, although not to the same extent throughout the region. This weakening has reduced the ability of trade unions to influence regulation of employment relations such as wages and working conditions – as well as matters of economic, employment, education and social public policy. Employers' organizations have, according to the general perception, not experienced the same loss of power and influence.

Although mixed types of regulatory approaches exist, there are basically three ideal-typical ways to regulate within and beyond the individual firm: the state can unilaterally regulate through legislation; regulation can be left open to market forces and the management prerogative; or trade unions and employers' organizations (the 'social partners'[1]) can jointly regulate through collective agreements and other forms of rule setting.

These ideal types of regulation tend to influence the content of regulation in different ways. State regulation is generally believed to lead to uniform rules and hence to equality, whereas market/management prerogative regulation provides flexible rules, but with a greater risk of inequality. Regulation in the hands of employers' organizations and trade unions leads to a compromise position between the two other types of regulation, that is, a medium level of uniformity/flexibility and equality. The three types also have consequences for cost-efficiency, although, in this case, it is less clear which regulation types lead to higher or lower efficiency. Hence, actor constellations are not interesting just because they illuminate 'who governs', but also because the actor constellations have an impact on the content of regulation and key societal features such as equity and efficiency.

The general weakening of trade unions since the 1980s might be expected to cause a rebalancing of the three ideal types of regulation in the direction of greater state regulation and market regulation. Because economic crises reduce the power of trade unions due to a reduction in labour demand, the Great Recession, that is, the economic crisis that started in late 2008, might have

1

been expected to further challenge the position of the trade unions for at least a time and thereby put additional pressure on social partner-based regulation.

However, the reduction in social partner-based regulation has not been experienced uniformly. Moreover, there are different perceptions about whether the direction of change is even the same everywhere. Before digging deeper into these differences, it would be useful to describe in more detail how social partner regulation works. Basically, social partner-based regulation can take two forms. The core form is the bipartite regulation (e.g., collective bargaining as a stronger form of regulation and employee involvement as a weaker form) that is mostly used in relation to the within-firm issues mentioned above. The research tradition of industrial relations (IR, aka employment relations) has provided in-depth up-to-date comparative knowledge of the state of collective bargaining and other forms of bipartite regulation in Europe (Dølvik et al., 2018; Marginson, 2016; Van Gyes and Schulten, 2015, to name just a few recent high-quality studies), some of which point to a degree of resilience in collective bargaining in at least some European countries, while others identify various levels of decay as the common trend.

The second form of social partner-based regulation is tripartite (with participation of both the state and the social partners and occasionally other actors) and often transcends issues related purely to employment relations. The tripartite form of social partner-based regulation is found in relation to economic policies and what can be labelled work and welfare policies in areas such as unemployment, education and training, work–life balance and labour migration. The social partners' involvement in these policies has often previously been studied under the label of 'corporatism' and – since the 1990s – also under the label of 'social pacts'.

This primarily tripartite type of social partner regulation has not, unlike the bipartite type, been studied very intensively in recent years. Excluding a number of highly influential studies where tripartite regulation is addressed, though not as a main issue (e.g., Baccaro and Howell, 2011; Martin and Swank, 2012; Thelen, 2014), only a limited number of English-language comparative studies of corporatism (Armingeon and Baccaro, 2012; Avdagic, Rhodes and Visser, 2011; Culpepper and Regan, 2014; Freyssinet, 2010; Padadakis and Ghellab, 2014; Welz and Broughton, 2014) covering the 2010s existed when work on this book was begun in late 2016. These studies paint, in most cases, a picture of reduced frequency of tripartite agreements since the mid-2000s – although some countries showed a short increase in tripartite activity after the outbreak of the Great Recession as a result of government attempts to involve the social partners in addressing the challenges from the crisis. This picture reflects what can be described as 'a swing in the pendulum' in studies of IR, political economy and other social science traditions in the first half of the 2010s, towards an emphasis on market mechanisms and strengthening of the management prerogative as a universal destination – and thereby a swing in the academic pendulum away from the emphasis on institutional diversity that dominated the 1990s and partly also the 2000s.

Fuelled by observations from my home country, Denmark, which did not seem to follow this pattern of reduced tripartite activity, and by the draft of a study (final version, Guardiancich and Molina, 2017) that pointed to several national cases of sustained bi- as well as tripartite institutions and decision-making processes in Europe, I decided to critically address this dominant picture. The way I chose to do this was by focusing on countries where the social partners post-2008 had *seemingly* not lost their roles in – and ability to influence – work and welfare policies. The aim was to discover whether, after a *closer* examination, their role and ability to influence had survived – and if so, why. If the social partners' roles and ability to obtain real influence turned out to be sustained in spite of the unfavourable conditions of the crisis, this would challenge the 'uni-destination' understanding of liberalization in both liberal market economics (LMEs) and coordinated market economies (CMEs), expounded by Baccaro and Howell (2017) (discussed further in Chapter 2, Section 2.2). If the opposite was the case, it would support the 'uni-destination' understanding, especially since the selected countries represented critical cases (e.g., Flyvbjerg, 1991), that is, cases where it can be argued that if the hypothesis 'is not confirmed here, it is not confirmed anywhere'.

The social partners, including the trade unions, are stronger here and have lost less power than similar organizations in most other European countries. Hence, if there was found to be a decline in corporatism due to weakening of the social partners in these countries, it could be expected elsewhere in Europe too.

Apart from the focus on the 2010s, this book will be different from most previous studies of tripartite policymaking in at least two ways. First, most studies of corporatism from previous decades focus mostly, or only, on the grand tripartite 'social pacts'. Although no common understanding exists of what a social pact is, most policy arrangements included in these studies are ad hoc tripartite agreements covering more than one issue of socio-economic importance. This book will also address these, but in addition include the often neglected single-issue corporatist decision-making processes. Without these, it is not possible to get a full picture of tripartite policymaking corporatism in a specific country. Second, the aforementioned studies tend to focus much more on the outcomes of tripartite agreements rather than on processes, whereas this book will include analyses of both. Including detailed analyses of the decision-making processes allows for a better understanding of why regulation ends up as it does and how, and to what extent, the social partners manage to impact work and welfare regulation. In addition to the focus on process and outcomes, the analyses will also – where possible – address the issue of the impact of the agreements.

Three countries were selected where – according to previous studies (Guardiancich and Molina, 2017; Mailand, 2016a) – a marked reduction in tripartite activity had not taken place: Denmark, the Netherlands and Austria. Hence, the three countries represent similar cases in this regard, although they display considerable variation in important dimensions such as trade union organizational densities, which could possibly yield some fruitful discussion of power dynamics. A further reason for the choice of countries was my extensive knowledge, based on previous research, of tripartite arrangements in Denmark and some, limited, knowledge of tripartism in the Netherlands.

Three partly overlapping work and welfare areas were chosen: unemployment insurance (UI); active labour market policy (ALMP); and continuing vocational training (CVT). These policy areas were chosen for the following reasons: because they cover large areas seen as important for work and welfare; because they are traditionally among the areas the social partners are involved in (if they are involved at all); and because I have previous research experience in these areas. The justification for the selection of policy areas is further elaborated in Chapter 2, Section 2.4.

1.2   RESEARCH QUESTIONS AND THE MAIN ARGUMENT

To fulfil the broadly formulated aim above, three more specific research questions will be pursued:

1. To what extent are tripartite arrangements still used in work- and welfare-related policy areas?
2. Are the social partners still able to influence the regulation of societal challenges through tripartite arrangements following the Great Recession?
3. Which factors best explain the development in the quantity and quality of corporatist arrangements?

The argument that will be developed is that the trade unions' power resources are, to a varying extent, weakened in the three selected countries, but least so in Denmark. The frequency of tripartite agreements has either been stable or has increased since the Great Recession. Hence, in these countries, the social partners are still strong enough, under the right conditions, to be included in corporatist arrangements. However, although the frequency of tripartite agreements has not declined in any of the three countries, corporatism is in trouble, particularly in the Netherlands and Austria. In the Netherlands, the core of the trouble is the organizational development, while in Austria it is the political development. It is furthermore argued that economic crisis is a stronger driver for corporatist arrangements than social partner strength, government strength and government ideology, although the importance of each of the four drivers differs between the three countries, and a certain level of social partner strength might be a necessary precondition for sustaining corporatist arrangements.

Before describing how the research questions will be addressed, the above-mentioned academic tradition of corporatism, followed by a number of other relevant research approaches, will be presented in Chapter 2.

NOTE

1. The term 'social partners' will be used as an umbrella term for employers' organizations and trade unions. In industrial relations research – which is one of the research traditions I personally feel most attached to – the phrase 'labour market parties' is sometimes used instead of 'social partners' in order to avoid the connotation of harmonious relations, which, admittedly, can be a problem with the latter term. However, I will use the term 'social partners' despite this, because it is the most commonly used umbrella term for employers' organizations and trade unions, and because the term, as I understand it, does not exclude conflictual relations – as will be illustrated in this book.

2. Theoretical framework and methods

The theoretical framework of our empirical analyses will be covered in this chapter. The studies of corporatism – with its strong focus on the state and interest organizations – are well suited to framing the attempts to answer the research questions presented in Chapter 1. Hence, this approach makes up the core of the theoretical framework and will be presented first in Section 2.1. Two other research approaches will supplement the corporatist approach: first, in Section 2.2, the political economy approach, including 'varieties of capitalism' (VoC), which focuses more on firms and more on comparison than the corporatist approach; second, in Section 2.3, various studies of power within and beyond the industrial relations (IR) approach, which can provide knowledge about how this key feature of relations between the state and interest organizations can be understood.

Whereas the corporatist approach and power approaches will be used to formulate hypotheses directly, the political economy approach is mainly included for the following reasons: to provide an understanding of the national variations in the labour markets and welfare states to be analysed in the empirical chapters; in order to understand what the uni-destination approach presented in Chapter 1 is a reaction to; and, finally, to contrast those power approaches emphasizing the role of labour with those emphasizing the role of capital. The hypotheses – together with a methodological section (Sections 2.4 and 2.5, respectively) – are presented at the end of the chapter.

2.1   THE CORPORATIST APPROACH AND THE SOCIAL PACT LITERATURE

As a research tradition, corporatism was formed in the 1970s and became an influential approach within state theory and political sociology as well as within IR. In the 1970s, a distinction was made between 'state corporatism', an authoritarian form found in Latin American and South European dictatorships where employers' organizations and trade unions in reality took the form of state-controlled monopolies, and 'liberal corporatism' or 'neo-corporatism', a democratic version mostly found in Continental European and Scandinavian countries. It is clearly 'neo-corporatism' that is in focus in this book. However, because 40 years or more have passed since the authoritarian versions of corporatism disappeared from Europe, the prefix 'neo-' will be left out in the present study.

In short, corporatism can best be understood as a political exchange between the state and interest organizations, where the state and the interest organizations can use each other to fulfil their own goals. More specifically, the state (government) can, through corporatist arrangements, obtain support for new initiatives and for the implementation of reforms. Moreover, the state can, through corporatist arrangements, share the responsibility for unpopular measures. In addition, the involvement of interest organizations may provide important new information that can lead to more adaptable or flexible regulation. Finally, the social partners may contribute to the financing of reforms, thus reducing budget pressure on the state. For the social partners, corporatist arrangements include the possibility of influencing policies affecting labour and welfare and of getting funding for initiatives, although corporatist arrangements can also be used to block initiatives and change. Furthermore, corporatist arrangements may improve the interest organizations' legitimacy by showing their willingness to take on responsibility for societal challenges. Finally (and potentially in the interests of both the state and the social partners), direct stakeholder involvement – such as social partner involvement – is positive from the point of view of participatory democracy (Mailand, 2011).

The Classic Corporatist Studies

Philippe Schmitter (1979) was one of the first to propose a definition of the concept of corporatism, and he became the most influential in the first generation of corporatist researchers. He defined corporatism as:

> a system of interest representation in which the constituent units are organized into a limited number of singular, compulsory, non-competitive, hierarchically ordered and functionally differentiated categories, recognized or licensed (if not created) by the state and granted a deliberate representational monopoly within their respective categories in exchange for observing certain controls on their selection of leaders and articulation of demands and supports. (Schmitter, 1979, p. 13)

Where Schmitter thus defined corporatism as a system of interest representation, Lehmbruch (1979), understood corporatism as a special political process:

> Corporatism is more than a peculiar pattern of articulation of interests. Rather, it is an institutionalized pattern of policy formation in which large interest organizations cooperate with each other and with public authorities not only in the articulation (or even 'intermediation') of interests, but – in its developed forms – in the 'authoritative allocation of values' and in the implementation of such policies. (Lehmbruch, 1979, p. 150)

Against this background, Schmitter later suggested that the term 'concertation' should be used to describe the political process Lehmbruch referred to, whereas 'corporatism' should be used to describe a system of interest representation that he himself had originally proposed (Schmitter, 1982, p. 139). Concertation has actually become a quite frequently used expression, but a clear separation between the two, as proposed by Schmitter, has never developed. Common to both approaches is that they see the corporatist arrangements as a form of political exchange between rational actors, so that the state will obtain better implementation of a given action in exchange for providing selected interest groups with influence in the area – perhaps even a monopoly of influence.

Perhaps the most important feature of the classic corporatist studies is the understanding – reflected in the quote by Schmitter's above – of *strong and hierarchical organizations* as a necessary, though not sufficient, condition for being granted the privileged access to the formulation and implementation of policies that corporatist arrangements include. However, developments in several European countries from the mid-1980s – as will be seen below – raised doubts about this assumption. Studies of these developments will be among the newer corporatist studies to be addressed below. In order to highlight the different scholars' understanding of what creates conditions favourable to corporatist arrangements, the studies will be divided into those that focus on endogenous drivers of corporatist relations (i.e., the actors and the relations between them) and those that focus on exogenous drivers.

Some of the classic studies of corporatism often included a presumed connection between social democratic or socialist government and corporatism. Whereas political parties did not figure in Schmitter's original contributions, Lehmbruch (among others) saw a close connection between interest organizations and political parties and even understood the *existence of a social democratic party* as a necessary prerequisite for the emergence of corporatism. He specified that neo-corporatism is most important in those countries where the working-class movement has obtained participation in political power through the channels of the party system (Lehmbruch, 1979, pp. 168–9).

The Social Pact Literature

The assumption that the existence of strong and hierarchical organizations is a necessary condition for corporatism was questioned by developments in several European countries from the 1990s onwards, specifically the tripartite peak-level agreements in the form of so-called social pacts that were signed in countries such as Portugal, Spain, Italy and Ireland that lacked these conditions (e.g., Baccaro, 2003; Compston, 2002; Fajertag and Pochet, 1997; Molina and Rhodes, 2002). According to most of these latter studies, the newer types of tripartite agreements, the so-called 'social pacts', were different from the classical arrangements on wage restraints and employment/social rights. However, the studies of the newer types of corporatism included different descriptions of the ways in which the newer types of tripartite arrangement differed from the old ones. An early study emphasized the fact that various welfare policies had become more important, but that the welfare reforms on the agenda often weakened the rights included in previous policies, and it was therefore difficult to see what benefit the trade unions got from participating in these (Ebbinghaus and Hassel, 1999). A slightly newer study suggested that, in a hard currency regime, trade unions could no longer expect the traditional quid pro quo that compensated them for wage restraint, because governments could threaten them with tight monetary policies. The choice the trade unions had to make under the new regime was to either engage in negotiated adjustment of welfare or suffer restrictions (Hassel, 2003).

A number of studies of corporatism of a more recent date than the classic studies will be presented below in order to develop hypotheses on the explanatory factors referred to in the third research question: 'Which factors best explain the development in the quantity and quality of corporatist arrangements?' Not all these studies of the drivers behind corporatist arrangements use the term 'corporatism', but they are nevertheless included if what they focus on is, de facto, the same as corporatist arrangements. The studies are divided according to whether the main explanatory factor is endogenous or exogenous in regard to the actors (the government and the social partners mainly) and their relations. Other studies could have been added, but those included are arguably among the most frequently referenced.

Newer Studies of Corporatism: Endogenous Factors

Hugh Compston is one of the newer corporatism scholars who reach back to classic explanations of corporatism. He tests the explanatory power of various factors by comparative analyses. In a study of 'social concertation' (leading to binding agreements as opposed to non-binding 'consultation') in seven European countries over more than 100 years, the organization's *implementing capacity* appears as one of three key explanatory variables. By an organization's implementation capacity, Compston understands the organization's ability to effectively implement decisions in relation to its members. It is the government's view of this capacity that is essential in his view. Together with the explanations of 'war and crisis' and 'shared perception of problems' between the key actors, the implementation capacity explains why binding corporatism is more prevalent in some European countries than others, both in the 1990s and in the rest of the century (Compston, 2002).

A number of studies of corporatism have contributed to the understanding of corporatism as a political exchange, but have also added other dimensions to the analysis. One of these studies is Jelle Visser and Anton Hemerijck's (1997) model for 'corporatist institutional change', which differs from many of the other corporatist studies by being deduced from developments in a single country (the Netherlands) and by having a dynamic dimension in that the model seeks to explain why corporatism either evolves into different forms or disappears. The core question, according to the authors, is whether political learning takes place or not. Their model of corporatist change has two dimensions. The first is the degree of societal support, understood as the representativity of the interest organizations and the organizations' support for the corporatist arrangements. The second dimension is the degree of institutional integration, that is, the extent to which public authorities award authority to bipartite and tripartite bodies, and in what areas this happens and does not happen. The two dimensions form four types of corporatism, illustrating different periods in the historical development of corporatism in the Netherlands. The model starts in 'innovative corporatism', where corporatism is initiated. In this, the perceived interests of the state and organizations coincide, and the social partners experience strong support from their members. If the innovative corporatism is maintained for a long time, the result will be a period of 'responsive corporatism', that is, an institutionalization of corporatism. Here, bipartite and tripartite relations provide flexible solutions to external challenges on a routine basis. Sooner or later, the responsive corporatism is likely to encounter problems, such as the inability to establish consensus on the way ahead, because there is no longer a common understanding of the nature of the problems or their causes, and/or because social partners block the reforms. This is 'immobile corporatism'. If the barriers are overcome, the responsive corporatism is restored; if not, the result will be 'corporatist disengagement', where the state chooses unilateral government control instead of corporatism. With regard to shifts between the four types, Visser and Hemerijck argue that corporatism exists 'in the hierarchy shadow' in the sense that the state always has the capacity to legislate without involvement of interests and without concessions.

Visser and Hemerijck's model includes several drivers, but *political learning* is central and crucial. The corporatist decision arena gives players a longer time horizon and opportunities to build trust, to learn from past experiences, continually to redefine interests and to seek 'win–win' situations. However, according to Visser and Hemerijck, learning is also related to power. For instance, trade unions in many European countries learned under the liberal governments in the 1980s that the price of non-cooperation is the loss of power.

Other researchers with an endogenous focus have sought explanations for the choice of corporatism on a more strategic level. A frequently asked question in studies of corporatism is what the parliamentary situation means for the involvement of social partners in policy formulation. Whereas the classic corporatist studies often focused on the strength of the interest organizations, newer studies often focus on the strength of the government. The presumption here is that majority governments, and governments that are otherwise strong, are less likely to involve interest groups than minority governments and weak governments. Kerstin Hamann and John Kelly are among the researchers who have pointed out such a relationship empirically. They have compared developments in the UK and Spain, both of which experienced a series of labour market reforms and increased involvement of social partners in the political process in the late 1990s. However, the reforms were more extensive in the UK than in Spain. Hamann and Kelly reject the idea that political ideology and labour market institutions are able to provide adequate explanations for the development in corporatism – the latter because neither of the two countries has a tradition of strong social partner involvement. The authors look instead for an explanation in politics, more specifically in the strength of the government. Tony Blair's New Labour government in Britain was a majority government and did not include the social partners much, while Aznar's first Conservative government in Spain was a minority government that did include the social partners. This gave the British government leaders more freedom and fewer incentives to involve the social partners (Hamann and Kelly, 2003). A more recent study, which also points to the strength of government as a key driver, is a three-country study by Philip Rathgeb with a focus on labour market 'outsiders'. Rathgeb finds that the weaker the government, the stronger the capacity of trade unions to influence policies (Rathgeb, 2018).

Strength and power are also included as causalities in corporatist studies in other ways. Power plays a significant role in a study on corporatism in the newer Central and Eastern European EU member states conducted by Sabina Avdagic (2006). Her point of departure is a critique of the perception that the outcome of a decision-making process can be deduced from the institutional set-up, as indicated in the different approaches that rely on path dependency. Avdagic sees this perception as particularly questionable in the case of young institutions, such as the corporatist arrangements in the post-communist countries. According to her, these institutions are just as much the effect of the decisions as the reason for them.

In Avdagic's study, the *actors' perceptions* of their own and other players' power positions are key for understanding the evolution of corporatist arrangements, in that the choices the actors make reflect their perception of their own ability to influence the outcome without compromising the actors' main objectives. More specifically, the government's perception of union power is influenced by three parameters: (1) the degree of trade union concentration (unified/fragmented); (2) the existence of formal ties between trade unions and political parties (strong/partial/non-existent); and (3) the type of relationships between the unions (cooperation/conflict). Avdagic argues that the government chooses to involve trade unions when the government is facing a united, collaborative trade union movement without party-political ties.

Other studies emphasizing endogenous drivers pay more attention to norms and values. The basic assumption of the path-dependency approach is that norms, values and routines are institutionalized and therefore will be difficult to break free of. In this way, historical traditions or 'path dependency' are created. Such notions are also found within the corporatist research tradition. Colin Crouch's (1994) book, *Industrial Relations and European State Traditions*, is an example. Drawing on, inter alia, the neo-corporatist literature – but surprisingly with no reference to Esping-Andersen's *Three Worlds of Welfare Capitalism* (Esping-Andersen, 1990; see below), Crouch identifies basically three different industrial relations models in Europe: state-controlled, liberal/pluralist and corporatist. Crouch describes how the economic, political and religious developments during the nineteenth and twentieth centuries have created various state traditions, corporatism being one of them. While he allows that state traditions in special cases can be broken or modified, the state traditions are strong, which means that a given corporatist arrangement can often be explained by a corporatist state tradition.

Newer Studies of Corporatism: Exogenous Factors

A number of both classic and newer corporatist approaches focus on issues outside corporatism as explanations for the choice of the corporatist decision-making arena. Peter Katzenstein has included drivers beyond the borders of the national economies. The key driver behind corporatism can, according to Katzenstein, briefly be described as the 'openness of the economy'. Like this book, Katzenstein focuses on small states. He argues in his book *Small States in World Markets* (Katzenstein, 1985) that use of corporatist strategies is more often found in smaller states than in large states, partly because of their more vulnerable position in the world market. Because small states are more dependent on exports, they cannot use protectionist policies to shield themselves from changes in the world market. Instead, they develop internal coordination between government, unions and employers. Corporatism provides, according to Katzenstein, an opportunity to activate social forces and promote flexible adaptations and responses to the challenges presented by the economies' openness. He distinguishes between two versions of this 'small-state corporatism'. Austria, Norway and Denmark have 'social corporatism'. This form is dominated by strong social democratic parties and strong trade unions, whereas 'liberal corporatism' is characterized by weaker and more divided unions, but stronger employers, and is found in Switzerland, the Netherlands and Belgium. Katzenstein found that Sweden combines elements from both types of corporatism.

Some of the newer corporatism theories also seek beyond the individual nation state for the drivers behind corporatism. Martin Rhodes is one of a number of researchers who state that *growing international competition* has encouraged national actors to come together in tripartite cooperation. He uses the label 'competitive corporatism' to describe and explain corporatist arrangements in relation to labour and welfare policies driven by increasing international competition (Rhodes, 1998). Also, Franz Traxler (2004) understands corporatist agreements on wage moderation as being key to minimizing costs in order to succeed in an internationally competitive environment. However, according to Traxler, the tripartite arena is not the only useful arena – bipartite agreements can also be used to reach agreements on wage moderation. Importantly, Traxler later questioned the beneficial effect of bipartite and tripartite agreements on wage moderation when he found a positive correlation between these and high total public expenditure (Brandl and Traxler, 2005).

A related type of explanation also emphasizes external pressure on the national actors, but here it is the political – as much as the economic – pressure that is in focus. The causality of this alternative explanation is that the EU member states' efforts to meet the Economic and Monetary Union (EMU) criteria during the 1990s provided incentives for national tripartite agreements. The EMU criteria not only provided incentives to ensure the private sector's competitiveness, but also to keep public budgets in balance via social policy reforms. The broad social pacts were well suited to meeting these requirements because they created a shared responsibility for meeting the challenges and included wages and various welfare issues in their reform packages (Ebbinghaus and Hassel, 2000; Fajertag and Pochet, 1997; Hassel, 2003).

A study by Anke Hassel (2009) also points to exogenous drivers, with specific emphasis on the macroeconomic context that she identifies as the factor 'largely determining' the social pacts. However, what makes this study especially interesting is that, despite its semi-deterministic point of departure, it leaves some room for actor strategies and points to an important difference between 'policy interests' and 'power interests' in social pacts. The former relates to policy content and the latter to process in the form of security for participation in decision making (for the trade unions) and electoral support and legitimization of initiatives (for the government). Different combinations, on the one hand, of governments/trade unions and, on the other hand, of policy/power interests leads, according to Hassel, to different relations between government and trade unions. For instance, tripartite relations in Central and Eastern Europe post-1989 have often taken the form of 'illusory corporatism' where both government and employers have emphasized power interests, whereas government in classic corporatism emphasizes policy interests while trade unions emphasize power interests.

Summing Up and Comparative Studies from the Present Decade

The plethora of ideas about what facilities tripartite negotiations has tended to create confusion rather than clarification. A major comparative study from the present decade – with the participation of some of the above-mentioned researchers – has tried to 'clean up the mess' by systematically testing a number of hypotheses, drawing on several drivers: Avdagic, Rhodes and Visser (2011) argue, on the basis of a six-country study over several decades, that most social pacts are concluded where there is pressure resulting from a major economic problem (corresponding to the 'crisis' in the vocabulary of Compston and Schmitter), where governments are weak, or where the labour movement is centralized to a medium degree. But the study also found that these three factors are far from being able to account for all social pacts concluded. Other factors such as the proximity to a general election, internal divisions in the government and special dynamics within and between unions and employers' associations (such as perceptions of the actors' own and other actors' power positions) also play a role. So even though the Avdagic et al. study improves our knowledge regarding the drivers of corporatism, it also makes it clear that it is still difficult to prescribe exactly what is needed for corporatist arrangements to be set up.

Table 2.1 summarizes the main drivers/facilitators from the various studies.

Table 2.1   *The main drivers/facilitators of corporatism in corporatist studies up to 2010*

Endogenous Drivers (Regarding the Actors and Their Relations)	Exogeneous Drivers (Regarding the Actors and Their Relations)
Strength and structure of organizations (Compston; Schmitter)	War (Compston)
Parliamentary situation (Hamann and Kelly)	Economic crisis (Compston; Schmitter; Hassel)
Policy learning (Visser and Hemerijck)	Path dependence (Crouch)
Perceived power (Avdagic)	Openness of economy (Katzenstein)
Political ideology (Crouch; Lehmbruch)	International competition (Rhodes)
Policy vs power interests (Hassel)	EMU criteria (Fajertag and Pochet; several others)

Measuring Corporatist Influence

Apart from the question of drivers for corporatist change, it is also important, for a thorough analysis of corporatism, to be able to measure the depth of social partner involvement in corporatist arrangements. Ebbinghaus (2002) has proposed a way to do that. Excluding unilateral state regulation in his study of social partners' involvement in pension reforms and employment policy across Europe, Ebbinghaus proposes 'four modes of societal governance' (Table 2.2), with social partner involvement varying from strong to weak state control. 'Consultation' provides the least loss of authority for the state. Here, the government may choose to confer with the social partners or be legally obliged to consult with them, but the government is free to diverge from the social partners' given opinions and recommendations. In contrast, 'concertation' entails an agreement between government and social partners, involving some concessions on the part of the government in order to reach a compromise that would bind the government. While consultation is routinely practised, concertation occurs, according to Ebbinghaus, more on an ad hoc basis. 'Self-administration' is the delegation of some (but not all) decision-making authority to an independent self-administrated agency that may be more or less independent of the state and may have a bi- or tripartite structure. 'Self-regulation', in contrast, results from voluntary agreements between collective bargaining partners without state interference (Ebbinghaus, 2002, p. 5). With regard to this book's focus on tripartism, it is primarily the concertation and consultation processes that are relevant. These concepts are also central to Compston's (2002) study mentioned above.

2.2   POLITICAL ECONOMY: VARIETIES OF CAPITALISM AND BEYOND

The literature on neo-corporatism has provided us with important knowledge about the relations between the social partners and the state. However, within the research tradition of political economy, the 'varieties of capitalism' approach (VoC) also has important things to say about these relations and can thus contribute to the theoretical framework of the present study.

VoC has, to a much larger extent than the corporatist studies, pointed to national variations in configurations, and among these configurations is the role of interest organizations. VoC is not focused on relations between state and interest organizations exclusively, as the corporatist tradition is, but these relations are nevertheless covered. The novelty of the VoC approach is compared to both the corporatist tradition and other political economy literature, both of which pay a great deal of attention to relations within and between firms. VoC, by contrast, pays more attention to the features of the capitalist state (an aspect that is largely ignored in studies of corporatism), namely that state policies are also influenced by – and formed to fit – the different ways in which companies are run in different countries.

In its original formulation (Hall and Soskice, 2001), a distinction is made between the liberal market economies (LMEs) (including USA, Canada, Australia, New Zealand, Ireland and the UK) and coordinated market econ-

Table 2.2   Ebbinghaus's four models of societal governance with social partners' (SP) involvement

	Consultation	Concertation	Self-administration	Self-regulation
Function	Deliberation of SP's view on legislative project	Negotiations of government with SPs	Delegation of partial authority to SPs	Voluntary agreement between SPs
State's role	Consideration of affected interest, but can divert from it	Negotiation with SPs; may offer side payments/threaten to intervene	Partial delegation of authority; remains 'principal': sets parameters	Facilitation: *erga omnes* extension; threaten to intervene
Social partners' role	(Joint) opinions, recommendations	Negotiate agreements; enforce compliance of members	Supervision; implementation	Bipartite agreement; implementation
Decision mode	Majority/minority positions	Voluntary agreement	Majority decision	Voluntary agreement
Potential threat	Voice/exit	Exit	Voice/exit	Exit
Advantage	Deliberation; process legitimacy	Public–private actor coordination; social consensus	Deliberation; process legitimacy	Internalization of costs; self-determination
Problems	Cumbersome; status quo defence; no deal making	Power decides; payments costly; danger of desertion	Status quo defence; lack of competences; bureaucratic	Danger of collusion; narrow interests; state excluded

Source: Ebbinghaus (2002).

omies (CMEs) (including Sweden, Austria, Germany and Japan). These two ideal types are anchored in different kinds of 'institutional complementarity'. LMEs rely to a large extent on market forces to support their growth models, whereas, in the CME countries, coordination between various actors is of prime importance. The institutional complementarities in the two ideal type models are found in five areas:

• industrial relations, including collective bargaining: CMEs have higher levels of membership in trade unions and employers' organizations than LMEs and bargaining takes place at the sectoral or national level, whereas in LMEs it takes place at the company level, if at all;
• vocational training and education: in CMEs, employees have specific skills that are limited to the firm or the industry where they are working. In LMEs, workers have more general skills that can easily be transferred to other workplaces or even other industries;

- corporate governance, including the availability of finance between firms and investors: companies in CMEs rely more on capital that does not depend on full financial openness and short-term returns on investment. LMEs tend to rely on public information about finances and short-term capital;
- inter-firm relations, including coordination between the firm, suppliers, clients and competitors: in CMEs, these are more collaborative, while in LMEs they are more competitive;
- employee relationships: in CMEs, managers often have to cooperate with employees to reach major decisions, while in LMEs there is often a more hierarchical relationship between management and employees.

The VoC approach has been very influential, but has also been criticized extensively (see Hancké, Rhodes and Thatcher, 2007 for a summary). What in Chapter 1 was labelled the 'uni-directional approach' within political economy has criticized VoC for placing too much emphasis on the variation between different capitalist societies and neglecting that all capitalist societies move in the same neo-liberalism direction (e.g., Baccaro and Howell, 2011; Howell, 2003). However, VoC has also been criticized for including too little variation and for lacking tools for moving beyond the LME and CME archetypes (e.g., Hay, 2005; Schmidt, 2002). Denmark, for instance, has been described both as a possible hybrid between an LME and a CME, and as a 'negotiated economy', a decentralized and social partner-wise inclusive subtype of a CME (Campbell and Pedersen, 2007; Pedersen, 2006). A more comprehensive critique is presented by Molina and Rhodes (2007), who find it difficult to extend the VoC dichotomy to 'deviant' cases where there is a high degree of institutional incoherence and an apparent absence of complementarities. This is the case in Mediterranean countries such as Italy and Spain.

The issue of variation within the CME model has been addressed – among others – by Kathleen Thelen (2014), who distinguishes between three 'varieties of liberalization'. She thus acknowledges the argument that all Organisation for Economic Co-operation and Development (OECD) countries are following a path towards liberalization, at the same time as she upholds the view that there are qualitatively important differences in the way different types of countries do this. 'Deregulatory liberalization' is an LME path and includes the active political dismantling of trade unions and employers' coordinating capacities and involves declining regulatory coverage, as seen in, for example, Australia and New Zealand. 'Dualization' involves continued strong coordination on the employer side, but also a reduction in the number of firms and employees covered by coordinating agreements. Hence, institutions and agreements are resilient in the core, but vanishing in the periphery. Germany is a prime example here. In 'embedded flexibilization', the liberalization path is embedded in 'supply-side solidarity', where risks are collectivized by focusing resources on enabling society's most vulnerable people to enter or re-enter the labour market. In this way, dualization is counteracted. Scandinavian countries are the prime examples here.

One of the latest contributions in the field of political economy within this debate is a clear example of what I labelled in Chapter 1 the 'uni-destination' approach. It is a critique by Baccaro and Howell (2017),[1] who take the liberalization theme further. They argue that liberalization of industrial relations is not just a characteristic of LMEs, but that liberalization has affected CMEs as well, although coordinating institutions such as centralized bargaining and employee involvement institutions still exist. There might still be institutions in some countries that on the surface are constructed to serve other models, but these have been reshaped in order to support the neo-liberal path. As an alternative to the imprecise term 'liberalization', their understanding of liberalization focuses on an expansion in employer discretion, as constraints on employers – in the form of labour law and collective regulation – diminish. Employer discretion is all about discretion in wage determination, discretion in personnel management and work organization, and discretion in hiring and firing.

2.3   POWER RESOURCE THEORY AND POWER IN INDUSTRIAL RELATIONS

Looking across the studies of corporatism, varieties of capitalism, and the labour market model approach above, it is evident that power relations between the key actors – which is addressed in the third research question, 'Which factors best explain the development in the quantity and quality of corporatist arrangements?' – explicitly or implicitly play an important role in the actors' interaction and the regulation that results from this interaction. However, in none of these three approaches is it clear how power is defined. Approaches that include more explicit power concepts are presented below to clarify.

Power Resource Theory

Among the approaches to studying state/interest organization relations, the power resource theory is one of the few that – as the name indicates – includes an explicit power dimension. It was developed around the 1970s within political science and political sociology following debates between Marxist and other elitist approaches on the one hand and pluralism on the other. Moreover, it is partly a response to the 'three-dimensional' approach to the study of power that was developed gradually from the 1950s to the 1970s.[2] These three dimensions are still referred to in recent studies of power.

The power resource theory emphasizes the working class and the role of the two organized groups associated with the working class: the trade union movement and the social democratic/labour parties. Korpi (1985, 2006) has been one of the main proponents of this approach. He argues that power resource theory provides the best approach for understanding the variation in institutions and outcomes. He sees the clustering of countries with regard to distribution and redistribution as a function of the organizational strength of the working class. The literature in this tradition documents how the size and structure of the welfare state is related to the historical strength of the political left, including the social democratic parties and the trade unions, and how it has been mediated by alliances with the middle classes.

In Korpi's version of power resource theory, power is understood as a resource that the actors intentionally use in conflicts as well as in exchanges. The types of power used by an actor A when facing actor B can be either 'reward' or 'pressure'. Actor B has the same options, and the possible outcomes in a disagreement between the two are, therefore, exchange, exploitation or conflict. The actors' choice of behaviour is influenced by how strong they are in terms of power resources. This is the micro-foundation of Korpi's macro-approach, where he contrasts his own approach with Marxist and pluralist approaches that were popular at that time. The pluralists claim, according to Korpi, that the development of the welfare state reflects the needs of the population, while the Marxists see the welfare state as arising from the needs of capital. According to both these traditions, party politics and parliamentary relations have played limited roles. Contrary to this, the resource power theory sees party politics and the relation to organized interests – especially trade unions – as being key to power relations.

Often included under the power resource theory umbrella are the (early) studies of welfare regimes. The book that started this research – and the most influential book in this tradition – is Gösta Esping-Andersen's *Three Worlds of Welfare Capitalism* (1990), in which three main concepts were used to place welfare state regimes into separate categories: (1) decommodification, which is the extent to which one can live without being dependent on the market; (2) social stratification, whereby states are key actors in the structurization of class and social order; and (3) the balance between publicly and privately financed and controlled social assistance and social insurance models. According to the author, comparison of the quantitative data sorted the welfare states into three types: liberal (heavy use of private, market-driven benefits); conservative (paternalistic regulation via employment history); and social democratic (universal rights to privilege). Liberal United States, conservative Germany, and social democratic Sweden typified the ideal models for each category.

More recently, a debate has taken place between the VoC scholars – who emphasize the role of employers and point to the interests of CME employers in coordination and welfare institutions – and Korpi, who maintains the class-based approach that focuses on working-class and centre-left policies, and rejects the idea of employers as first drivers behind any welfare institutions (Iversen and Soskice, 2009; Korpi, 2006).

Power in Industrial Relations Studies

Power relations between actors are of great importance for the questions that are addressed in the academic discipline of IR. However, the IR discipline has contributed surprisingly few explicit frameworks for studying power. Those few frameworks of power that exist within IR tend to focus on trade unions. One of these is John Kelly's framework. Kelly (2011) points to five different models of power in the IR literature. The first is what Kelly labels a *market theory of union power* that draws on the economist Alfred Marshall and emphasizes the importance of competition in product and labour markets for union bargaining power. The second is the *resource mobilization* perspective in which union power is, first and foremost, influenced by union membership, and where the decline in this since the 1980s is seen as resulting in a similar decline in trade union power and influence (as indicated in, for instance, the moderate wage settlements and decline in days lost to strike actions). Third, there is an *institutionalist* perspective, in which unions' powers are influenced by both the structure (including membership) of unions themselves and by collective bargaining, especially the extension clauses. Fourth, there is a *labour process* perspective, where union power is linked to the production process and the degree to which this creates strategic groups of workers with great disruption capacities. Finally, there is a *mobilization theory* argument, which points to ideas of injustice.

Kelly himself uses Lukes's (1974) approach to power (the third dimension of power), and finds that if the mobilization theory perspective is applied, the loss of union power is less marked than commonly perceived. According to him, trade unions throughout Europe have, since the 1980s, shown a remarkable capacity to mobilize large numbers of people in general strikes in order to protest against government policies. The period from 2009 to 2010, with its protests against government austerity policies in many countries, illustrates, according to Kelly, a sense of injustice in the populations and a source of power for trade unions. Kelly sees the weakening of parties and governments as part of the explanation for the success of some union-organized anti-austerity protests and strikes in recent years (Kelly, 2011).

Recently there seems to have been a re-emergence in IR researchers' interest in power. An example[3] is the Schmidt et al. (2018) power resource typology, which they have applied to a study of trade union power in the public sector with inspiration from researchers such as Wright (2000) and Hyman and Gumbrell-McCormick (2013). These authors distinguish between the trade unions' structural power (workers' position in the labour market due to vocational skills etc.), organizational power (organizational density, economic resources, etc.), institutional power (rights established by law and collective bargaining), societal power (the legitimacy and support the trade unions have in the society as such) and political power (the presence of trade union-friendly governments).

2.4   OPERATIONALIZATION AND HYPOTHESES

Following from the presentation of the four theoretical approaches to the study of state-interest organization relations above, this section will operationalize core concepts and perceptions from the theoretical approaches and formulate hypotheses, before, in Section 2.5, describing the methods used in the empirical analysis.

Which Definition of Corporatism and Tripartite Arrangements to Apply?

Because the focus of the present study is on corporatist arrangements, it will be Lehmbruch's understanding of corporatism as an 'institutionalized pattern of policy formation' rather than Schmitter's more system- and actor-focused understanding that will be used as an interpretation of corporatism.

Moreover, it should be emphasized that the focus in the book is on tripartite arrangements, which admittedly is only a part of what corporatism is about, regardless of which definition is used. The fact that I have chosen to focus on the tripartite type of social partner-related regulation, has, as mentioned in Chapter 1, to do with the lack of attention paid to this type of regulation compared to the bipartite type. Although touched upon, bipartite regulation and delegation of power to either trade unions or employers' organizations will not be analysed in any depth. Hence, the book provides only a partial picture of corporatism. Another reason for this partial focus is obvious: the aim of getting deeper into systems and processes. A complete study of both sides of corporatism might have run the risk of being superficial.

Which Policy Areas to Focus On?

Active labour market policy (ALMP), unemployment insurance (UI), and continuing vocational training (CVT) were chosen as the three policy areas to focus on. These areas were chosen because they cover large areas seen as important for work and welfare, because these areas are traditionally among the areas the social partners are involved in (if they are involved at all), and because I have research experience in these areas. The three areas are partly overlapping in the sense that both UI and CVT have extensive overlap with ALMP, whereas UI and CVT do not have any notable overlap. Hence, the three areas could be illustrated with three partly overlapping circles next to each other with ALMP in the middle.

During the research process, an unforeseen weakness in the choice of policy areas appeared: whereas ALMP and UI are large and high-priority areas in all three countries, the size and priority given to CVT turned out to be somewhat larger and higher in Denmark than in the Netherlands and Austria. This makes the study vulnerable to the criticism that it does not compare like with like, and moreover made it difficult to find suitable cases. However, although being a 'smaller' policy area in the Netherlands and Austria than in Denmark, CVT is not peripheral in either of these countries and, as will be illustrated by the country chapters, a comparison with Danish CVT was manageable.

What Processes to Focus On?

As stated in Chapter 1, the book includes analyses of both the process and outcome (content) of tripartite agreements. In the analyses of the decision-making processes, the focus will be on policy formulation and – to some extent – agenda setting (Ham and Hill, 1993). Other phases in the policy process will only be included to a limited extent. Agenda setting is the process before policy formulation. In agenda setting, the actors attempt to form and influence the discourse on a specific issue. The two processes following policy formulation have largely been excluded. 'Transformation to legislation' is the phase where a political agreement is transformed into actual legal text. This phase is often in the hands of civil servants in the relevant ministries, but might also include some involvement of politicians, social partners and other actors who have formulated the tripartite agreement and/or political agreement that has led to the new piece of legislation. 'Policy implementation' is the next step where the legislation is implemented and 'transferred' to the users. This phase will also only be included sporadically in the empirical analyses.

What Definitions of Power and Resources to Focus On?

When addressing the issue of resources, most political science studies of relations between state and interest organizations (including social partners) focus on the resources of the interest organizations that make them relevant for the state in terms of involving them in corporatist arrangements. This perspective will also be pursued in the analyses in the following chapters. The types of power resources in focus will be those proposed by Schmidt et al. (2018), especially organizational power (organizational density, economic resources, etc.), institutional power (rights established by law and collective bargaining), and political power (the presence of trade union/employer-friendly governments).

In addition to these power resources, it is relevant to include a number of other resources by focusing more directly on the policy exchange between government and the social partners taking place in corporatist arrangements. Most of these resources are either implicitly or explicitly addressed in the corporatist studies and power-related studies presented above. The resources of the state that the social partners can use include legitimacy. This legitimacy is created when the social partners take part in corporatist arrangements that deliver goods to their members and/or solve societal challenges. A related resource is blame avoidance/credit taking, that is, the avoidance of being blamed for an unpopular initiative by pointing to another actor as the real source of the initiative or, conversely, taking credit for an initiative whose real source is another actor (e.g., Trampusch, 2005, 2006). Moreover, the state can deliver financial resources for initiatives that the social partners cannot afford. However, the most general, and perhaps the most important, resource of the state that the social partners are interested in, is the ability to influence policy formulation and/or policy formulation itself.

Also, most of the social partners' resources that the state can use to facilitate policy information or implementation are implicitly or explicitly addressed in the corporatist and power-related studies presented above. These include the legitimacy the social partners deliver if their organizational density is high. What is 'high' depends on subjective judgements by the actors and on contextual factors such as the existence of competing organizations. Another resource is the social partners' knowledge, based on the fact that they have greater proximity to the work-related realities of their members than the state/public authorities. A third resource is blame avoidance/credit taking, mentioned above, and a fourth resource is the financial resources the social partners can provide (though having less of these than the state). The financial resources are of at least two types. One type is the money the social partners unilaterally or jointly use to provide social benefits, training or other goods that could or should be provided by the state if the social partners did not provide them. Another type – not addressed in the various analytical approaches presented above – is the financial resources the social partners respectively use to support various political parties, including those in government. These might be used to influence the voting behaviour of the organizations' members (e.g., Christiansen and Nørgaard, 2003).

How to Measure Influence?

Ebbinghaus's (2002) four types of societal governance presented above will be applied in order to measure the depth of the social partner involvement. The present study focuses on policy formulation processes in recent times that imply that the concepts of *consultation* and *concertation* are most relevant. However, *self-administration* and *self-regulation* will also be relevant – for instance, in relation to the role played by the social partners' collective agreements (self-regulation) and the trade unions' role in the unemployment benefits system, which includes self-administration in some of the countries analysed.

Hypotheses

In this section, a number of hypotheses – drawing on insights from the theories and models presented above – will be formulated.

Related to the first research question 'To what extent are tripartite arrangements still used in work- and welfare-related policy areas?' is:

Hypothesis 1: Tripartite arrangements are still frequently used in work and welfare policies in the three selected countries.

The justification for this hypothesis, as described in Chapter 1, is based on the various studies (e.g., Guardiancich and Molina, 2017; Mailand, 2016a) indicating that a marked reduction in tripartite activity has not taken place in the three selected countries. It would therefore be surprising if the present study showed that corporatism does not play a role in these countries. However, it is still interesting to analyse to what *extent* this is the case. If the hypothesis is confirmed, it would challenge the 'uni-destination' approach, although only to a limited extent because this approach does not suggest that institutions such as tripartite arrangements have necessarily disappeared. They might instead have changed function so that they support neo-liberal policies and the management prerogative. If the hypothesis is rejected, it would to some extent support the 'uni-destination' understanding, especially given that the selected countries are 'critical cases', that is, cases where it can be argued that if the hypothesis 'is not confirmed here, it is not confirmed anywhere'.

The second research question was worded 'Are the social partners still able to influence the regulation of societal challenges through tripartite arrangements following the Great Recession?' This research question is related to the first research question, but it is different as it aims to dig deeper: it is possible for the social partners to sign tripartite agreements without having any real influence through these on work and welfare policies. This might be the case if the social partners strike the agreements for reasons other than influencing the content and/or if the social partners are simply rubber-stamping government policies through the agreements because they are too weak to influence the content. The expectation here will be:

Hypothesis 2: The social partners in the three countries will still be able to exercise decisive influence on work and welfare policies through tripartite arrangements from the Great Recession onwards.

A situation where the social partners – both the employers' organizations and the trade unions – are not getting substantial concessions through their participation would not be sustainable throughout a whole decade. It would lead to some kind of erosion of the institutions and this has not taken place and is not foreseen – see Hypothesis 1. That being said, however, the expectation will be that these three countries with corporatist traditions are not immune to the forces that weakened corporatist arrangements in other European countries. Hence, it is likely that some impact from these will be seen.

The factors weakening – as well as strengthening – the tripartite arrangements are dealt with in the third research question and accompanying hypothesis. The third research question asked: 'Which factors best explain developments in the quantity and quality of corporatist arrangements?' Analyses and discussions of all the drivers presented above will not be possible within the framework of this book. One possibility here would be to take the most recent large-scale analyses of corporatism (in the form of social pacts), Avdagic et al. (2011), as a point of departure. It could be argued that there is no reason to believe that the factors Avdagic et al. found to be the most important facilitators of corporatism – major economic challenges, weak governments and moderately centralized unions – are not still the most important facilitators across Europe, although the authors do not see them as the only facilitators. However, this book will examine only two of these: major economic crisis and the strength of government. These are two of the most frequently mentioned drivers. As described in Section 2.1, weak governments are always hypothesized to impact positively on the involvement of the social partners, whereas economic crisis has been pointed to as an obstacle (in some of the more recent studies) as well as a driver (in some newer and several older studies) to the involvement of social partners. In studies of the Great Recession, economic crisis has most often been pointed to as a barrier to social partner involvement, and that is also how it will be hypothesized in this book. Two of the other most frequently mentioned explanatory factors will also be addressed. One of these is the ideology of the government, which, especially in the classic corporatist studies, was viewed as being important because left and centre-left governments were seen as being associated positively with – or even as a prerequisite for – corporatism. Finally, the strength of the social partners in terms of power resources will, as indicated above, also be analysed. Here the literature is unanimous in finding a positive correlation between strong social partners and the extent of governments' willingness to involve them. Thus:

Hypothesis 3: Tripartite arrangements will be facilitated by strong social partners and weak government as well as left or centre-left governments, whereas the Great Recession is expected to have functioned as a barrier to tripartite arrangements.

Although the book includes analyses of three different countries that will be compared, no hypothesis aiming to explain their differences has been formulated. The reason for this is that, when it comes to corporatism, the countries represent very similar cases in the sense that the social partners in all three countries have played strong roles and tripartite relations in various forms have been crucial in the regulation of work and welfare. Still, not surprisingly, the empirical analyses in the forthcoming chapters will show important differences between the three countries and their types of corporatism.

2.5   METHODS

The sources of information for the analyses in the book are a combination of interviews and text analysis. More precisely, 42 semi-structured interviews were conducted with key decision makers from government and social partners and with researchers in the three countries. The interviews focused mostly on decision-making processes in the three selected areas in general and in relation to selected cases more specifically (see below). Most interviews were conducted face-to-face, but some were conducted as phone interviews (see the Appendix). The interviews about Denmark were conducted in Danish, whereas the Dutch and Austrian interviews were conducted in English. Where needed, specific questions were followed up in telephone conversations with the interviewees. In addition to these interviews, ongoing telephone conversations were conducted with some of the key Danish decision makers who were interviewed about the three rounds of tripartite negotiations during the period 2016–17.

   The text analyses include analyses of draft and final key policy documents, studies of secondary literature (i.e., academic studies of the social partners, the labour market models and corporatism in the three countries) and – to a limited extent – descriptive statistics.

   In many cases, the different methods and data sources have provided information on the same decision-making processes and their outcomes and effects.

This has opened up the opportunity for triangulation in order to improve the reliability of the findings.

Due to the different timing of the interviews in the three countries, the period in focus is not entirely, but is very nearly, the same. In all three countries, the main focus is on the period following 2008, but with the inclusion of previous decades as a comparison with the post-2008 period. However, in Denmark, the analyses cover only the period until the first half of 2018, in the Netherlands until the end of 2018, and in Austria until the first half of 2019.

With regard to the presentation of the findings, each national chapter includes, first, a presentation about the market model and, second, a short cross-sector description of tripartite agreements during the last 30 years, which, first and foremost, is used to discuss the frequency of tripartite agreements. Third, that section is followed by the core of the analyses – the analyses of the three policy areas. These include: a general presentation of basic features within the areas and tripartite arrangements before the Great Recession; a general presentation of basic features and tripartite arrangements from the Great Recession onwards; and, finally, one or two cases from 2009 or later in the form of tripartite decision-making processes that focus on the preparations (the agenda-setting phase), the policy formulation process, an evaluation of the process and outcome, and – where possible – the effect of the agreements.

Although all three country studies follow the same structure, they are not equal in length. The Danish chapter is the longest because it was possible for me to collect more high-quality data and information from Denmark than from the Netherlands and Austria. The reasons for this include, not surprisingly, the fact that I am a Danish researcher situated in a Danish university. Moreover, I am a native speaker of Danish with limited competence in German and none in Dutch. This has, of course, complicated the research process and made it necessary to translate key Dutch and Austrian texts. However, although more information has been provided in the research process and communicated in the book regarding Denmark than regarding the two other countries, enough Dutch and Austrian data and information were provided to allow for a deep and structured comparative analysis.

NOTES

1. Their argument was more or less already fully developed in their 2011 publication (Baccaro and Howell, 2011).
2. *Direct power* is the power exercised directly in decision making. This means that A can get B to follow A's will, as formulated by Robert Dahl (1958). The second dimension is indirect power, which has been labelled 'non-decision making' and has been formulated by Bachrach and Baratz (1970). *Non-decision making* involves suppressing challenges to the status quo and suppressing the addition of new issues to an agenda. Issues are excluded from an agenda because they are

threatening in some direct way, or because of the competition for the limited space for agenda items. Steven Lukes emphasizes that power analysis must also include the consciousness of controlling power, which occurs when A can affect B's preferences so that B thinks they are following their own interests, but in reality they are following A's. Lukes's distinction in this regard is between B's *objective interests* and B's *perceived interests*, which are subjective (Lukes, 1974).

3.   Other recent examples include, for instance, the Hansen and Seip (2018) study of potential power of public employers in Sweden, Denmark and Norway; Carstensen and Schmidt's (2016) attempt to theorize ideational power and the use of it; Keune's (2018) study of trade union power and occupational pensions; and Ibsen's (2015) study, which shows that cooperation between social partners is conditioned by power relations.

3. Denmark: informal tripartism and few social pacts

3.1 THE INSTITUTIONAL SET-UP OF WORK AND WELFARE REGULATION

According to Visser (2008), Denmark is an example of the organized corporatist labour market model, but often the country has either been excluded from the analyses of corporatism (because Norway and Sweden have been seen as clearer cases of corporatism in Scandinavia and therefore there has been a greater focus on them), or, as in most welfare state research (e.g., Esping-Andersen, 1990), it has been placed outside the corporatist model.

There are several reasons why researchers have at times been reluctant to use the term 'corporatism' to describe work and welfare regulation in Denmark. One is that social pacts – the peak-level tripartite agreements spanning several issues and areas – have been rare in Denmark. Another reason is that the state has traditionally played a limited role in the regulation of wages and working conditions, and some industrial relations (IR) researchers have therefore found Danish IR to be closer to the pluralist/liberal/voluntaristic model known from the UK and Ireland than to the corporatist model from Continental Europe.

However, the voluntarism found in the regulation of wages and conditions of employees is not found in other welfare- and work-related areas. Here, the state plays a much greater role and involves social partners through processes of consultation or concertation. These areas show some form of corporatist regulation. They include, for instance, health and safety at work, active labour market policy (ALMP), vocational education and training (VET), continuing vocational training (CVT), (occupational) pensions, and labour migration. Many of these areas are related to welfare as well as to labour market issues (Mailand, 2008).

Like the other two country study chapters, this chapter will be introduced by a short description of the development of the labour market regulation model and an overview of the last (approximately) 30 years of corporatist agreements (to compare the pre- and post-2008 periods), before the analysis digs deeper into three policy areas.

The Historical Development of the Labour Market Model

The Danish model of industrial relations was born out of extensive industrial conflict between employers and unions around the turn of the twentieth century. The 'September Compromise' in 1899 between newly founded confederations of trade unions and employers created the foundation for an institutionalized collective bargaining system. Conflicts, however, continued and there was no formal legal system to handle these. This led to the establishment of a comprehensive labour law system in 1910, which was prepared in a tripartite committee in 1908. The labour law system included a new labour court and a National Conciliator. From the 1930s onwards, a gradual centralization of the negotiations and a process of concatenation between the different sector collective bargaining areas took place (Madsen, Due and Andersen, 2016).

The third quarter of the twentieth century was the 'golden age' of the collective bargaining model, as regular highly centralized collective bargaining rounds took place between the trade union confederation, LO, and the employer confederation, DA. The public sector expanded gradually as the welfare state was developed from the 1960s onwards. Collective bargaining was also introduced in the public sector and gradually replaced the old civil servant system (ibid.).

However, this highly centralized industrial relations model ran into difficulties in the 1980s when the government had to intervene three times because negotiation and arbitration had failed. Under pressure from international competition and changing power relations, a partial decentralization or 'centralized decentralization' of the system took place from the early 1990s so that the sector level became the most important level (Due, Madsen and Jensen, 1993).

Due and Madsen (2006) have summarized the six main features of the Danish model across time: (1) high organizational density of social partner organizations and high collective bargaining coverage – although debated, an estimate of the coverage rate for the whole labour sector (private and public) stands at 83 per cent (Jørgensen and Bühring, 2019); (2) a nationally connected bargaining system where the National Conciliator plays a role in transferring collective agreements in key bargaining sectors to other areas; (3) a coherent regulation system connecting sector level to company level; (4) a system where the relations are based on consensus seeking and trust between the parties and where the possibilities of conflict between the collective bargaining rounds are limited; (5) a voluntaristic system with extensive social partner self-regulation and limited legislation, and where social partner involvement in legislation regarding IR procedures is based on the 'consensus principle', that is, consensus between the social partners; and (6) involvement of social partners in other labour market and welfare state issues, often, but not always, based on the consensus principle.

Who Are the Danish Social Partners and How Representative Are They?

On the *employer* side, the largest of the two remaining employers' confederations is the Confederation of Danish Employers (Dansk Arbejdsgiverforening, DA), established in 1896. Since the end of the 1980s, its 150 member organizations have, as part of the process of centralized decentralization, been reduced to only 13. The changes of the 1990s also led to the creation of one dominant member organization (Confederation of Danish Industry, Danske Industri, DI) which in 2014 accounted for 62 per cent of DA's total payroll. DI was originally only responsible for representing manufacturing companies but is now also present in the private service sector. In 2012, a third employers' confederation – the Danish Confederation of Employers' Associations in Agriculture (Sammenslutningen af Landbrugets Arbejdsgiverforeninge, SALA) – became a member of DI. DA's member organizations have around 25 000 member companies and represent companies employing 49 per cent of the employees in the private sector (Jørgensen and Bühring, 2019; Madsen et al., 2016; Navrbjerg and Ibsen, 2017).

Since 2012, the only other employers' confederation apart from DA has been the Danish Employers' Association for the Financial Sector (Finanssektorens Arbejdsgiverforening, FA). FA has around 200 members and represents around 3 per cent of the Danish labour market. The overall organizational density in the private sectors stands at 74 per cent and has, in contrast to the trade unions' organizational rate, not been reduced in recent years (Jørgensen and Bühring, 2019).

It is also worth mentioning one of the public sector organizations. Around 30 per cent of all employees in Denmark work in the public sector, and the majority of these are employed in the municipalities, represented by their interest organization Local Government Denmark (Kommunernes Landsforenging, KL). The large number of responsibilities, the relative autonomy of the municipalities, and the high number of municipal employees means that Local Government Denmark is a relatively strong organization. This is true even though it may have lost power during recent decades due to the centralization of political power in the Ministry of Finance.

On the *employee* side there were, at the time the interviews were conducted, three confederations. The largest and oldest of the three, the Danish Confederation of Trade Unions (Landsorganisationen i Danmark, LO), was founded in 1898.[1] Most of LO's member organizations started at the local level as craft unions, but developed over time into nationwide associations (Madsen et al., 2016). The craft base continued to be important for the unions for a long time and is still reflected today in the structure and demarcation lines of the unions. LO members represented both manual and non-manual workers in the private and public sectors. LO's member organizations, who used to be formally linked to the Social Democratic Party and now retain only informal links, had, at the time of the interviews, around 822 000 members (see Table 3.1). Because of the decentralization process described above, LO is no longer directly involved in collective bargaining, but continues to be involved in the coordination of it and in the processes of arbitration and consolidation. However, LO was still the main organization regarding inter-sectoral issues and involvement in tripartite arrangements.

The second largest trade union confederation was, at the time the interviews were conducted, the Confederation of Professionals in Denmark (Funktionærernes og Tjenestemændenes Fællesråd, FTF), with around 350 000 members (see Table 3.1). FTF for the most part represented unions whose members are public sector employees like civil servants, teachers and nurses, but FTF also included some private sector non-manual workers, particularly in banking and finance. FTF was also involved in tripartite arrangements, whereas collective bargaining was the prerogative of its member organizations.

In spring 2018, LO and FTF decided to join forces to strengthen their position with regard to the employers and the government (Andersen and Hansen, 2018). The two organizations merged in January 2019 into the Danish Trade Union Confederation (Fagbevægelsens Hovedorganisation, FH). Since this chapter only focuses on the period up to the end of 2017, the possible consequences of this merger are not analysed, and LO and FTF are referred to by their old names.

The third confederation still exists. It is the Danish Confederation of Professional Associations (Akademikerne, AC), with around 200 000 members (Table 3.1) (320 000 if students and other non-employed members are included). AC represents graduate-level employees in the public and private sectors.[2] Unlike LO and FTF, AC is directly involved in collective bargaining and also takes part in tripartite arrangements.

Beyond the umbrellas of these three confederations, ideologically alternative – or 'yellow' – unions such as the Christian Union have increased membership steadily during the last ten years. These unions are involved in intense competition with LO's member organizations for recruiting members. In 2012, some 220 000 employees were members of the ideologically alternative unions.

The level of trade union density (including the 'yellow unions') in Denmark stood at 67 per cent in 2013 (Ibsen, Due and Madsen, 2015), but has since then dropped to 64 per cent in 2018 (Andersen and Arnholtz, forthcoming). The union density, however, is still comparatively high. The density has been steadily declining since 1996 from around 75 per cent (Figure 3.1). The decline has mostly taken place among the unions of skilled and unskilled workers, as well as among unions representing clerical and commercial employees, that is, the members of LO. FTF's membership was stagnating at the time when

Table 3.1   The Danish social partner confederations and their organizational densities (2014–15)

	Members	Organizational Density
*Employers (private sector)**		77%
DA	25 000 companies	
FA	200 companies	
*Employees***	1 812 000	67%
LO	822 000	
FTF	345 000	
AC	235 000	
LH (Ledernes Hovedorganisation)	100 000	
Alternatives	253 000	
Outside the confederations	57 000	

Sources: *DA (2014); ** Ibsen, Due and Madsen (2015) (2015 figures).

the interviews were conducted, whereas AC's and the yellow unions' memberships have increased in recent years (Madsen et al., 2016). These developments are of importance for tripartite cooperation because the leadership of LO (or the legitimacy of it) during the last decades gradually became weaker. Moreover, although still comparatively high, the overall organizational density of the trade unions has been reduced, which challenges their legitimacy to some extent. Contributing to this problem is the fact that, because the yellow unions are not represented in tripartite fora, the organizational density of the participating trade unions' confederation stood at only 58 per cent in 2014 (Ibsen et al., 2015).

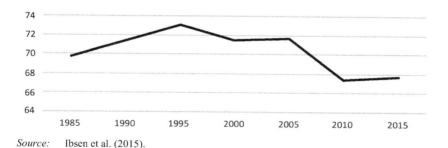

Source: Ibsen et al. (2015).

Figure 3.1   Trade union density in Denmark, in percentages

Since the 1990s, another important development has taken place. As part of the 'centralized decentralization' process described above and as a reaction to technological development, a move – similar to that of the employers' organizations' – towards fewer organizations – has taken place on the employee side. This development has been most notable in LO, where the number of member organizations was reduced from 40 in 1980 to 18 in 2017. In FTF, the number only decreased in the years 1980–2000 from 133 to 104 and to 69 in 2017, while the number increased in AC in the years 1980–2000 from 19 to 22 and further to 25 in 2017 (Due and Madsen, 2001; see also the confederations' websites).

3.2   CORPORATIST AGREEMENTS IN A 30-YEAR PERSPECTIVE: AN OVERVIEW

Denmark has never had a permanent inter-sectoral forum for social partner involvement that has played an important role in tripartite decision making of the kind found in the Netherlands, Spain, Portugal and elsewhere. The closest might be the Economic Council. The Economic Council has 25 members representing unions, employers, the Danish Central Bank and the government. The members of the Economic Council meet twice a year to discuss a report prepared by the council's 'Chairmanship'. The council's Chairmanship is staffed with independent economists and is responsible for the analyses of and conclusions on the economic situation in Denmark, and for supervision of the sustainability of public finances and the productivity and competitiveness.[3]

The involvement of the social partners at national level in Denmark primarily takes two forms (when excluding lobbyism). One is through national tripartite fora limited to one policy area. These exist in a number of policy areas, including employment policy, work environment policy, vocational education and training (VET), further training, and labour migration. They play a greater role in the implementation and administration of policies than in the formulation of them. These bodies sometimes take the form of 'pure' tripartite bodies, with the participation of only government representatives and social partners, whereas others are what has been labelled 'tripartite+' (e.g., Guardiancich and Molina, 2017), with participation of other interests such as voluntary sector organizations. The other form of involving the social partners is ad hoc involvement.

Table 3.2 provides an overview of tripartite agreements for the last 30 years. Only one of the agreements – the Common Declaration from 1987 – takes the form of what is known in the international literature as a social pact, that is, a tripartite agreement spanning more than one policy area/issue. All other agreements focus mainly on one policy area.[4] Other features of tripartite agreements will be discussed in Section 3.6.

Tripartite Agreements Until 2008

In the mid-1980s, the Conservative-led Schlüter government – supported by the employers – saw a need for wage moderation and increased saving in society. This perceived need was increased by an 'expensive' collective agreement round in 1987, where the trade unions gained substantial wage increases. The trade union movement, for its part, was interested in employment growth and occupational pensions (although the latter was not a high priority among their members). With the Common Declaration, the social partners' peak organizations, DA and LO, committed themselves to wage restraint in order to secure a competitive wage level – 'Job party, not wage party', as it was formulated by LO's former chairman (Due et al., 1993). While the agreement on wage restraint had an impact in the following collective bargaining round in 1989, the situation was a bit more complicated with the labour market pensions. An occupational pension committee was set up to reach consensus on a model for occupational pensions, but such a consensus could not be established. However, the committee work was not wasted. Among the four models of occupational pensions crystallized in the committees, one was used as a basis for the final breakthrough that came to pass during the 1991 collective bargaining round. It was an occupational pension model that tied the pensions closely to the collective agreements (Due and Madsen, 2003).

The Common Declaration was terminated in 1998, but a new bipartite agreement on wage restraints was reached the same year in the form of the so-called Negotiation Climate Agreement ('Klimaaftalen'). Following the Common Declaration, permanent general tripartite structures were set up. However, the so-called Tripartite Forum and its affiliated Statistical Committee never acquired any important role for tripartite agreements. The bodies were not useless though, since the Statistical Committee has made economic forecasts that have been used in the private sector collective bargaining rounds (Due and Madsen, 2006, 2012).

All tripartite agreements – and attempts to reach them – in the 1990s and in the first decade of the 2000s were focused mainly on one policy area, as seen in Table 3.2. These tripartite agreements were mainly found in the ALMP and CVT areas and will be described in the sections below on tripartite agreements in these two policy areas.

Whereas this attempt to picture the state of tripartism from the mid-1980s to the late 2000s focuses on the decision making of new policy agreements only, a number of Danish researchers have conducted research on the development of corporatism in Denmark across policy areas that also include policy implementation and other channels of influence (e.g., Binderkrantz and Christiansen, 2015; Binderkrantz et al., 2014; Christensen, Mouritzen and Nørgaard, 2009; Mailand, 2008). The large majority of these studies conclude that the influence

Table 3.2   *Overview of tripartite agreements in Denmark, 1987–2017*

Year	Name	Head of Government	Areas
1987	Common Declaration	Conservative	Wages, pensions and savings
1991	Zeuthen Committee	Conservative	ALMP (unemployment insurance, UI)
1998	Labour Market Reform 3	Social Democrats	ALMP (UI)
1999	Continuing Training Reform	Social Democrats	CVT
2002	Four-partite negotiations on integration	Liberals	ALMP and integration policy
2003	East Agreement	Liberals	Labour migration
2004–05	Globalization Council	Liberals	CVT, education, research, entrepreneurship, etc.
2006	Continuing Training Reform	Liberals	CVT
2007	Quality Reform	Liberals	CVT (work environment, elderly in labour market)
2008	Laval Committee	Liberals	Labour migration
2012	Acute Agreement 1	Social Democrats	Unemployment insurance (ALMP)
2013	Vocational Education Reform	Social Democrats	Vocational education
2014	Unemployment Insurance Commission	Social Democrats	Unemployment insurance
2016	Tripartite negotiation labour market integration (round 1)	Liberals	ALMP and integration policy
2016	Tripartite negotiations sufficient and qualified labour power (round 2)	Liberals	Vocational education (ALMP)
2017	Implementation of Enforcement Directive	Liberals	Labour migration
2017	Tripartite negotiations CVT (round 3)	Liberals	CVT

Note: Secondary subjects are in brackets. Working environment agreements are not included.
Source: Mailand (2010) and the present chapter.

of the interest organizations has diminished since the 1970s or 1980s, but not so much in relation to the implementation of policy as in the formulation of policies. In particular, it is the use of pre-legislative committees with interest group representation that has diminished. Variations in the studies are found regarding the extent to which corporatism has weakened, which depends on the areas and processes analysed.

Tripartite Agreements After 2008

Tripartite agreements were not – as indicated in Table 3.2 – directly used as an instrument in Denmark to meet the challenges of the Great Recession that hit the country relatively hard and more than doubled the unemployment rate to 7 per cent. One of the reasons that no tripartite agreement was used had to do with the previously mentioned tradition that wages and most working conditions are nearly exclusively regulated bilaterally between the social partners. In line with this tradition, the government would have faced strong resistance from the social partners (see also Ibsen, 2016). Moreover, the government trusted the social partners' ability to strike responsible agreements in both the private and the public sectors. These agreements resulted in very limited or no pay increases, but no direct wage reductions (Refslund and Lind, 2019).

However, although no tripartite agreements can be shown that directly address the Great Recession, an attempt to sign a social pact was made by the Social Democratic-led government in 2012 that could be seen as indirectly addressing the economic crisis. The context for this attempt was the Social Democratic-led government plan for financial policy, 'Fair Solution', formulated in 2010 while in opposition. The plan included a proposal to increase labour supply by increasing the working day by 12 minutes. This was an alternative to the then Liberal government's proposal to increase labour supply and improve the budget by dismantling the voluntary early retirement scheme. The Social Democrats promised that they would initiate tripartite negotiations if they could form a government after the general election in June 2011, which they did. However, in the meantime, the voluntary early retirement scheme had (de facto) been phased out as part of the pension reform 'Later Withdrawal from Labour Market' (Regeringen, 2015), which neither the Social Democrats nor the social partners had been involved in. Due to this reform, the need for increasing labour supply and improving the public budget was reduced. The government and the trade unions nevertheless still wanted to initiate tripartite negotiations in order to formulate a new socio-economic path. In spite of the new circumstances resulting from the de facto elimination of the voluntary early retirement scheme, the government set a target of increasing the labour supply by 20 000 people, with an increase in public spending of approximately 0.6 billion euros. These financial resources were then able to be used for, for example, labour market policy and education initiatives (Due and Madsen, 2014).

In April 2012, the government and the parties agreed on broad terms of reference that – in addition to longer working hours achieved through the cutting of bank holidays – also included issues such as the lack of practical training places in vocational education, continuing vocational training (CVT), the economic framework conditions for trade unions, social dumping/labour migration, occupational health and safety, employment policy, modernization of the public sector, and initiatives to stimulate growth in the private sector. However, resistance from the trade union rank and file to working longer and reducing holidays at a time of high unemployment led the Danish Metalworkers' Union to withdraw from the negotiations. Hence, the tripartite negotiations ended before they really started (ibid.)

After this defeat, the Social Democratic-led government did not attempt to reach any other social pact-like agreements. The expectation after the defeat was that it would take quite a number of years before a Danish government would again embark on them. However, a tripartite+ pre-legislative committee was set up in 2014 to lay the groundwork for an unemployment insurance (UI) reform (see Section 3.3) and during the run-up to the election, the Liberal opposition leader promised broad-based tripartite talks in the event that he was elected to office – just as the previous prime minister had done before she was elected four years before. In the new government's work programme that started in June 2015, the government repeated the invitation to peak-level tripartite negotiations. It resulted in three rounds of tripartite agreements. The processes and outcomes of these will be analysed below.

3.3   UNEMPLOYMENT INSURANCE (UI)

From the Introduction to the Great Recession

The first UI funds were established in the 1880s, partly to ensure basic living conditions for unemployed workers and partly to create an effective remedy for wage pressure. In this earlier phase, the funds were self-financed and pro-posals from the Social Democrats in Parliament to grant public support for the funds were repeatedly rejected (Due and Madsen, 2007).

The first UI act was adopted in 1907 and was inspired by the Belgian Ghent system (ibid.). Hence, the law established self-governing UI funds divided according to occupation and affiliated to the unions, but under public super-vision and with a ceiling for the total government grants from municipalities and state of a maximum of 50 per cent of total expenditure (Pedersen, 2007). It is surprising that such legislation, which gave unions a significant part of the control of UI and led to wide-ranging double membership of UI funds and trade unions, could be unanimously passed through Parliament with a right-wing majority. But it was important for the right-wing majority that as many union members as possible joined the UI funds to make them economically sustainable. Possibly, the right-wing majority trusted the state control of the system and hoped that formal separation between trade unions and UI funds would be a real separation (Due and Madsen, 2007).

The Labour Exchange Act from 1913–14 tightened control of available unemployment funds and established national and local tripartite fora in connection with unemployment benefit (Nørgaard, 2007). The number of UI funds grew steadily and reached 65 in 1920 (Pedersen, 2007). A review of the UI legislation in 1927 under a Liberal government opened up the opportunity for cross-occupational UI funds, which paved the way for the Christian UI fund (Due and Madsen, 2007). It became the first of a series of cross-occupational UI funds, but it was years before they could seriously threaten the established UI funds. Based on recommendations from a tripartite commission established in 1964, legislative amendments were introduced in both 1967 and 1969, which, inter alia, made part-time employees eligible for UI. The rule, which is still in existence, that UI should amount to 90 per cent of the previous income, but with a fixed ceiling, derives from these legislative changes. The legislative changes also established the Public Employment Service (Arbejdsformidlingen, AF). AF took over the role of matching available jobs and job seekers from quasi-municipal public employment offices and from trade unions, UI funds and other non-governmental actors.

Finally, in 1979, the Voluntary Early Retirement Scheme gave 60–66-year-olds the opportunity to retire from the labour market with 80–100 per cent of the maximum UI if they had been members of a UI fund for ten years (Pedersen, 2007). The introduction of the scheme increased membership of the UI funds. Later, it became possible for self-employed people to be members of UI funds.

From the mid-1970s – when it turned out that the economic crisis and rising unemployment were persisting – more and more ALMP initiatives came into being (see Section 3.4). Participation in these schemes gave the unemployed the opportunity to regain the right to UI up until 1994. In 1994, a reform set the maximum benefit period at seven years. Previously it had de facto been unlimited. In the following years, the Social Democratic-led government continued to shorten the maximum benefit period, which in 1999 was placed at four years. The shortening of the maximum benefit period was in many cases 'traded' with the trade union movement and the opposition in the form of extensions of activation efforts. A reform of the Voluntary Early Retirement Scheme introduced a requirement of 25 years of UI membership out of the previous 30 years and reduced the pension age from 67 to 65. The reform was introduced without much political debate and without the involvement of the social partners, and it became a political problem for the Social Democratic-led government and its prime minister, who shortly before had insisted that no reductions in the scheme would take place (Refslund and Lind, 2019).

Whereas the Social Democratic-led governments of the 1990s succeeded in reducing the maximum benefit period, the Liberal-led governments, in the following decade, had little luck in their attempts to continue this development and to change the UI level. One of the first attempts was made in the autumn of 2003. The proposed law would have had consequences especially for the UI of high-paid employees. After massive criticism from the opposition and trade union movements, the government withdrew the proposal. In addition, repeated attempts to extend the lower benefit rate for the young to 25–30-year-olds failed. Instead, new interventions in unemployment benefits were primarily targeted at groups of unemployed people other than the insured unemployed. The initiatives included the Social Assistance Ceiling and the introduction of Start-Aid (reduced social assistance) for new immigrants. The fact that the Liberal prime minister, in the mid-2000s, often praised the Danish flexicurity model (which as one of its three main components has 'generous unemployment benefits') perhaps reflects the fact that the Liberal-Conservative government in this period did not have further UI reductions high on their agenda.

What the Liberal-led government was able to introduce in 2002 was the opportunity for the UI funds to recruit beyond their main occupation by introducing cross-occupational UI funds. A side-effect of the 2002 law was a weakening of the so-called 'Ghent effect', that is, the widespread 'double membership' of trade unions and UI funds due to the fact that the UI funds were administered by the unions. The 2002 law clarified that it was possible to choose alternative UI funds (Due and Madsen, 2007).

Since the Great Recession

Since 2008, a number of important changes have taken place, some made without the involvement of the social partners and some with their involvement. In the autumn of 2007, the Liberal-Conservative government tried to strike an agreement informally on a quid pro quo basis with the social partners and the Social Democrats on increasing the compensation rates (which several studies had shown had decreased) and a shorter maximum benefit period, which had been the aim of the government since it took office in 2001. However, LO and the Social Democrats rejected the offer. Immediately thereafter, in December 2007, the government set up a Labour Market Commission, an expert commission without the participation of the social partners. The main recommendations of the commission, published in August 2009, were to increase the employment threshold from six months to one year and to shorten the maximum benefit period from four to two years. The commission forecast that these changes would increase job-seeking activity and thus increase employment and improve public finances (Arbejdsmarkedskommissionen, 2009). The emphasis on a positive effect from an increase in the labour supply on employment and public finances was repeated in several of the following years' social and employment policy reforms.

At the time of the publication of the Labour Market Commission's report, there was no majority in Parliament to support their main recommendations. This changed when the right-wing populist Danish People's Party changed their position. In May 2010, the government was therefore able to agree the Unemployment Insurance Reform 2010, whose main content was identical to the two main recommendations from the Labour Market Commission but with no increases in the compensation rates. No notable involvement of the social partners took place. The de facto veto power in relation to UI, which the trade unions had exercised more or less successfully throughout the 2000s, was apparently gone. It was controversial to shorten the benefit period for several reasons, one of them being the downturn in the business cycle. The Danish People's Party – which has a large share of working-class voters – defended their position on the grounds that the business cycle was expected to shift soon. Moreover, the government estimated that only between 2000 and 4000 people would exhaust their right to unemployment insurance before they had found a job. However, the government was proved to be wrong on both estimates: the employment level only started to rise in 2013 and at least ten times as many people than estimated exhausted their right to unemployment insurance before they had found a new job (AK-Samvirke, 2013).

The surprisingly high number of people exhausting their right to UI developed into a major political problem for the Social Democratic-led government that was in power from September 2011 to June 2015. In order to deal with this problem, the government made no less than five different adjustments to the reform between 2012 and 2014. The Social-Liberal government partner had supported the 2010 reform and refused to support any new reform that included permanent changes. Hence, only temporary adjustments were possible.

These changes were a series of de facto temporary extensions of the maximum benefits periods and ALMP measures for those at risk of exhausting their right to unemployment insurance, not real and permanent changes to the reform measures. This should be seen in the context of the Social-Liberals' support of the 2010 reform that, from a short-term perspective, prevented them from supporting a new reform that included permanent changes. It is worth taking a closer look at the two of these that included involvement of the social partners.

The 'Acute Agreement 1' was a political agreement reached in August 2012 based on a small and rapidly drafted tripartite agreement (including Local Government Denmark and AK-Samvirke, the interest organization of the unemployment benefit funds), which allocated 332 million DKK to various active measures to address the issue of those at risk from exhausting their right to unemployment insurance. Apart from specifying various active measures, the agreement also defined the responsibility of each of the actors signing the agreement. Finally, the agreement committed the actors to setting up a working group to support the implementation of the agreement. The agreement did not include any changes to UI itself. According to one of the trade union interviewees, the role of the social partners was also – apart from supporting the implementation – to make sure that the government did not promise anything too unrealistic during the speedy decision-making process. Another trade union interviewee pointed out that the level of commitment from the social partners was not high, in spite of the list of responsibilities. This seemed to be confirmed by the fact that there were no quantitative targets set and no actual signing of the agreement.

The 'Acute Agreement 2' followed very soon after, in October 2012. This agreement included not only standard active measures like those under the first agreement, but also a job-creation measure in the form of the set-up of 12 500 'acute jobs'[5] that could be within the private as well as the public sector and be open-ended as well as fixed term. The employers would receive a bonus of between 12 500 and 25 000 DKK for each acute job. Interestingly, this second agreement was not a tripartite agreement in that it did not include the trade unions, but only the private and public employers. The reason for this, according to several interviewees, had to do with the unwillingness of the trade unions to commit themselves to the acute jobs and the targets for them. The private employers in DA and DI, on the other hand, showed a strong degree of commitment to the measure and allocated substantial resources to implement the agreement by persuading individual member companies of its benefits. The reason that the employers' organizations made such a great effort to help the Social Democratic-led government was, according to all interviewees addressing the question, that the employers' organizations were willing to make major concessions in order to avoid the alternative – a new unemployment insurance reform including a permanent extension of the maximum benefit period.

CASE: UNEMPLOYMENT BENEFIT REFORM 2015

Preparing the Process

Yet another temporary de facto extension of the maximum benefit period (although on a reduced benefit level) for the target groups was introduced in May 2013 in the form of the Labour Market Allowance (Arbejdsmarkedsydelsen), and finally in November 2014, the Cash Allowance, targeting those who had already exhausted their right to unemployment insurance but were not eligible for social assistance.

However, in June 2014, before the introduction of the Cash Allowance, the government announced that they would set up an Unemployment Insurance Commission to put an end to temporary solutions and propose a real reform of the unemployment benefits system. By waiting until the end of its term to set up the commission, the government ensured that the commission would only report its recommendations after an election and that the government would therefore not be bound by the promises made in its previous term.

Although, in a certain sense, the Unemployment Insurance Commission could be seen as the first tripartite pre-legislative commission in years, it was still not a 'classic' tripartite commission in that the social partners (DA, Local Government Denmark, LO and FTF) were only granted four of the ten seats. Five were given to academic experts (three economists, one legal expert and one political scientist) and one to a civil servant from the Ministry of Employment. The secretariat was staffed mainly with civil servants from the Ministry of Employment, but also with some participation from the Ministry of Finance. According to interviewees from the Ministry of Employment, the relative weight between the two groups was a deliberate choice and signalled that the outcome should be more expert than interest based.

The terms of reference for the commission were relatively open. They emphasized, inter alia, that a future UI system should meet the challenges posed by more open borders, new employment types and new types of payments. Moreover, the terms stated that the proposals from the commission should not lead to increased unemployment, decreased employment or represent a worsening of public finances.

Decision-making Process

LO gave a high priority to the commission from the outset and – like FTF – appointed their president to the commission. After the failure to strike a tripartite agreement in 2012, it was important to demonstrate that they were still a relevant actor in the labour market and the formulation of welfare policies. Moreover, the issue of UI was a core issue for the confederation. The same two explanations could be given for the high priority accorded to it by FTF. The role of the DA in the commission was – according to a DA interviewee – not to come up with new suggestions but to be defensive, and make sure that LO supported a model based on a two-year maximum benefit period without changing the system created in 2010 in too many other ways. DA was, for various reasons, forced to change their representative several times, the last time in July 2015 when DA's CEO was appointed Minister of Employment. Some interviewees felt that this lack of stability in its representation on the commission negatively influenced DA's performance. However, none of the interviewees pointed to any specific influence on the outcome resulting from this.

Early on in the process, there was a discussion among the representatives about which groups should be prioritized most in terms of benefiting from the changes. The decision was that the groups with the highest unemployment risk should benefit most. This meant that increases in the replacement rate were taken off the agenda, because low compensation rates were primarily a challenge for the mid- and high-income groups, which were also the groups facing the lowest risk of unemployment. Hence, at an early stage, discussion could focus on issues other than replacement rates.

Having to deal with experts in at least two different fields as well as the social partners was a challenge for the chairperson (one of the economists), but she did well according to all the interviewees evaluating her performance. Several dimensions of UI were discussed at the meetings and over time a few alternative models were developed. In August 2015, an internal report was completed. It included three main models. The first model extended the maximum benefit period from two to three years but reduced the benefit level gradually after the first year. The second model included the possibility for the individual to 'earn' the right for a third year of benefit if the person worked for at least half a year during the first two years' benefit period. This model also included a reduced benefit level in order to finance it, but with lower reductions than in the first model. A third model was a continuous model for 'earning' the right to UI, where one month of work would give the right to two months of benefit over a maximum of two years.

Towards the end of the period, several interviewees found that the analytical work was side-lined to some extent and interest-based politics became more marked. For the employers, the experts' suggestion of increasing the number of employer-paid days of UI (which until the reform was only the first day of unemployment) was controversial and DA tried to avoid it. LO on their part tried to avoid having their members pay for the changes through reduced UI for the newly educated or in other ways.

The Outcome and Effects

The commission's report and recommendations were published in October 2015 (Dagpengekommissionen, 2015). The main recommendations are shown in Table 3.3 and compared to the political agreement.

Focusing first on the commission's recommendations, it seems that these come close to the second model of the three models suggested in the August report (see above). However, importantly, in the commission's recommendations there were no general reductions of the benefit level included. Instead,

Table 3.3   *The UI Commission's agreement compared with the following political agreement*

Commission Agreement	Political Agreement, Deviations from Tripartite Agreement
Extension of maximum UI period up to one year. One hour of employment in an individual employment account gives two hours of UI	One waiting day every four months UI for new graduates is reduced to 71.5% of UI maximum, but only for
Use of UI in hours (previously in weeks)	persons without dependent children
Calculation of eligibility to UI benefit from hours to income: 212 400 DKK, with a maximum of 17 700 DKK per month	Additional funding needed: 300 million DKK
Two waiting days (without benefit) every third month (only for those who have not been employed for at least 15 days within the last three weeks[a]	
UI benefit for new graduates reduced from 82 to 78% of maximum UI benefit	
Employer pays UI benefit for the first two days of unemployment	
Supplementary UI benefit: previously all supplementary UI benefit had to be used before a new period could begin where more could be earned through employment. It is proposed that this rule should now be dropped[b]	
One waiting month (without benefit) for any person who within the last eight years has received benefit for four years[c]	

Notes:
a. LO and FTF suggest one day every fourth month.
b. This feature was also included in the political agreement, but never implemented due to technical challenges.
c. LO and FTF did not support this recommendation.

it was suggested that the period extension be financed by four elements: (1) two waiting days (without benefit) every third month; (2) one waiting month (without benefit) for any person who has received benefit for four years or more within the last eight years; (3) reduced benefit for new graduates (from 82 to 78 per cent of the maximum level of benefit); (4) employer payment of the two first days of unemployment (previously one).

It took only three days from the signing of the tripartite agreement for the political agreement (Regeringen et al., 2015) to also be signed. The reason for the speed of the process was that the government – as well as the social partners – wished to prevent any possibility of mobilization against the fragile consensus of the tripartite agreement. The main opposition parties accepted this. But to secure broad support for the reform, the Liberal-Conservative government needed some changes in the tripartite agreement. The government seems to have listened to the Social Democrats and Danish People's Party (who regretted their support for the 2010 reform). Moreover, LO and FTF managed to secure a reduction in the number of waiting days from two per three months to one per four months. On the other hand, LO and FTF were unable to avoid a substantial further reduction in the benefit level for new graduates. They were unhappy about this, but it was especially disappointing for the confederation of the professions in AC (which was not part of the commission and whose members would first and foremost be affected). However, according to an interviewee from the Ministry of Employment, the government wanted deeper cuts for new graduates, but this was blocked by the trade union representatives. Finally, LO – who was consulted informally during the short political process – had to accept special conditions for insured unemployed people with dependent children. This kind of more lenient treatment for carers is familiar in the social assistance system but had not previously been seen in the UI system. LO and FTF were afterwards criticized for allowing this blurring of the boundaries between the two systems and warned that it could be a Trojan horse.

By and large, however, the political agreement followed the commission's recommendations. The social partners, and not least the trade unions, managed to exercise considerable influence in the commission. However, it should also be noted that the reforms did not fundamentally change the 2010 reform, but rather adjusted it. This shows the limitations of the social partners' – and more precisely in this case the trade unions' – influence. The reforms, nevertheless, included important new features and effects. The most important could be said to be:

- more flexible eligibility criteria by counting short-term temporary jobs;
- an opportunity to extend the maximum benefit period by 12 months if the person has worked for at least six months during the two benefit periods;
- reduced benefit levels for new graduates without children and other minor groups.

In addition, some of the government interviewees found that an important side-effect of the reform was that discussions and criticisms of UI were reduced substantially. Although the overall effect of the reform could be said to be higher employment security, especially for non-standard employees, media cases confirmed by one of the interviewees found that there were other groups apart from new graduates who had unintentionally had their UI reduced. Moreover, several interviewees found that the system was not simplified, as intended, to any notable extent. Furthermore, apart from increasing the economic incentives to accept short-term jobs, the challenges of non-standard employment were not addressed in the report. The commission decided that they did not have the time to work on this highly complex issue and a decision was made that a working group in the Ministry of Employment with some kind of social partner involvement should look into the issue (see the following case).

CASE: TRIPARTITE WORKING GROUP ON UNEMPLOYMENT INSURANCE FOR THE SELF-EMPLOYED 2017

Preparing the Process

The Unemployment Insurance Commission's proposal to set up a working group with the aim of analysing the UI system for self-employed and freelance workers (in the following labelled 'the working group of self-employed') was confirmed in the political agreement on the UI reform of October 2015. The agreement took effect in February 2016 with the set-up of two groups: a ministerial committee with staff from the Ministry of Employment, and a 'follow-up group' with representatives from the social partners. DA, Local Government Denmark, Danish Regions,[6] LO, FTF and AC each appointed one member to this group, which also consulted UI funds, including those for the self-employed. As in the case of the Unemployment Insurance Commission, the terms of reference stated that proposals from the working group should not lead to increased unemployment, decreased employment or worsening of public finances.

The aim of the working group was, according to the terms of reference, to cover self-employed workers according to the same principles under the UI system as wage earners. Part of the aim was to address the challenges from persons combining self-employment and employment. The terms of reference included four focus points regarding: definitions of self-employment and self-employment as a secondary job; special conditions for fee earners and freelancers; termination of self-employment; and self-employed access and rights to UI (Beskæftigelsesministeriet, 2016a).

Decision-making Process

Whereas the Unemployment Insurance Commission was a high-profile group, which commanded a lot of attention from both politicians and the media, the working group on UI for self-employees was low profile. Nobody really noticed the working group beyond certain narrow circles. The interviewees found this lack of attention to be beneficial for the decision-making process.

Employers were concerned that the working group might suggest changes to the definitions of self-employment and employment or make proposals to introduce an intermediary category between self-employment and employment. However, it became clear early on that the working group would come up with no such suggestions. For the trade unions – especially FTF, which was the organization that had pushed most for the set-up of the working group – a fair and non-bureaucratic solution for the self-employed (many of whom are trade unions members) was of great importance. Government interviewees found that the social partners – unlike their focus in the Unemployment Insurance Commission, but in line with their role in a separate 'follow-up group' – focused more on the overall principles and engaged less in formulation of the specific models.

All interviewees found the decision-making process to be marked by a high level of consensus between the representatives and an effective chairing by the Ministry of Employment. One factor that facilitated the decision-making process was the recent development of an e-income register for all citizens. This register makes no discrimination between sources of income, whether from employment or self-employment. Hence, it is well suited for the exact purpose of the working group and was used as a base.

Outcome and Effects

The working group reported in April 2017. The main message of the report was that a person should no longer be defined as either employed or self-employed. It should be the economic activity – not the person – that is defined as either employment or self-employment. Moreover, register-based information should be used instead of manual case work to create fairer decisions and more transparency, and the new unemployment benefit system for the self-employed should to a larger extent support full (self-) employment. The report included six more specific proposals:

- new definitions of activities, with a greater dependence on definitions used by the tax systems – rather than those used by the UI systems;
- earning the right to unemployment benefit should be based on total earnings (e-income);
- new digital model for self-employment as secondary employment based on e-income;
- the possibility for the self-employed to work part-time and receive UI should be harmonized with the rules for employees;
- better opportunities to start up a self-employed business while receiving UI;
- a simpler and digitally based model for winding up a self-employed business (Arbejdsgruppen om selvstændige i dagpengesystemet, 2017).

A month later, in May 2018, a political agreement was signed by all parties in Parliament apart from two left-wing opposition parties. The main elements of the new law are:

- the categorization of employed employment vs self-employed/ self-employment to be related to the economic activity and not the person, thereby facilitating combinations of the two;
- a partial harmonization of regulations for employees and the self-employed based on the former;
- harmonization of categories used in the tax system and the UI system;
- more use of objective information and data in the UI system for both employees and the self-employed and less use of case-worker judgements (Law No. 1670 of 26 December 2017; Regeringen et al., 2017).

The law was not implemented until October 2018 and therefore, at the time of writing, it is too early to evaluate the agreement. With regard to the social partners' impact on the agreement it is difficult to estimate this precisely. On the one hand, the decision-making process was clearly driven and dominated by the Ministry of Employment and none of the main elements in the agreement have strong footprints from the social partners. On the other hand, the agreement included no challenges to the social partners' interests and the initiative to set up the working group came from the trade unions.

3.4   ACTIVE LABOUR MARKET POLICY

From the Introduction Until the Great Recession

In Denmark, active labour market policy (ALMP) has a long history. In 1919, public employment projects were initiated with the aim of combatting unemployment, and also in the years around World War II a few ALMP-like initiatives were introduced. However, as late as the 1950s, still only 5–10 per cent of unemployed people took part in ALMP schemes (Rosdahl, 2003, p. 128). Many scholars consider the set-up of the Public Employment Service (Arbejdsformidlingen, AF) in 1969 as the initiation of ALMP in Denmark.[7] AF was established after the unemployment benefit funds had been criticized for being unable to secure a sufficient level of geographical and vocational mobility during the 1960s' economic boom (e.g., Jørgensen, 1986).

From the outset, the social partners had a strong formal role through representation in tripartite fora. The Ministry of Labour's tripartite Labour Market Policy Committee (Det Arbejdsmarkedspolitiske Udvalg) was supplemented with another tripartite forum, the National Labour Market Policy Committee (Landsarbejdsmarkedsnævnet) and accompanying tripartite councils connected to the 14 regional Public Employment Service departments (PESs). The role of the National Labour Market Committee was to advise the Minister of Labour, but the committee had no real decision-making power.

The content of ALMP was, until the mid-1970s focused on increasing labour supply. When the oil crisis hit in 1974, the Social Democratic-led government's first response was to relax the eligibility criteria and expand the numbers of people eligible to participate in ALMP schemes (Brüniche-Olsen, 1996). However, the rapid increase in unemployment led to pressure on the state budget, and the levels of UI were, accordingly, somewhat reduced. Furthermore, during the late 1970s, it became clear that the unemployment problem might not be as temporary as first expected and that more ALMP measures were needed. A number of ALMP measures – especially targeted at young people – were therefore introduced in the form of targeted traineeships in counties and municipalities, wage-subsidy jobs in the private sector and job creation in the public sector (Ibsen, 1985). The influence of the social partners on policy formulation at this time was not as strong as their tripartite representation would indicate. For instance, the Job Offer Initiative from 1978 was prepared without any involvement from the social partners. Both DA and LO were critical of the content of the reform and remained so after implementation, having attempted to exert their influence through joint statements (Winter, 2003). The Job Creation Initiative of 1982 created jobs in the public sector for the unemployed to work on important social projects. In this case, LO supported the initiative (which they were involved in the preparation of), whereas DA, along with the opposition parties, were concerned that it would have the effect of distorting competition (Jensen, 1990; Mailand, 2008).

Later, in 1982, a Conservative-led government came into office, abandoned the existing ALMP initiatives that involved subsidized jobs and job creation and, instead, introduced new initiatives with a stronger emphasis on education and entrepreneurship. Importantly, the social partners were not involved in the policy formulation process of these changes and both the Social Democrats and LO were strongly against them (Jensen, 1990; Jørgensen, 1986). In 1989, the Youth Package was introduced. This initiative could be seen as the pilot for the work-first approach (e.g., Lødemel and Trickey, 2000) of activation policies, and it obliged 18–19-year-old social assistance recipients to take part in activation after only two weeks of unemployment, on a 'youth allowance' that was lower than social assistance (Rosdahl and Weise, 2000).

One last important initiative of the Conservative-led government was taken in 1991 when they set up a pre-legislative committee with a social partner majority. When formulating the resulting reform, the Social Democratic-led government that took office in 1992 followed the recommendations of the committee, although no further involvement of the social partners took place. Among these recommendations was the decentralization to the regional level of some responsibilities, more involvement of the social partners, a balance between individual and labour market needs, and choice between several options in activation. The social partners in the pre-legislative committee also succeeded in blocking a reform of the financing of unemployment benefit that would have increased the social partners' financial contribution (Mailand and Due, 2003).

These labour market reforms increased the influence of the social partners by upgrading their competences in the Regional Labour Market Councils. However, by 1996, a process had begun that partly recentralized activation policy and rolled back some of the influence of the social partners. This development included the bypassing of the National Employment Council in adjustments to activation policy, which increasingly were decided in conjunction with the annual budget negotiations in the Parliament, which the social partners have a limited ability to influence. However, the social partners attempted to maintain their influence by formulating joint proposals and using the media to promote their views. This strategy had some success, particularly in the case of the 1998–99 revision of the 1994 reforms. Nonetheless, in general, the social partners' influence in policy formulation was weakened during the 1990s (Jørgensen and Larsen, 2003; Mailand and Due, 2003; Winter, 2003).

Following the election of a new right-wing government in 2001, a new labour market reform was formulated in 2002. This reform reduced upskilling of the unemployed and placed more emphasis on guidance and control, and on job training in the private sector. Moreover, social assistance and UI were dealt with under the same legislation and the tripartite and multipartite bodies at the central level were amalgamated. Finally, the reform opened up opportunities for the increased use of new private actors such as temporary work agencies, private training institutions and consultancies in delivering the activation measures (Larsen and Mailand, 2007; Mailand, 2005). The social partners were invited separately to a consultation meeting, but only after the government had carried out detailed preparations for the reforms and already knew the direction they wanted to go. This form of 'social partner involvement-lite' did not result in strong social partner influence. However, the social partners did, nonetheless, have some influence on the reform, especially in the agenda-setting phase. Nevertheless, regarding governance, the regional tripartite councils with some decision-making power were replaced with local multipartite councils with a purely consultative role with regard to the municipalities and the job centres (Mailand, 2008).

The broken consensus between DA and LO was re-established in connection with the Structural Reform agreed in 2005. The government plan – as part of a larger reform of the local and regional administrative structures and division of labour – was to decentralize the responsibility of the ALMP from the 14 state-controlled PESs to 99 newly formed municipalities. Despite concern among opposition parties and joint written statements from social partners arguing against the changes, PESs and the local authorities' employability service departments were amalgamated within 91 municipality-level one-stop-shop 'job centres'. Local Employment Councils connected to the 91 job centres now only advised on local employability strategies. However, because of the objections to the reform, the municipal ownership was only secured for a trial period – no definite decision about where to place the responsibility would be made before a further evaluation had taken place (Lindsay and Mailand, 2010).

But the evaluation of the municipal-governed ownership never took place. In December 2008, likely as a payback for the unwillingness of the social partners to support a UI reform (see Section 3.2), the Liberal-led government provided the municipalities with full and permanent responsibility for the job centres. The government did so during the negotiations on the annual budget for 2009 without any consultation with the social partners or the opposition. This led to strong protests, especially from some of the trade unions (Mailand, 2010). This 'municipalization' was a de facto weakening of the social partners' regional-local influence. There was also, according to the interviewees, a gradual weakening of the social partner influence in the only national-level permanent tripartite forum. The National Employment Council never had an important role in relation to policy formulation processes but was initially quite influential in the implementation of policies. However, during the decade, the council lost some of its influence although its competences remained the same. As a result, it moved its focus to more technical issues and away from broader lines of policy. The interviewees point to different reasons for that, including the reawakened DA–LO consensus in the area and the aim of the Ministry of Employment to limit, but not abandon, the involvement of the social partners.

All in all, the social partners' influence on ALMP in the period up until the Great Recession has been reduced, something that has, to varying degrees, been confirmed by other studies in addition to those referred to above (e.g., Jørgensen and Larsen, 2013; Klitgaard and Nørgaard, 2010).

Since the Great Recession

With the Job Centre Reform of 2009, the municipalities were given the task of addressing the consequences of the economic crisis at the local level. However, there were no new large-scale ALMP initiatives taken as a response to the crisis, although a series of smaller initiatives were introduced in 2009–10, such as the More Young People in Education and Jobs initiative to combat long-term unemployment, as well as a short-term work arrangement initiative. It seemed that most efforts in these years were directed towards the UI reforms. The Social Democratic-led government that took office in October 2011 introduced a serious of UI adjustments, some with ALMP elements (see Section 3.3). The ALMP policy content of these adjustments included a number of actions targeting the unemployed, with an immediate risk of exhausting their right to benefits (Mailand, 2015).

From 2012 onwards, the Social Democratic-led government was very active when it came to reforms in areas partly overlapping with ALMP. Common to all these reforms was a double aim: to increase the labour supply and to improve public finances by cutting the budgets on the various schemes (Mailand, 2014). They all also shared a 'make work pay' or 'work-first approach' where cutting the level of benefits (directly or indirectly) were believed to increase the labour supply and employment rates among the target groups, but they also combined this philosophy with other ALMP instruments of the more 'human capital'-oriented types (Bredgaard et al., 2017).

To reduce the number of early retirees, the Early Retirement and Flexi-job Reform agreed in 2012 made it nearly impossible for anyone under 40 years old to receive early retirement benefit, which is a permanent benefit. Instead, people with a reduced capacity to work would, as a rule of thumb, have to go through so-called 'resource processes'. At the same time, the flexi-job scheme (wage-subsidy jobs for people with a reduced capacity to work) was changed to allow for flexi-jobs under 12 hours a week and for paying below the normal rate for the job (Regeringen et al., 2012). The Sickness Allowance Reform followed shortly after and also combines reduced benefit levels and intensified activation efforts. The previous 52-month maximum for receiving sickness benefit was reduced to 22 months, but with options for an extension or for continuing on a lower Job-Possibility Allowance for two years. Moreover, the reform emphasized early intervention and the job-possibility process reflected stronger efforts to get the sick/injured person back into work, that is, an activation approach (Regeringen et al., 2013b). Also, in 2013, the government introduced a Social Assistance Reform. Again, a combination of reduced benefits and new active measures were introduced (Regeringen et al., 2013a).

The social partners were, to varying degrees, involved in the consultation and hearing processes, but – according to the interviewees – they had no significant involvement in any of these reforms. There were no invitations to tripartite negotiations and no ad hoc tripartite bodies were set up. However, there is no tradition of strong involvement of the social partners in the social policy area.

In contrast to these reforms, the focus below will be on three reforms that are fully or partly in the employment policy area and have significant involvement from the social partners.

CASE: THE EMPLOYMENT POLICY REFORM 2014

Agenda Setting

The Employment Policy Reform agreed in 2014 was a 'real' ALMP reform. Like the two cases in the UI area, a mix of tripartite and non-tripartite preparation was used. In the case of the Employment Policy Reform, two working groups were set up: an expert group with academic experts and a few selected civil servants, and a working group for the social partners, which was clearly secondary to the expert group. Expert groups with such a clear aim of doing the preparation work for a particular reform had not previously been used in the Danish ALMP.

The expert group published its report in February 2014 with a large number of recommendations, which mainly focused on five issues: (1) a more individualized and early intervention approach to job seekers, including assistance to fired employees already in the notice period and more intensive counselling during the first six months of unemployment; (2) a more targeted use of education as an activation tool, including limiting it to the unemployed who are motivated to gain more education; (3) more focus on the needs of companies; (4) enhanced economic incentives for the authorities, less bureaucracy and fewer process demands; (5) restructuring of subnational organizations and increased involvement of interest groups, including a replacement of the 94 local and four regional councils with 8–12 regional councils to align better with real regional labour market boundaries, and the provision of these councils with decision-making competence regarding funds for education for the unemployed (Ekspertgruppen om udredning af den aktive beskæftigelsesindsats, 2015).

The social partners' response to the recommendations was included in the report. LO and FTF made a joint written statement in which they voiced their support for most of the elements in the report. They gave particular emphasis to, for example, the more simple and early approach to activation and the stronger focus on education, but stated that the unemployment insurance funds should be responsible for the insured unemployed and that education as an early activation tool should still be part of the employment policy. DA was somewhat less positive in their response. They stated that they supported evidence-based policies but forecast that if the expert group's recommendations were implemented in their totality, activation policy would no longer take the form of the 'work-first' approach. Job search, close contacts between job centres and the unemployed, and sanctions were the right measures according to DA, and education should only be used if there was a very specific need for that particular training in the labour market. Local Government Denmark's response was perhaps the most positive. They emphasized especially the expert group's recommendation for the municipalities to continue to be the centre of gravity in employment policy and that positive results could be expected from less bureaucracy and giving more choice to the municipalities (ibid.).

It is notable that the responses were not joint social partner responses, but separate. This is contrary to the situation in the 1990s and part of the 2000s, where joint DA–LO responses in the employment policy area were common practice. Since then, trade unions and employers have argued for different versions of activation policies. Put simply, the trade unions have argued for a human capital approach while the employers have argued for the work-first approach.

The social partner interviewees said the process around the expert group functioned well, although some of them also emphasized that, to some extent, they felt side-lined from the 'core' group – which was in line with the purpose of the government. This should be seen in light of the fact that the expert group was set up in February 2013, which was less than one year after the failure to reach a social pact-like tripartite agreement (see Section 3.2). Hence, the political-administrative system's trust in the social partners' ability to contribute positively to tripartite arrangements was limited. However, the chairperson of the expert group – who also chaired the National Employment Council – was reported by the interviewees as having had support from the social partners.

The Decision-making Process

The social partner involvement in the actual policy formulation of the reform took an ad hoc form and was mostly of the lobbying type, where the social partner organizations contact the ministers, the civil servants and the politicians. Still, at least LO seems to have had some influence, particularly on the educational elements of the reform. The problem with education as an activation tool is that a large number of evaluations have questioned its employment effect. However, LO maintained their belief in education as an activation tool and wanted to protect the six weeks of 'education by your own choice', which was a right for the unemployed prior to the reform but which was in considerable danger of being excluded in the reform. LO managed to keep it in by reframing it as 'job-targeted education', meaning that it was directed towards areas with high labour demand. That was difficult for DA and the government to reject. The six weeks of education were saved. The agreement included regional lists of approved educational programmes. According to the social partner interviewees, the six weeks of education and the greater role for the UI funds mirrored the fact that the trade unions – or more specifically LO, whose members were the only ones to benefit from the education – had stronger influence on the reform than the employers. However, trade union interviewees also felt that their aim of providing the UI funds with a greater role in the activation policy had failed.

The Outcome and Effects

The main elements of the political agreement were:

- a regional fund for short vocational education as an activation tool to improve the skill levels of employees with few or outdated competences;
- six weeks of 'vocationally targeted education';
- right-and-duty to one activation offer; repeated activation is abolished;
- improved job counselling for companies;
- changes in the wage-subsidy job scheme: wage subsidy in the private sector reduced from 12 to six months and in the public sector reduced from six to four months, the aim to avoid abuse of the system;
- new Regional Labour Market Council replaces the Local Employment Councils;
- more choice for the municipalities and less bureaucracy (Regeringen et al., 2014).

Because the Social Democratic Minister of Employment prior to the reform had criticized the activation policy quite strongly for including too much meaningless activation, some observers (e.g., Bredgaard et al., 2017) and several of the interviewees had expected greater changes and felt the reform was mainly a mild correction of previous policies, including an insufficient reduction in bureaucracy. However, among the interviewees there was also one who saw a major change in it from a work-first approach towards a more education-friendly human capital approach, due to the regional fund for short vocational education and the abolition of repeated activation. A further effect of the reform was that criticism of activation policy was reduced substantially. In particular, some of the ministerial interviewees – who described the criticism as at least partly unfair – felt that to be a very important effect.

Finally, an unintended consequence can be identified. In recent years, a drop in the so-called 'activation degree' (the time a job seeker is actually taking part in an activation activity) has been seen across groups and activation measures. For the insured unemployed the decline was, between 2012 and 2017, from 31 to 12 per cent (Danske A-kasser, 2017). The question is to what extent the drop can be explained by the Employment Policy Reform of 2014. Some observers felt that this reform might be part of the explanation. What could have happened, according to this scenario, is that the reduction of 'meaningless activation courses' has developed into a more general reduction in activation activity. Another possible explanation for the drop in activation activity is the introduction of a 2015 reform of remuneration to the municipalities (which was mentioned by some of the interviewees as being as, or more, important than the Employment Policy Reform). Due to the remuneration reform, the municipalities are no longer paid differently for different types of activation measures and the remuneration is gradually reduced over time. Therefore, it will be expensive for the municipalities to keep people in activation that is not leading to employment in the short term (Frandsen, 2016).

CASE: TRIPARTITE AGREEMENT IN RESPONSE TO THE REFUGEE CRISIS 2016

In June 2015, the Social Democratic-led government lost the election and a Liberal government (made up of only the Liberal Party of Denmark with 25 per cent of the seats in the Parliament) came into power. The new government introduced, as one of its early legislative initiatives, the so-called Job Reform in November 2015. The label 'reform' might be a bit of an exaggeration, because it only included two elements: a reintroduction of the 'Social Assistance Ceiling' (placing a maximum on the total social assistance benefit an individual/couple can receive); and a '225-hours rule' (the number of hours a social assistance recipient has to work to receive the maximum social assistance), both regulations that the previous government had removed. This was clearly a strengthening of the already strong 'make work pay' element in the activation policies. The reform was formulated without any notable involvement of the social partners – their positions on the issue were well known, and the government had no intention of making concessions to the trade unions.

The Job Reform was basically a social assistance reform and not an ALMP reform. The Liberal government did not actually introduce any 'pure' ALMP reforms, but ALMP was part of two out of three rounds of tripartite bargaining rounds that took place within just 18 months – from February 2016 to October 2017. The first of this will be analysed here.

Agenda Setting

The refugee issue was not included in the new Liberal government's work programme of June 2015, in which the government hosted peak-level tripartite negotiations (with the social partners, i.e., trade unions and employers' organizations). On the agenda for the tripartite negotiations were predictable issues such as the competitiveness of companies, education, labour migration and the transfer of citizens from various forms of transfer income to employment (Regeringen, 2015). However, during the summer and autumn, the inflow of refugees had increased. It peaked in November, when 5000 – equal to 0.1

per cent of the Danish population – applied for asylum in Denmark during only one month. For 2015 as a whole, Denmark received 3.7 asylum seekers per 1000 inhabitants, the ninth highest number among the EU's 28 member states (Frandsen, 2016). This transformed the political landscape, so that, when the tripartite negotiations started in February 2016, the refugee issue had side-lined all planned issues for the negotiations. Now, the refugee issue was identified by the government as the 'greatest current societal challenge' and 'a threat to the future of the welfare state' because of the potential burdens on public finances. Moreover, the government made an agreement on the issue a prerequisite for any subsequent negotiations on other issues.

When the leader of the opposition, in May 2015, proposed tripartite negotiations towards the end of his electoral campaign (to be undertaken should he win the general election), it was probably because he could foresee that his government would be of the weak minority type and therefore would need support from extra-parliamentary forces, and because he would like to demonstrate the ability to do what the Social Democratic government failed to do in 2012 – reach a broad agreement with the trade unions. Moreover, it would be impossible for the government to integrate the increasing number of asylum seekers into the labour market without the help of the social partners.

Unlike previous broad tripartite negotiations, the negotiations were divided into phases related to the different issues being dealt with. The government insisted that the refugee issue should be the only issue on the agenda for the first round and made an agreement on this issue a prerequisite for any further negotiations.

All three parties had procedural interests as well as substantive interests in the first phase of the negotiations. For the government, it would, as mentioned, be a major political victory to accomplish what the previous government had not been able to: a tripartite agreement on an issue of great societal importance. Regarding the substantive interests, the government needed – according to their own understanding – the social partners' help to employ the refugees in order to avoid large cuts in welfare issues or increases in taxes.

The trade unions, too, had a strong interest in the negotiations. After their power base had weakened somewhat in recent years and after the failed 2012 negotiation, they needed to show that they were still a relevant actor when major societal challenges were addressed. Moreover, they needed an agreement to get to the next phases of the tripartite negotiations, which were expected to include their priority issues. Regarding their substantive interests, their main interest in the first round of negotiations was defensive: to avoid an agreement that would replace trade union members' jobs with jobs for refugees – or just provide the refugees with assistance and benefits above the level the trade unions' unemployed members could expect. The trade union interviewees explained that their interest in the agreement was that the core of it should be collective agreement based, but that it was also in their interests that refugees were employed rather than on benefits that would be paid by tax payers, including trade union members. However, the trade unions' interests were also clearly rooted in their usual 'watchdog' function in ALMP: to protect the wages and working conditions of ordinary employees from pressure from the ALMP initiatives.

The employers' organizations had the least to lose and were – in line with tradition – the least enthusiastic about entering tripartite negotiations. Regarding their procedural interests, they could, just like the trade unions, use an agreement to show their societal relevance (by trying to solve a major challenge to society), but they needed this less than the trade unions. Regarding the substantive interests, as is often the case, the employers had a defensive interest in avoiding burdens being placed on companies. However, there were potentially also some benefits for employers, if a solution could be found that reduced wage levels for some groups of refugees and immigrants. The employer interviewees also emphasized that a well-functioning integration policy was in their interests. One of the reasons for this was to avoid the stigmatization of immigrant labour, which could follow from a situation where a very large group of refugees was concentrated in a particular form of employment. Moreover, the employers also had – as is often the case in ALMP initiatives – an interest in increasing the supply of low-cost labour, depending on the qualification level of the workers.

The division of the negotiations into separate phases and the prerequisite of a refugee agreement put pressure on the social partners to reach an agreement if they wanted to discuss anything other than refugees. This pressure was especially felt by the trade unions, who for procedurally related reasons were very eager to reach an agreement since they also wanted to discuss education and labour migration as well as other issues with the government and the employers.

The tripartite negotiations started in mid-February 2016, but preparation started several months before. Important in this phase was a discussion about the possibility of using the tripartite negotiations to allow newcomers in the labour market a lower wage for at least a period, so-called 'introductory pay' (*indslusningsløn*), to overcome the above-mentioned barrier of the universally high collectively agreed minimum wage. Introductory pay had been discussed before, in relation to other target groups apart from refugees, but the initiatives had never materialized due to resistance from, especially, the trade unions. In addition, this time, the proponents of introductory pay – mostly labour economists, the largest refugee non-governmental organization Dansk Flygtningehjælp, right and centre-right politicians, a centre-right newspaper and some employers' organizations – were met with strong resistance. However, only when DA and LO, in a joint letter, refused to accept an entrance wage, did the debate cool off somewhat, probably because the proponents could see that introductory pay in a pure form was not realistic with the dominant labour market organizations being opposed to it. The common concern of these two dominant social partner organizations was process related: pay was not a matter for tripartite negotiation and subsequent legislation, but for bipartite collective bargaining. Moreover, and related to the content, LO's resistance was also grounded in the fear of replacement of those already employed. One of the two large general workers' member unions added that they were never going to sign any tripartite agreement that included introductory pay.

The Decision-making Process

Apart from the government and the social partners, the negotiations also included the organizations Danish Regions and Local Government Denmark (KL) – the latter being responsible for accommodation and integration of refugees as well as for the activation policies delivered through the job centres. Very little time was allowed for the negotiations.[8] An agreement was expected at Easter. The terms of reference stated that, in 2015 alone, 25 000 refugees were expected, and more were expected to arrive in the following years. Moreover, the terms of reference stated that, in general, the efforts to integrate refugees had not previously been successful.

The terms of reference divided the negotiations into three themes: (1) 'a closer focus on employment in integration initiatives', focusing on language-related initiatives and the role of the public authorities in employment initiatives; (2) 'better opportunities for companies to employ refugees', which became the core of the agreement; and (3) 'simpler and more flexible initiatives involving companies', which basically was about reducing administrative burdens and other limitations for the companies' involvement in the activation policies (Beskæftigelsesministeriet, 2016a).

The discussion on the first theme was mainly focused on the existing activation measures for immigrants and on language training. According to the interviews, the parties did not have strong disagreements on how to address this theme. Twenty-one initiatives were agreed upon that could be summarized as: better assessment of the refugees' competences; a priori expectation that the refugees are ready to work (unless the assessment of competences show otherwise); and more vocational focus on Danish-language courses for refugees and immigrants (including the possibility of courses taking place at workplaces).

The discussion on introductory pay indicated that the second theme, on the role of the companies, could be the most difficult one – and so it became. Several approaches to this were discussed during the negotiations, including a more legislation-based approach that the social partners could 'follow up'. However, things started to move when DA and LO, after bilateral 'side negotiations', suggested building the initiative on a collective bargaining-based training scheme for young people (see below for details). There were several controversial issues regarding the second theme that had to be addressed before an agreement could be reached. One was how binding it should be. Local Government Denmark – who would have to deal with the refugees in the organization's capacity as a public authority – pressed for quantitative measures, but LO and DA refused. They pointed to a lack of knowledge about the target group as the explanation for this. However, the bad experience of promising a quantitative target from the second Acute Agreement (see above) might also have played a role. A second controversial issue was the balance between work and education. The trade unions placed a great deal of emphasis on education. One of the reasons for this was to avoid being accused of supporting a scheme that was just the provision of cheap labour or introductory pay in disguise. The employers emphasized workplace presence. A third controversial issue was the age span. LO wanted to limit measures to young people (below the age of 30), while DA preferred not to have an age limit at all. Until the very end of the decision-making process it was unclear whether LO could agree internally on supporting the deal. In the end, only one member organization was not able to accept the deal (described below), possibly because the collectively agreed rate was lower than that the member organization had agreed with their respective employers.

The third theme on 'simplified and more flexible measures' was negotiated at the end of the process, but the negotiations failed to end up in an agreement. This part of the bargaining process was described by some of the interviews as 'chaotic'. The core of the discussion was adjustment of the so-called 'fairness demand' (*rimelighedskrav*). The fairness demand required companies with up to 50 employees to have five employees on ordinary contracts for each person in the company on active measures. Above this threshold, the company could have one on active measures for each ten employees.

Some of the interviewees stated that they were surprised that what, in the terms of reference, was described as de-bureaucratization, de facto turned out to be about relaxing the fairness demand, whereas others stated that although the fairness demand was not mentioned, all the bargaining parties were very well aware that this was what it was all about. In any case, LO ended up not being able to support a relaxation of the fairness demand. After having agreed to special measures for refugees (see below) some of the trade unions' representatives felt that they could not give further concessions that included the danger that refugees might supersede existing employees. The Minister of Employment was of the opinion that an informal 'backstage' agreement on the issue had been settled. Hence, he was, according to several interviewees, not very happy.

In the end, there was no agreement on the third theme of the negotiations. However, none of the interviewees felt that this put the rest of the agreement in danger and none of the representatives mentioned it when the agreement was presented.

The Outcome, Process Evaluation and Effects

The agreement was reached in mid-March 2016 and included no less than 32 initiatives all connected to the first two themes of the terms of reference. The most important of these could be said to be:

- better assessment of the refugees' competences;
- an a priori expectation that the refugees are ready to work (unless the assessment of competences shows otherwise);
- stronger vocational focus on Danish-language courses for refugees and immigrants (including the possibility that courses take place at workplaces);
- a new 'basic education for integration' (*integrationsgrunduddannelse*, IGU; Regeringen og arbejdsmarkedets parter, 2016a).

The IGU was the core of the agreement. The initiative was agreed between LO and DA, with the other actors waiting on the side-lines. IGU is an up to two-year-long combination of work and education/language courses. The eligible group is refugees of 18–40 years old. They are paid a student allowance for the 20 weeks on education/language courses, and a wage according to the collective agreements' rates for trainees, the 'vocational basic education' (*erhvervsgrunduddannelserne*, EGU),[9] which the IGU was modelled on. The wage rates for trainees vary between the collective agreements. The companies that hire IGU trainees receive a bonus of approximately 2700 euros per trainee when the IGU is initiated and another 2700 euros when it is completed. Importantly, the IGU is not the only measure in the Danish activation policies that could be used to support the refugees' labour market integration. It is a supplement to existing measures (Beskæftigelsesministeriet, 2016b). A few of the interviewees felt that the IGU was just 'introductory pay' by another name, whereas the majority of the interviewees emphasized that it was very different because it was time limited, limited to a target group and included a strong educational dimension.

Evaluating the process, some interviewees reported that it was a challenge with a brand new LO leader team and also that several of the other trade union representatives had no collective bargaining experience. This made it difficult for the trade unions to establish the necessary intra-organizational consensus on the IGU, because the low-skilled worker unions feared that some of their employed members would be replaced with refugees. It was clearly the trade unions that were under pressure in this first round of the tripartite negotiations.

Regarding the effects of the agreement, several interviewees pointed to the shift towards helping the refugees to prepare for work as an important step. By itself, this change is not sufficient to get the refugees into employment, but it is a necessary precondition to improving their employment rate. However, most attention was paid to the IGU. After a slow start, the number of IGU trainees reached 1200 in December 2017 (Udlændinge- og Integrationsministeriet, 2018), which the actors found encouraging. Since then the number has increased to 2067 as of April 2019.[10] It is also important to note that, following the signing of the tripartite agreement, Denmark received a much smaller number of refugees than expected. Hence, the pressure on the municipalities and the social partners was therefore less severe.

In December 2017, the whole agreement was put in danger when the immigrant-sceptical allies of the government, the Danish People's Party, put the government under pressure to reject the tripartite agreement as part of a political quid pro quo. However, the social partners gave a strong public warning that such a step would undermine the trustworthiness of the government and all future opportunities to strike tripartite agreements, and the government refused to resign.

CASE: TRIPARTITE AGREEMENT ON LABOUR SUPPLY 2016

According to the interviewees, the government explicitly made a successful first round of tripartite bargaining on refugees and integration a precondition for any further rounds of tripartite negotiations, where issues that were more important to the social partners could be addressed.

Agenda Setting

The government did not wait long before setting up the second round of the negotiations. Only one month after the first tripartite agreement was signed, the terms of reference for a second round were ready. Again, three themes were formulated: (1) prevention of barriers to recruitment; (2) practical training places – more skilled workers; and (3) continuing vocational training (CVT). The aim of the first theme was to improve the already high level of geographical and vocational mobility. For the second theme, the justification was a (long-lasting) problem of providing a sufficient number of practical training places for the dual vocational education system and for the third, to address a notable decrease in the use of CVT, which had always been at a comparatively high level in Denmark. It was the second theme that was the core theme of the negotiations. What made this theme especially important was that the dual vocational education system (where school-based training is combined with long periods of practical training in 'real' firms) is the backbone of Danish vocational education.

The various actors had different reasons for their interest in the core issue of the negotiations – that of expanding practical training places. LO had a strong interest in increasing the number of practical training places because this would improve the quality of their young members' education and most likely improve their employment opportunities later in life. In addition, they had a strong interest in the negotiations for procedural reasons, in that this second phase of the negotiations was supposed to include issues of greater interest for LO. The employers also had a strong interest in expanding the number of practical training places but, with no additional public funding for it, the fact that some of their members would have to deliver more than previously in one way or another, naturally made this an area of particular interest for them. The government's interests also included a greater supply of practical training places.

As with the first round, the prime minister indirectly framed the negotiations by promoting the government's message in the media and using the phrase, 'practical training places guarantee', which led DA to announce repeatedly that they were not able to deliver a guarantee. According to some of the interviewees, the prime minister aimed to put the parties under pressure by sending the message that if you do not agree to deliver, we as a government will force you to deliver – a clear case of what Scharpf (1993) has labelled 'negotiations in the shadow of hierarchy'.

Decision-making Process

The ALMP measures were mostly found under the first theme, 'Prevention of barriers to recruitment'. An important point for discussion under this theme was the government's aim of extending the geographical demand for job seeking to the whole country. Previously, such a demand only existed for people with medium to high levels of education or professionals (persons with academic degrees). However, this suggestion was met with strong opposition from trade union representatives. LO as well as FTF argued that the labour market as well as the wage levels for skilled and unskilled workers were very different from those for professionals and pointed to research that forecast very limited employment effects from the extension that the government had in mind. Furthermore, they made it clear to the Minister of Employment that there would be no agreement at all if the geographical extension was part of it. Another important issue under the first theme was the list of educational programmes approved for the 'six weeks of job-focused education' (see case on Employment Policy Reform, 2014). But the most controversial issue was the level of unemployment benefit an unemployed person would receive when in education. The trade unions pushed to lift this from 80 per cent to 100 per cent of the UI maximum if the education was connected to jobs in areas with labour shortages.

With regard to the core second theme, DA's stated inability early in the process to deliver a guarantee de facto excluded this option. With the exclusion of a guarantee from the agenda, the decision-making process focused at an early stage on models for economic incentives to stimulate the companies to set up practical training places. Three major challenges had to be addressed. First, the fact that economic incentives were being introduced without adding additional public funding meant that some companies were going to have to pay for not providing their quota for practical training places, and the employers' organizations therefore had strong and diverging interests in the negotiations according to whether their members, on average, were over- or undersupplying practical training places. Second, the government wanted to provide more favourable conditions for vocational education within areas of high labour demand. However, since this demand fluctuates over time, some kind of forecasting was needed – and accurate forecasting is difficult. Third, diverging interests between LO, FTF and AC were also a challenge, though perhaps not so big as the two others. For obvious reasons, LO wanted a focus on low-skilled workers, whereas FTF and AC (also) wanted to focus on further training, which could be of benefit to their members.

The interviewees described the process as being long and difficult. The employers – who in this round were the actors most under pressure – took a long time to agree amongst themselves on an economic incentive-based model, and it was, unsurprisingly, difficult for them to reach the necessary consensus between the parties. Some of the trade union interviewees reported that DA communicated directly with government representatives, so that the close DA–LO process from the first phase was not repeated. However, other trade union interviewees found themselves closely involved, but added, in line with other interviewees, that in the end the employers were allowed to decide themselves how the model for practical training places should be constructed.

The employers suggested very detailed mathematical models, including forecasting, which did not get support from the other two actors who found the models too complicated. However, there was an understanding among the other two actors that it was basically about internal distributions of the economic burden on the employers' side. At some point in the process, the government informed the employers that they could decide on the model, but that they had to finance it themselves.

With regard to the third theme, it was clear, early on in the process, that it would not be possible to achieve much within the time frame of the second round of tripartite negotiations, but that preparation for a Commission might be the possible outcome.

Outcome and Effects

The agreement was signed in August 2016 and was divided into three headings echoing the three themes of the negotiations (Regeringen og arbejdsmarkedets parter, 2016b). Most features of the agreement were included under the second heading, 'More Practical Training Places – More Skilled Workers'. The most important features of the agreement could be said to be:

- allocation of resources to improve qualifications of the unemployed for jobs in areas of high labour demand;
- more flexible use of the six weeks of vocationally targeted education;
- increase from 80 to 100 per cent of UI maximum if an unemployed person starts vocational education in areas with labour shortages;
- vocational education in areas with high labour demand to receive a bonus of 5000 DKK for each practical training place they set up;
- a target for establishing 8000–10 000 more practical training places within four years;
- reduction of the contribution to the Social Partners Educational Contribution (AUB) for those companies that reach their target for practical training places, and an economic penalty (27 000 DKK per training place) for those that do not;
- bonus to companies that are increasing their numbers of practical training places, to be agreed during 2017 with the social partners.

The issues of bonuses to companies was de facto postponed. The reason for this was that DA's largest member organization, DI, on the last day of the negotiation, found the formulation of a bonus of 'up to 15 000 DKK' (2000 euros) to be too low. The employers were able to reopen this part of the agreement in phase 3 of the tripartite negotiations (see Section 3.5).

The smallest section of the agreement was found under the heading, 'Adult Education and Further Training'. The most important element here was the set-up of an expert group on CVT – and a 'follow-up group' with participation of the social partners – with the aim of strengthening the content and use of CVT.

One way to evaluate the agreement is to look at who got what. All parties were (potentially) able to benefit from an agreement that had the potential to increase the number of practical training places. However, as expected, it was the employers who had to pay for the economic incentives in the case of underperformance, and some employers more than others. The government got some of the ALMP measures they had proposed, but the trade unions got 100 per cent of the UI maximum they requested for education as a means of activation in areas with labour shortages and also avoided the demand for extended job search activities. The more flexible use of the six weeks of vocationally targeted education was in the interests of all three parties.

The interviewees' evaluation of the negotiation process differed between and within the three parties. All three parties felt that the agreement was important, despite their above-mentioned scepticism with regard to its immediate effect. However, all three parties were also critical of the other parties' actions. Some of the social partner interviewees felt that the government representatives clearly showed they were not 'in practice' with regard to negotiations with the social partners and felt that the Ministry of Employment 'muddled through' the process. More specifically, it was reported that the government representatives did not acknowledge that social partner organizations are political organizations too, which means that getting clear mandates takes time. Moreover, the pressure applied by the government's 'guarantee rhetoric' was criticized. However, the social partner organizations also criticized each other. Most likely as a result of the fact that the greatest pressure was on the employers in this round, they were criticized for having difficulty in creating the necessary intra-organizational consensus and for not sufficiently being able to communicate a common position.

3.5   CONTINUING VOCATIONAL TRAINING

Continuing vocational training (CVT) in Denmark has, to a larger extent than in most other EU countries, been publicly financed. With 27 per cent of employees participating in CVT within the last four weeks in 2017, Denmark ranks third among EU countries, and somewhat higher than the Netherlands (18 per cent) and Austria (17 per cent) (Eurostat, 2019b). However, longitudinal measurement shows a downward trend. The annual indicator of 'adult participation in learning' has been reduced from 32 per cent to 27 per cent in just three years between 2014 and 2017.

The interaction between the state and the social partners in CVT is directly related to relations in vocational education that have a longer history.

From the Introduction to the Great Recession

In 1937, the role of the social partners was institutionalized, when the so-called 'occupational self-governance' (*det faglige selvstyre*) was consolidated as the governance model for vocational education. This mode of governance – in a similar way to the 'self-governance' in Ebbinghaus's (2002) typology – granted the social partners decision-making power in a large number of tripartite 'occupational committees' at national as well as sector and local levels. In these bodies, the social partners were entitled to a majority of the seats, while the remaining seats were occupied by state representatives. These bodies had the responsibility of developing the content of the courses. The occupational committees covered specific branches or sectors (Nielsen, 1993).

This governance structure of vocational education has had a major influence on CVT. CVT took off when the 'labour market course centres' (AMU centres) were established in the 1960s. AMU was triggered by the economic upturn in the late 1950s and the 1960s, which brought about a growing demand for (trained) labour, and by the increasing wage level for unskilled workers, which meant that fewer unskilled workers than hitherto felt inclined to undergo a vocational education.

During the years, many kinds of further education and training have been developed, some more vocational than others. The numerous shorter as well as longer courses can be divided into vocational adult education and training (in which AMUs are one of the cornerstones), general adult education and training and general education (*folkeoplysning*). The social partners are involved and take an interest in all three areas, but the interest and involvement are greatest in relation to vocational adult education and training.

The institutional set-up of continuing training includes tripartite bodies at all levels: an inter-sectoral tripartite council advising the minister; sector-based tripartite bodies called 'Further Training Councils'; and boards of the individual schools. In general, even though the overall design of the courses has remained at the national level, the tripartite boards at the schools have been granted more and more responsibilities regarding the schools' budget and supply of courses since the late 1980s due to a decentralization of competencies, at the same time as market-simulating ways of steering the schools were introduced.

A reform in 1995 – which was prepared in various ad hoc committees with social partner involvement – increased the role of demand management and targeting of the courses to local demand. Other important changes from the 1990s onwards meant that the vocational schools were allowed to supply AMU courses, that CVT developed into the most used ALMP policy tool, and that rights to CVT were introduced in a large number of collective agreements. Moreover, a new general secretary in LO emphasized the role of the social partners in the provision of welfare, including CVT (Mailand, 1999; Mailand et al., 2008).

A major CVT reform in 2001 was prepared in a pre-legislative committee without the participation of the social partners. During the committee's work there were reports that ministers were increasingly accusing the social partners of being defenders of 'yesterday's industrial society' and hence an obstacle to implementation of new and modern education schemes (Mailand, 2008).

However, the committee's white paper concluded that the involvement of the social partners was necessary because, as user representatives, they knew what the new qualification demands were. Still, the division of labour between the social partners and the public authorities was described in the white paper as 'not appropriate in all cases' (Arbejdsministeriet, Undervisningsministeriet and Finansministeriet, 1999). Although not in itself a product of tripartite work, the white paper was discussed in the then newly established tripartite committee, 'Tripartite Forum' (see above). During the negotiations, the social partners agreed on most elements of the reform as proposed in the white paper, including, after some time, the guidelines for the Labour Market Financing of Education and Training that later became one of the new features of the reform. Hence, what started out as a process the social partners were excluded from, ended up in a concertation process (Mailand et al., 2008).

The reform of CVT was agreed upon in Parliament in 2001 during the last year of the Social Democratic government. It merged some of the tripartite bodies but did not fundamentally change the structure of consultative bodies. However, a new tripartite Board for the Labour Market Financing of Education and Training was set up. The board was asked to advise on the overall scope of continuing education and financing of the activities and how the different activities should be weighted. If the predicted activities exceeded the budgetary limit, the board had the opportunity of requesting additional funding from employers (Mailand, 1999).

After, confusingly, having cut public expenditure for continuing training and increased it again in 2004, the Liberal-Conservative government's statements seem to have stabilized around the consensus that education, training, research and innovation are the way forward in order to sustain Denmark's competitiveness. Because the government was busy winding up knowledge centres, councils, committees and similar bodies in their first year in office, it came as a surprise to many when the prime minister announced a 'tripartite+' (government, social partners, researchers) Globalization Council. The council was a de facto think tank where research, education and training made up a great part of what was discussed. The council's agreement and a number of sub-agreements were incorporated into the government's globalization strategy from April 2006, which contained 350 different actions. Thus, the Globalization Council did not make decisions on new initiatives themselves, but some of their proposals were picked up on in the 2007 private sector collective bargaining round (Mailand et al., 2008).

The Liberal-Conservative government also initiated tripartite cooperation more directly focused on further training. Early in 2004, contacts between stakeholders identified a common interest in ensuring lifelong learning for all. The government's agenda in this area coincided with LO's strategic interests but was also sufficiently consistent with many employers' ideas about the need for competence development under the new conditions created by intensified competition. Preparation of new initiatives took place in a tripartite committee in September 2004. The committee completed its work in February 2006, after which the parties and the government in March 2006 signed a tripartite agreement in the form of the so-called 'Lifelong Learning and Acceleration of All in the Labour Market'. The prime minister compared the presentation of the final document of the tripartite lifelong learning agreement directly with the situation in the late 1980s and early 1990s, where the collective agreement-based occupational pension schemes were developed, and stated that the new decision on lifelong learning could prove equally significant for the labour market and for Danish society. The government itself contributed 1 billion DKK extra (approximately 130 million euros) in the form of the so-called Globalization Fund. The social partners took on the task at the 2007 private sector collective bargaining round, where 'competence development funds' were set up. A similar tripartite agreement and follow-up process took place in the public sector in 2008 (Due and Madsen, 2008).

Since the Great Recession

Until 2017, the post-2008 period did not provide many CVT initiatives, either with tripartite processes or without. One of the few was an amalgamation in 2009 of the two national tripartite advisory councils for general adult education and for CVT respectively into the National Council for Education and Continuing Training. They were amalgamated in order to strengthen the links between the two areas.

One single tripartite agreement from the period can be mentioned. In February 2013, the Liberal-Conservative government introduced Growth Plan DK. One of several aims of the plan was to strengthen CVT. The use of publicly funded CVT – especially the AMU – was declining at the same time as the business cycle was improving. Taken together this could have contributed to a situation where companies could not receive sufficient qualified labour.

The growth plan aimed to strengthen CVT through initiatives under eight different headings at a total cost of 1 billion DKK, including, inter alia, the introduction of the opportunity for adults to take vocational basic education (not only further training), more flexibility in the AMU system and up-qualification of more skilled workers to qualifications at a professional level. The specific initiative was agreed with the social partners, whereas the Growth Plan itself was a political agreement. Hence, it was a tripartite agreement on the implementation but not on the policy formulation, and the government and the social partners did not consider it to be a 'tripartite agreement'.

While the period did not provide a great deal of new CVT initiatives, a major vocational education reform was agreed upon in 2014. The aim was to increase the quality of vocational education and to increase the share of the youth cohort choosing this kind of education. In 2013, the government set up negotiations on a 'Vocational Education and Competency Education in the Adult and Further Education System' with strong social partner (DA and LO) representation to prepare for reform, but disagreement about how the quality of the education should be improved prolonged the discussion and did not achieve a consensus. Nevertheless, LO and DA later published a paper (LO and DA, 2013) on how they believed the reform should look. This plan was more ambitious than the government's. The government's subsequent reform proposal included several of LO and DA's main recommendations (Carstensen and Ibsen, 2015, 2019). Thus, a form of tripartite consensus was obtained in the end, and one of the basic features of the Danish model, that it can be difficult to ignore joint ideas from LO and DA, was confirmed.

CASE: CVT TRIPARTITE AGREEMENT 2017

The 2010s had revealed several problems with regard to CVT in Denmark. Although the use of CVT opportunities remained at a comparatively high level, a 50 per cent reduction in AMU activity took place from 2010 to 2015. Several possible explanations were suggested, including too much bureaucracy and very complicated rules for companies who wanted to use the courses, too little relevance to the needs of the companies in terms of the content of the courses, and a 2011 reduction in remuneration that companies received when their employees took part in the courses (Jørgensen et al., 2017). As described above, the issue was planned to be included in the second round of tripartite agreements in 2016, but, in fact, not much was included on the issue. Therefore, a third round was planned.

Agenda Setting

A break in the stream of tripartite negotiations was necessary between the second and the third phases for two reasons. First, the collective bargaining round in the private sector needed to be completed. It was completed as planned in April 2017. Second, the Expert Group on Adult and Continuing Training – the set-up of which was part of the round 2 tripartite agreement – first had to complete their work. This they did in June 2017. The expert group included five members, four from universities and other knowledge producing units, and one from the Ministry of Employment. The social partners were consulted through a 'reference group'. The expert group's final report pointed to a number of challenges in the CVT system, among them a high level of complexity in the supply of CVT, lack of coordination and coherence between different levels in the system, a mismatch between supply of and demand for

CVT, and a lack of evaluations of the learning-related benefits of the courses. To meet these challenges, the expert group's report mentioned recommendations under 13 headings. These included, inter alia: one entrance for all to the CVT system; individual learning accounts; improved basic competences; targeting of the publicly financed supply of participants towards core courses (and reducing the supply of the number of courses from 3200 to 800); and new roles for the social partners, including actions as 'ambassadors for education' and contributions to the financing of the individual learning accounts (Ekspertgruppen for voksen-, efter- og videreuddannelse, 2017).[11]

The tripartite negotiations started in June 2017. The terms of reference mentioned a focus on 'basic adult education and vocational further training', and two broad themes in connection to this: (1) a stronger, more coherent and more flexible CVT system; and (2) more balanced employer contributions to the financing of CVT. The latter included questions about what to do with unused employers' contributions to CVT, which the drop in the demand for CVT courses had caused. It was furthermore clear from the terms of reference that the focus would be on further training for people with little or no basic education.

Policy Formulation

Between the second and the third phases of the tripartite negotiations, the Minister of Employment was replaced, not out of dissatisfaction with the minister, but due to a change in the make-up of the Liberal-Conservative government to include yet another Liberal Party. The new minister, Troels Lund Poulsen, did not have his predecessor Jørn Neergaard Larsen's long experience in the labour market field. In fact, the interviewees found the new minister to be much more personally involved in the negotiations and much less reliant on his staff than the former minister. However, there was no agreement between the interviewees on whether this was a good or a bad thing. Another difference between the third round of tripartite negotiations and the two other rounds, was that the government, prior to round 3, did not attempt to put pressure on social partners by proposing measures via the media that would be extraordinarily difficult or impossible for the social partners to deliver.

The expert group's recommendations were – according to the interviewees who reported on this issue – not used directly for the most part, although a couple of the recommendations were discussed, including reducing the number of courses supplied (which related to the expert group's recommendation on targeting) and the individual learning accounts. Individual learning accounts were only addressed very briefly. Trade union representatives, in particular, were very sceptical about these.

Three themes dominated the decision-making process. The first of these was the unused financial resources, which became the most debated issue. DA wanted the unused resources transferred back to the employers, whereas LO wanted the resources to be used to boost CVT activity. The unused resources had, according to the government, been re-budgeted for other purposes for the coming years and, because this was the case, Danish budget legislation (on the public budgets) meant that a transfer of the money back to the companies was not possible. By mid-October – the initial deadline for the negotiations – this problem was still not solved – to the frustration of the social partners. In the end, the problem was solved and a part of the unused resources was transferred back to the companies. According to some interviewees, the real barrier was not the budget legislation but that some politicians wanted to use the unused resources for other means.

The second dominant theme was the question of a reduction in the number of courses. This theme was mostly debated in the early phases of the decision-making process. The government wanted a reduction in the number of courses but, unlike the expert group, they never specified the number of courses they had in mind. The social partner representatives, on their part, did not see a reduction in the number of courses as an aim in itself. Part of the explanation of why the issue gradually became less pressing was that both DA and LO were of the opinion that courses for which there was a demand should be supplied.

Third, the issue of stimulating and qualifying demand for CVT was also much in focus in the negotiations. It was easier for the three parties to agree on this than on the other two issues. Measures to improve basic competences, screening of competences, the set-up of one digital entrance to all types of CVT and more flexibility in courses with regard to the needs of the companies were all discussed in connection with this issue.

Similar to the first round of tripartite negotiations (on refugees), a substantial part of the decision-making process was a bipartite process between DA and LO. DA and LO delivered a proposal two weeks before the end of the negotiations for the main elements of a tripartite agreement. What they asked for was more expensive than the Ministry of Employment had a mandate to deliver. The challenges in this regard contributed to last-minute problems in the negotiations. An interesting part of the DA–LO draft for an agreement was that the bonus companies received for setting up individual training places – settled in phase 2 for 'up to 15 000 DKK' per student – was increased to '25 000 DKK'. This was a DA/DI priority. As a quid pro quo for supporting this, LO secured an agreement that the vocational education schools should receive 150 million DKK for the annual budget for 2018 to improve the quality of the education.

At the end of the process there turned out to be some disagreement between the Ministry of Employment and the Ministry of Education on one side, and the Ministry of Finance on the other. This was a traditional disagreement in the sense that it regarded the overall financial resources that the ministry thought should be on a lower level than the two other ministries.

The Outcome and Evaluations

The tripartite agreement on CVT was signed at the end of October 2017. Under the two headings from the terms of reference, 81 initiatives were listed. The agreement was for four years and included expenses totalling 3.5 billion DKK. The most important of the initiatives could be summarized as follows:

- a Conversion Fund: 400 million DKK to lift the unskilled to the skilled level;
- improved basic competences: 200 million DKK to improve basic competences in writing, reading, maths, English and IT and to improve knowledge about the courses;
- an increase in CVT remuneration from 80 to 100 per cent of UI maximum for all AMU courses;
- 420 million DKK to improve the quality of AMU courses;
- more flexible use of AMU courses; better opportunities to tailor-make courses to the needs of companies;
- one entrance to the CVT system, including one national advisory unit for companies and individuals;
- transfer of unused resources (680 million DKK) back to companies and a new budgeting model – based on actual CVT activity – to avoid unused resources piling up again;
- continuous termination of courses with no activity during the previous three years;
- bonus to companies for the setting-up of one practical training place increased from 'up to 15 000 DKK' to 25 000 DKK;
- government set-up of a working group regarding CVT for persons with longer initial education (Regeringen og arbejdsmarkedets parter, 2017).

The reactions to the agreement were mixed. While DA and LO and their member organizations, not surprisingly, welcomed the agreement, among the trade unions' confederations participating in the negotiations AC and, to some extent, FTF felt that the agreement included too little of relevance for their member groups. This criticism was also aired publicly (e.g., Birkman, 2017). In addition, other interviewees found the agreement to be very unambitious and did not feel that the lack of employee incentives to participate in CVT was sufficiently addressed. However, this position was questioned by others, who thought that a tripartite agreement would never be able to solve all the major problems in the CVT system, including the employees' lack of willingness to take up training. Some of the social partner interviewees furthermore appreciated the fact that the government refrained from presenting a 'quick fix' prior to the negotiations in order to put the social partners under pressure, as they did in rounds 1 and 2 of the tripartite negotiations.

It is still too early to evaluate the effect of the agreement, since part of it was implemented as late as 2018. So far, it seems that the drop in the AMU-related CVT activity level has been changed to a small increase (Bay, 2019). With regard to the question of who got what, all three parties will benefit from a CVT system with higher levels of activity and higher quality in the courses; and from courses that are more targeted to the needs of companies and employees (if the initiatives work as intended). Focusing on the different dimensions of the agreement separately, first and foremost, the government got a third tripartite agreement, which in itself was a major achievement, although the price in financial terms was higher than planned. Additionally, the agreement takes some small steps towards targeting their priorities. The employers were successful in getting part of the unused resources returned, as well as a new economic model to prevent the piling up of unused resources in the future, and greater flexibility in the courses to meet the needs of companies. Moreover, they got increased bonuses for companies setting up practical training places. The trade unions got the Conversion Fund, the increased remuneration rate and extra funding to improve the quality of the vocational schools. Furthermore, the social partners avoided the large-scale reduction in course supply, which the expert group proposed, and had to accept only a limited reduction. Moreover, they avoided the individual learning accounts, which the trade unions especially disliked.

3.6   DISCUSSION

In this section, Danish developments will be discussed. The discussion will be linked to the research questions and the hypotheses.

To what extent are tripartite arrangements still used?
First, it is noteworthy that the frequency of tripartite policy formulation has increased rather than decreased since the Great Recession. Although only a rough indicator, this is illustrated by the list of major tripartite agreements (Table 3.2), which includes ten agreements in the 22-year period of 1987–2008 and seven in the ten-year period of 2009–18. Although these agreements vary with regard to the influence of the social partners and their impact, there is

no systematic difference pointing in the direction of greater involvement or impact in the first period as compared to the others – or vice versa.

However, there are, in the post-2008 period, examples of the side-lining of the trade unions that can only be interpreted as major defeats. After the trade unions had, with some success, defended the UI system during the 2000s (so only the uninsured unemployed really felt the government's 'make work pay' policy) they could no longer protect the system in 2010. And contrary to the reductions in the maximum benefit period during the 1990s, the 2010 reduction: (1) had no trade-off with improvement in ALMP; (2) did not include consultation or negotiations with the social partners; and (3) was accompanied by an increase in the threshold for regaining UI from six months to one year of employment. Also, the Job Centre Reform of 2009, with its full municipalization of the activation policies, was a defeat for the trade unions and partly also for DA, which, like LO, had been very critical of full municipalization.

However, these two examples are the last obvious cases of trade union defeats. There have been no newer decision-making processes, indicating that corporatism has been further weakened in the present decade in the three areas under examination here. There have been a number of reforms without any notable involvement of the social partners with regard to issues closely related to ALMP, namely social assistance and sickness/disability benefits. However, the social partners' involvement in these issues has always been weaker than in ALMP, so the recent lack of involvement in these areas does not represent any notable change.[12] When the increased tripartite frequency is added, the general picture is that the social partners' influence has not been further reduced in the post-2008 period in the three areas analysed. This is the case both with the trade unions' influence, and, even more so, with the employers, given that there are fewer examples of their lack of influence.

Second, focusing on the last 30-year period, it appears that tripartite agreements (concertation) were more common in the CVT and ALMP areas than in the UI area, as indicated by Table 3.2. As for UI, the tripartite agreement behind the UI reform in 2015 is the only major tripartite agreement in the area where UI was the main focus, although UI was a secondary issue in two other tripartite agreements. However, applying Ebbinghaus's (2002) typology, in the UI area self-organization also played a role and secured the trade unions' strong influence without tripartite agreements, at least on implementation issues.

In terms of the depth of involvement, there might be a difference between the ALMP and the two other areas. Apparently, although this is not always the case, governments in this area more often use 'social partner involvement-lite' than in the other two areas. By using this type of involvement, the government seeks to control the influence of the social partners by involving them separately and late in the decision-making process and/or placing them in separate consultation forums away from the core decision-making processes. One of the reasons for the government to use this lighter form of involvement in the ALMP area might be previous experiences where the social partners, through joint positions and proposals, have gained more influence than the government planned, as happened, for instance, in the 1998 'Labour Market Reform 3'.

Are the social partners still able to influence the regulation?

Third, looking deeper into the social partners' influence, the analyses show that social partners are still able to exercise decisive influence on work and welfare through tripartite agreements. In other words, the decisions are of importance and the social partners are not only rubber-stamping the initiatives of various governments and are not (only) taking part in tripartite negotiations for procedural reasons. The fact that the social partners are still able to influence policy formulation through tripartite agreements is illustrated by numerous examples. In the UI area, although the trade unions were excluded from the major 2010 reform, their influence was strong (and stronger than the employers) on the 'medium-sized' 2015 reform, where the employers were satisfied with protecting the 'core' of the 2010 reform. Also in the 'minor' 2017 reform, which was limited to solo self-employed people and hybrid employees, the social partners were able to influence the outcome through a tripartite arrangement, although the social partner 'footprints' might be less strong here than on the 2015 reform. In the ALMP area, the Employment Policy Reform included few, but nonetheless important, concessions to the trade unions. In the tripartite agreement on refugees in 2016, the social partners managed to prevent an introductory salary and LO and DA formulated the core of the agreement, the IGU. LO furthermore avoided changes in the maximum ratio for 'activation employees'/ordinary employees and, somewhat under the radar, DA seemed to manage unilaterally to influence the part of the agreement about the municipalities/job centres approach to refugees as such. The 2017 tripartite agreement on labour supply again included small changes that the social partners had asked for. All parties had an interest in achieving changes to the system for practical training. Although some employers' organizations had to pay more into the system than previously, the agreement could not be said to be 'employer unfriendly'. Also in the CVT area, the social partners have managed to influence policy through tripartite arrangements in the last decade, although the agreements have been fewer here, and they have largely been able to sustain the strong influence they have had for decades in the administration and implementation of CVT policies.

Fourth, this chapter shows that the employers and the trade unions are far stronger when acting jointly and shows the DA–LO axis is still strong, although it might have been stronger previously. Although the DA–LO consensus is no longer always a sufficient condition for strong influence – as the

Structural Reform of 2004–07 and the Job Centre Reform of 2009 illustrate – it certainly helps for the two major confederations to join forces, as a number of the employment policy areas from the 2010s illustrate. The three phases of tripartite agreements of 2016–17 clearly show that.

Fifth, the way the social partners as well as the government seek to obtain influence has changed. However, this is not a brand new development. Studies from the 2000s (e.g., Christiansen and Klitgaard, 2008; Mailand, 2008; Torfing, 2004) have illuminated the fact that the agenda-setting phase (prior to the formal decision making) has become increasingly important and that the social partners, partly as a response to this, have upgraded their external communication efforts with newsletters and a stronger presence in the media. Cases such as the UI reform of 2015, with its extremely long agenda-setting phase, and the first and second rounds of the tripartite negotiations of 2016–17 with their push for an introductory wage and practical places' guarantee, as well as DA's early and detailed proposals during the first round, illustrate that the observations from researchers in the 2000s are still relevant.

Sixth, yet another finding confirms a development that has been pointed out in studies from the 2000s (e.g., Andersen and Mailand, 2002; Bredgaard and Larsen, 2009; Torfing, 2004): the social partners increasingly have to share the decision-making arena with other actors. This development is seen in the pre-legislative bodies where the social partners (if they are represented at all) always have to share their representation with academics and other experts, as the Unemployment Insurance Commission illustrates; or they are placed in secondary groups, as in the case of the Employment Policy Reform of 2014 and the UI reform for the self-employed. This differs from previous practice in the 1990s. Furthermore, primarily in the ALMP area, tripartite bodies of all forms from the 2000s and onwards have stronger and more frequent participation of, not only Local Government Denmark and Danish Regions, but also a number of voluntary organizations, changing them from pure tripartite fora to 'tripartite+' or multipartite fora. A plausible explanation for this development is primarily that in the ALMP area, to a greater extent than in the two other areas, the trade unions share their implementation role with other actors, such as the municipalities and representatives of specific target groups, such as disabled people.

Which factors explain best the development?
Finally, when discussing the four explanatory factors from the theoretical section on the Danish empirical analyses only, the short answer is that the Great Recession has not, to any great extent, influenced the frequency of tripartite agreements, while from a 30-year perspective, there is a clear tendency for right-wing/centre-right governments and weak governments to strike more tripartite agreements. However, the tendency is not strong, which indicates

that the actors' content-specific choices are decisive. This short answer is elaborated below.

There were no tripartite agreements, nor any attempts to strike any for around three years after the Great Recession began. This could indicate an effect of the crisis. However, first, the period is not especially long, as can be seen from Table 3.2. Second, if there was such an effect, it has proved temporary. The frequency of tripartite agreements has increased rather than decreased since the Great Recession. Moreover, the impact of the Great Recession itself was not explicitly a subject of tripartite negotiations (Refslund and Lind, 2019). The only tripartite negotiation in the crisis period (late 2008 to 2012) of the Great Recession was the failed tripartite negotiation on a 'social pact' in 2012 and the first Acute Agreement from the same year. However, although the Great Recession was only addressed in a few tripartite negotiations, it has formed the context for tripartite agreements and other political agreements due to the demand for budget savings or freezes on spending.

The power of the social partners is another of the key potential explanatory factors for the quantity and quality of tripartism. Although still comparatively strong, the Danish trade unions have been weakened by gradually declining membership (a weakening of their organizational power resources) and loosening links with the Social Democrats (a weakening of their political resources), at the same time as fragmentation has occurred, in the sense that the biggest confederation has lost power relative to the member organizations, and that a new single dominant organization did not develop as it did on the employer side, before 2019. The failed 2012 tripartite negotiation was a clear illustration of the trade unions' problem with fragmentation. It remains to be seen whether the trade unions, following the creation of a new confederation in 2019, will be able to act in a less fragmented fashion. The employers' organizations have not lost power to the same degree. Their organizational power resources in terms of membership and organizational density have been stable, and the structural development of the employers' organizations has produced one dominant member organization of the confederation in the form of DI. Moreover, their political powers might actually have increased since their contacts with, and influence on, Social Democratic governments seem to have become stronger in the 2010s.

With regard to the ideology of the government as an explanatory factor, Table 3.2 illustrates that, in the 30-year period in focus, governments with a Liberal or Conservative leader have signed 12 tripartite agreements over the 18 years they were in power, and Social Democratic-led governments have signed five agreements over the 12 years they were in office. Hence, the Liberal/Conservative-led governments have signed more tripartite agreements per year in government than the Social Democrats, although the difference is not huge. An explanation for this could be that since the trade union movement is more eager to participate in tripartite agreements than the employers' organizations, the former are likely to strike agreements with both Social Democratic as well as Liberal/Conservative governments, while the latter are more selective and prefer only to strike agreements with Liberal/Conservative governments.

The fourth explanatory factor, the strength of the governments, is more difficult to test, because the classification of strong and weak governments is not always straightforward. I have, however – based on various other Danish researchers' classifications – made such an attempt (Mailand, 2019), which will be used here. The strong–weak classification is primarily, but not only, based on whether the government represents a majority in Parliament and whether it is internally united or divided. The Conservative-led government of 1982–87 was strong and excluded the trade unions in some policy areas (Christiansen, Nørgaard and Sidenius, 2004) but nevertheless signed one of the most important tripartite agreements – the Common Declaration – in 1987. The Conservative-led governments 1988–91 were weak and laid the groundwork for another important tripartite arrangement by setting up the ALMP (and UI) pre-legislative Zeuthen Committee. The Social Democratic-led government of 1992–94 was strong and did not sign any tripartite agreements (but did include the Zeuthen Committee's recommendations in their Employment Policy Reform), whereas the Social Democratic-led governments of 1994–2001 were weak and achieved two tripartite agreements (the one 'involuntary' on the government side). The Liberal-led government of 2001–07 was strong and did challenge the trade unions, but nevertheless signed four tripartite agreements, whereas the strong Liberal-led government of 2007–09 was, in general, more open towards the social partners and signed two such agreements. The strong Liberal government of 2007–11 again challenged the trade unions and signed no tripartite agreements. The Social Democratic-led government of 2011–15 was weak (due to internal tensions). This government's tripartite activities included a failed attempt at a social pact, but three successful attempts at tripartite agreements (although one of them was only concluded after the government lost power). The following Liberal-led governments of 2015–17 were (very) weak and signed four agreements (and completed the agreement of the UI Commission). Summing up, in the 35-year period between 1982 and 2017, there were around 19 years with weak governments that, altogether, signed ten tripartite agreements (0.53 agreements per year) and around 16 years with strong governments that signed six tripartite agreements (0.38 agreements per year). Hence, in Denmark, weak governments seem to be slightly more likely to sign tripartite agreements than strong governments, although the difference between the two types is small, especially considering the uncertainty over the classifications.

Summing up the four explanatory factors, the analysis showed a possible, limited effect from the Great Recession and some limited effect from government ideology and government strength, whereas the continued loss of trade union power has not prevented them from being invited to tripartite negotiations and being able to influence work and welfare policies through tripartism, just as the employers' organizations have. However, this does not exclude the possibility that the trade unions' loss of power has had a longer-term effect on their tripartite role and abilities.

The fact that the four selected explanatory factors only have limited explanatory power in the Danish case could indicate either that other factors – such as those presented in Chapter 2 – could be at play or that the context-specific choices of the actors are what is of most importance. Specifically, the context-specific choices of the government might be important in responding to the following scenario: in the given political situation and with the given nature of the content of the initiative, what are the pros and cons of involving the social partners, including the likelihood that they will support it without too many concessions? Also, what are the pros and cons for the social partners in terms of asking for tripartite negotiations or accepting invitations to them?

NOTES

1. In January 2019, LO and the Confederation of Professionals in Denmark (Funktionærernes og Tjenestemændenes Fællesråd, FTF) merged into the Danish Trade Union Confederation (Fagbevægelsens Hovedorganisation, FH) – see below.
2. See https://www.worker-participation.eu/. Accessed 5 October 2018.
3. See https://dors.dk/english. Accessed 6 January 2018.
4. The Globalization Council 2004–05 included several issues (CVT, VET, entrepreneurship, etc.) and could be seen as another exception. However, its agreement was mainly made up of a catalogue of aspirations and did not lead to any specific policy initiative as such. It was, nevertheless, instrumental in establishing consensus in the areas mentioned and is therefore included in the table.
5. Wage-subsidy jobs targeted at persons risking their right to unemployment insurance in the near future.
6. Danish Regions's overall mission is to safeguard the interests of the five Danish regions, at national and international level, assisting them with services and relevant information.
7. Although the Labour Exchange Act from 1914 established a national public employment service as well as national and local tripartite forums (Nørgaard, 2007), it is common to see 1969 as the beginning of a real ALMP system, where ALMP was not just an appendix to the unemployment benefit system.
8. Actually, there were two tracks in the negotiations: a bipartite track between the government and Local Government Denmark and Danish Regions and a tripartite track between the government and the social partners, including Local Government Denmark and Danish Regions.

9.   The EGU is a special type of vocational education with longer periods with an employer and shorter periods at school, compared to the standard dual vocational education.
10. See https://integrationsbarometer.dk/. Accessed 4 February 2019.
11. During the winter of 2017, the chair of the expert group resigned because DA and LO were not willing to deliver information about the competence funds for CVT that are linked to the collective agreements in the DA–LO area. DA and LO explained their lack of willingness to provide the information as a way to avoid disturbing the (at that time) ongoing collective bargaining round in the private sector (Fris, 2017). A new chair was found shortly afterwards.
12. In one area clearly beyond the focus of the present book, trade unions have been challenged very directly. During the collective bargaining round of 2013 in the public sector, the public sector employers and the government – after failed bargaining and arbitration and a legal intervention – removed working time from the collective bargaining arena and made it a management prerogative (Mailand, 2016b).

4. The Netherlands: formal tripartite structures and weakened trade unions

4.1 THE INSTITUTIONAL SET-UP OF LABOUR MARKET REGULATION

In most of the labour market and welfare state regime studies, the Netherlands is placed in a continental 'corporatist', 'conservative' or – in the case of Visser (2008) – 'social partnership' cluster. In Visser's understanding, the social partners have a great deal of influence, but not as much as in the Nordic corporatist cluster. In the social partnership cluster, the social partners' autonomy exists in the shadow of the state.

The Dutch version of corporatism is often labelled the 'polder model'. Polder refers to the low-lying tracts of land enclosed by dikes, which are widespread in the Netherlands. In the polder model, the trade unions and employers' organizations have, for many decades, played a key role in the design and implementation of social and labour market policy (Keune, 2016; Visser and Hemerijck, 1997). Through social pacts, collective agreements, national bi- and tripartite institutions and a whole plethora of implementation and consultative functions, they have established themselves as key players in the economy and welfare state.

The Historical Development of the Labour Market Model

According to Keune (2016), a large number of authors claim that collaboration, seeking compromises and sharing political power are historical characteristics of Dutch society, and that these characteristics originate from the joint struggle to hold back the water and drain the polders in the late Middle Ages. This tradition of cooperation has lasted and is still a feature of the contemporary Dutch model. Prak and van Zanden (2013) indicate that the model has undergone fundamental changes over the centuries in main three periods: first, the agricultural economy, then the trade economy and finally the industrial economy. After World War II, the polder model was initially characterized by a centralized wage policy, but since the Wassenaar Agreement in 1982 (see below), the state has had a more limited role in industrial relations and employ-ers' organizations while the role of the unions has increased.

The involvement of social partners has also taken place in ad hoc nego-tiations as well as in permanent bodies. The Social and Economic Council (Sociaal-Economische Raad, SER) has an advisory and consultative role with regard to the government. It is not tripartite in the normal sense of the word in that it has no government representatives. There are 33 members appointed by employers' organizations, trade unions and the Crown (de facto the gov-ernment). The so-called 'Crown members' are mostly academic experts from university departments of economics, finance, law and sociology. SER has, in addition, a sizeable secretariat with around 100 employees. Important for the production of advisory reports and other publications and activities are the issue-specific committees. According to the interviewees, most processes in SER are initiated by the government, although there are exemptions from this general rule. One of them is a recent initiative on refugees (see Section 4.4).

In recent years, SER has broadened its activities. The classic issues SER have been dealing with for decades are the labour market, social security (including pensions), and health and education. But, recently, issues such as energy and refugees have been added, which – among other things – resulted in an Energy Pact in 2013. The broadening of the agenda has also meant a broad-ening with regard to the actors and stakeholders involved, including various voluntary organizations, although this has not led to changes in the permanent representation in SER. In other words, the organization has become a bit less tripartite and a bit more multipartite.

While SER is a large tripartite public organization, the other impor-tant general/cross-sector consultative organization, the Labour Foundation (Stichting van de Arbeid, STAR), is bipartite and is smaller, with a staff of only four people. STAR was established in 1945. There is no formal, straight-forward division of responsibilities between the SER and STAR and there are extensive overlaps with regard to both representatives and the processes that the two organizations advise about. However, according to some of the interviewees, SER tends to give more general advice primarily addressed to the government, whereas STAR's advice tends to be more specific. Moreover, the decision-making processes in STAR are closer to bargaining than in SER (see also Stichting van de Arbeid, 2010).

Who Are the Social Partners and How Representative Are They?

On the *employers'* side, there are three main organizations, VNO-NCW, MKB-Nederland and LTO, which are all members of SER and STAR and which all take part in collective bargaining. Although not the largest in terms of member organization, VNO-NCW, the Confederation of Netherlands Industry and Employers (Vereniging van Nederlandse Ondernemers-Nederlands Christelijk Werkgeversverbond), is the largest in terms of the wage sum of their member companies, because these on average are larger than the members of MKB-Nederland. According to VNO-NCW, they represent 80 per cent of the medium-sized companies and nearly all the large Dutch companies. MKB-Nederland (Koninklijke Vereniging MKB-Nederland) is an organization that organizes entrepreneurs – especially small and medium-sized enterprise (SMEs) – in construction, industry, retail, chainstore trade, recreation and tourism, business services and healthcare and medical services. The Dutch Land and Horticultural Organization (Land en Tuinbouworganisatie Nederland, LTO) is the organization for employers in the agricultural sector. There is some uncertainty about the membership figures, but LTO claims to represent 50 000 employers (Van het Kaar, 2019).

There are some doubts about the organizational density on the employers' side. This density is best measured as the member companies' share of the wage sum. However, high-quality estimates point to more or less stable organizational densities during recent decades of between 60 and 80 per cent in the private sector, most likely around 70 per cent (de Beer, 2016). The estimate from Jelle Visser's oft-quoted analysis was 71 per cent (Visser, 2013).

On the *employees'* side, there are also three main organizations. The Netherlands Trade Union Confederation (Federatie Nederlandse Vakbeweging, FNV), is by far the largest organization (see Table 4.1), and could be seen as a special type of trade union confederation. The FNV was founded in 1976 as a federation of two unions, the Catholic NKV and the Social Democratic NVV. The organization's main development over the past years has been the internal restructuring process that took place in 2014–15. There are now 14 unions that are members in addition to 26 FNV sectors. The restructuring process also established the so-called 'FNV parliament', with 108 members as the main decision-making body.[1] The change could be argued to strengthen trade union democracy, but the new structure has been criticized (among others, by some of the interviewees) for making the trade unions' decision-making processes slow and the decisions conservative. The second-largest organization is the National Federation of Christian Trade Unions (Christelijk Nationaal Vakverbond, CNV) (Table 4.1), founded in 1906. It has Protestant origins and deliberately stayed out of the 1976 merger that created FNV. Eleven trade unions are affiliated.[2] Few new trade unions have been established in recent years. However, in 2017, a new trade union, POinactie, was set up in the primary education sector. This trade union started as a Facebook group (Van het Kaar, 2019).

Union presence at the national level has been strong since World War II, but has – with some exceptions – been relatively weak at the company level. Trade union density has been halved since 1975, where it peaked at 32 per cent. In

Table 4.1   The Dutch social partner organizations and their
organizational densities

	Members	Organizational Density
Employers (private sector)		71%[a]
VNO-NCW	115 000	
MKB-Nederland	186 000	
LTO	50 000[b]	
Total	–	
Employees		15%
FNV	1 060 200	
CNV	262 400	
VCP (Vakcentrale voor Professionals)	151 200	
Other	228 800	
Total	1 702 600	

Notes:
a. Share of active employees employed by employer member companies (Visser, 2013).
b. Claims to represent, but no figures on actual membership exist.
Source: van het Kaar (2019).

2015, it stood at 16 per cent (de Beer, 2016) (Figure 4.1). The decline has naturally caused some worry among the trade unions themselves and fuelled a long-lasting discussion of their legitimacy. In the eyes of some employers and politicians, trade unions are not sufficiently representative of the employees, which some employers and employers' organizations increasingly prefer to address directly. In this connection, it is noteworthy that, in more and more cases, FNV is not signing agreements that CNV is signing and increasingly is seen by employers as following an activist rather than a cooperative line (see Section 4.6 for a further discussion of this).

The declining trade union density has, however, not been accompanied by a reduction in collective bargaining coverage. This feature of the Dutch collective bargaining model is also found in a number of other countries. The collective bargaining coverage is high and is estimated to have been around 80 per cent over the last half-century. It has even shown an increasing trend in the present decade (de Beer, 2016).

In addition to the traditional social partner organizations, the Association of Netherlands Municipalities (Vereniging van Nederlandse Gemeenten, VNG) should be mentioned, as it plays an important role in relation to active labour market policy (ALMP) and also a role in relation to unemployment benefit – although not directly in relation to unemployment insurance (UI), but rather to social assistance. VNG represents all municipalities. The VNG facilitates municipalities with an exchange of knowledge and experience regarding the

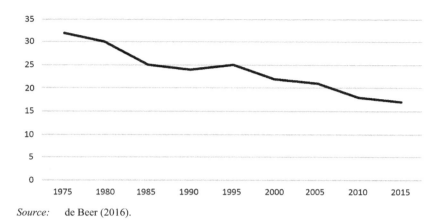

Source: de Beer (2016).

Figure 4.1   Trade union density in the Netherlands, in percentages

implementation of national and local policies.[3] VNG also lobbies on behalf of the municipalities on numerous platforms and is represented in some of the same consultative bodies as the social partners, although not in SER or STAR. The organizational density of the VNG is 100 per cent, though this can hardly be compared to the organizational density of the social partner organizations. But, like the trade unions, VNG is, according to one interviewee, also facing organizational challenges, in that the bigger municipalities increasingly act independently of the organization – one of the developments caused by the extensive decentralization in many policy areas.

4.2   CORPORATIST ARRANGEMENTS IN A 30-YEAR PERSPECTIVE: AN OVERVIEW

Until the Great Recession

The bipartite so-called 'Wassenaar' Agreement of 1982 contained a political compromise on wage moderation and working-time reductions and represents the first step towards decentralized bargaining within a framework of centralized coordination. Wage moderation and the introduction of part-time work contributed significantly to the employment growth in the late 1980s and the 1990s (Hemerijck, Unger and Visser, 2000). Other important agreements followed in the 1980s and 1990s – for instance, 'Agenda 2002' in 1997, which aimed at enhancing the employability of older workers and paid particular attention to disadvantaged groups such as ethnic minorities, and the so-called

Flexicurity Agreement of 1996 that improved the terms of temporary agency workers. These have been said to have contributed to the so-called 'Dutch employment miracle' of sustained employment growth and reduction in unemployment during the late 1980s and the 1990s (Ebbinghaus and Hassel, 1999; Visser and Hemerijck, 1997).

Including the Wassenaar Agreement, in the period from the 1980s until the beginning of the Great Recession, there were seven social pacts (the last in 2004), which each covered several policy areas. Almost as many were made by centre-right as by centre-left governments. Six of the pacts included wage moderation, but working time, unemployment benefits, employment policies, early retirement pensions and conditions for atypical employees were also negotiated as part of the pacts. The diversity of the reforms' content is also found in their drivers. Some of them addressed economic crises directly, while others aimed at equalizing conditions for different groups on the labour market (Visser and van der Meer, 2011).

Some of the pacts have not been purely tripartite, in the sense that the core of them was bipartite bargaining between the social partners with the government playing a facilitating or pushing role, so that the bargaining took place 'in the shadow of hierarchy'. This was the case with the Wassenaar Agreement in 1982 and also with the pacts of 1993 and 1996 (ibid.).

Since the Great Recession

The Netherlands suffered greatly from the consequences of the collapse of Lehman Brothers and its subsequent bankruptcy in September 2008. The economy went into deep recession with a –4 per cent annual growth rate in 2008–09 (Van der Meer, Hemerijck and Karremans, 2019). However, unemployment growth was initially more moderate than in Denmark. It started from the same level of 3.7 per cent in 2008 and increased to 5.0 per cent in 2010, but continued to increase and only peaked in 2014 with 7.4 per cent unemployment (Eurostat, 2019).

After four years without social pacts, a tripartite social pact was signed in 2008. It started out as a bipartite agreement, which was negotiated and signed in September 2008 just after the collapse of Lehman Brothers under the heading 'Doing Together What Is Possible'. The agreement included measures such as wage moderation, stimulation of employment measures for vulnerable groups, promotion of part-time employment and stimulation of mobility. The centre-left Balkenende-IV government joined the negotiations and promised additional funding, lifting the bipartite agreement to a tripartite agreement. When the consequences of the Great Recession became evident in 2009, this tripartite agreement was followed up by a bipartite Crisis Pact with further wage-moderation measures (to keep wage increases below inflation), extension of short-time work arrangements and calls for action regarding training, productivity and pensions. Unlike the 2008 agreement, the Crisis Pact was not transformed into a tripartite agreement, although this had been the intention. The social partners were invited to tripartite talks that started in July 2009 but did not finish before the Balkenende-IV government fell in February 2010 (Van der Meer et al., 2019; Visser and van der Meer, 2011).

Instead of increasing the retirement age, the Crisis Pact obliged SER to come up with alternative solutions for improving the pension system and improving the public budget within six months. This turned out not to be possible within the time limit, to the regret of all three main actors. Instead, two advisory committees were set up to prepare the way for a pension agreement. They managed to do this, and a bipartite agreement was signed in STAR in June 2010, three months after the Balkenende-IV government had resigned and the Liberal-Christian Democrat Rutte-I government had come into office. The agreement included, inter alia, an increase in the pension age by linking it to life expectancy. In March 2011, a tripartite pact was signed that, in terms of its content, was similar to the STAR agreement. However, it became clear during 2011 that both left-wing political parties and FNV's two largest member organizations were opposed to the pact. Even though a small majority for the pact could be established in FNV, the disagreement plagued the organization for years afterwards (Van der Meer and Hemerijck, 2019).

The Mondriaan Pact, signed in 2013, was the last broad social pact in the Netherlands in the period focused on here. It lasted until 2018 – although there was a renegotiation of one element of the pact in 2015, this did not count as a whole new pact. This pact is selected as one of the cases and therefore analysed below.

In 2016–17, attempts were made to strike another pact, as described in the social security case about the Mondriaan Pact below. However, a number of so-called ad hoc pacts in untraditional areas and partly also with unconventional actors were signed, such as the Energy Pact (with the aim of reducing total energy consumption and increasing reuse of energy resources and renewable energy), the Education Pact (with the aim of improving the content and quality of primary and secondary education by strengthening teachers' knowledge and skills), the Technology Pact (with the aim of ensuring that all children aged 4–18 would learn how to work with technology) and the Housing Pact. The social partners are included in these pacts, but since the content of the pacts is beyond the work and employment focus in the present book, they are not included in the overview in Table 4.2.

Although, strictly speaking, most parts of the decision-making process took place after the period in focus for this chapter, and therefore have not been addressed in the interviews, the table nevertheless includes the Pension Agreement of June 2019. The 2019 agreement included: (1) more flexible

Table 4.2   *Overview of tripartite agreements in the Netherlands*
                   1982–2019[a]

Year	Name	Government	Areas
1982	Wassenaar Agreement	Centre-right	Wages, working hours
1989	Joint Policy Framework	Centre-left	Social benefits (indexation), social security, budget
1993	New Course Agreement	Centre-left	Wages, decentralization
1996	Flexicurity Agreement	Left-right	Temporary agency work, temporary work
2002	Mini-pact	Centre-right	Wages, job subsidies (ALMP)
2003	Half-pact	Centre-right	Wages, social security
2004	Museum Square Pact	Centre-right	Wages, early retirement, disability pensions
2008	Doing Together What Is Possible	Centre-left	Wages, ALMP, UI
2009	Crisis Pact	Centre-left	Wages, part-time, unemployment, public investments, pensions
2011	Pension Pact[b]	Centre	Pensions
2013	Mondriaan Pact	Left-right	UI, job protection, ALMP
2019	Pension Agreement	Centre-right	Pension

Notes:
a. The table includes only work- and welfare-related agreements. Other (multipartite)
agreements include the Energy Agreement (September 2013).
b. The Pension Pact 2011 should have been ratified in 2011 by the members of FNV, but the
two largest of their member organizations did not ratify it.
Sources: van der Meer and Hemerijck (2019); van der Meer et al. (2019); Visser and van der
Meer (2010, 2011); Appendix interviews.

rules concerning occupational pension fund solvency; (2) the abolition of
the 'average contribution rate' (under which all employees pay the same
contribution rate, regardless of salary), which was heavily criticized because
it benefited older employees more than younger ones; (3) slow scheduled
increases in the pensionable age (currently 66 years and four months) by
freezing it for two years and slowing the rate of adjustment to increases in life
expectancy, meaning the retirement age will now reach 67 in 2024; and finally,
(4) introduction of changes in tax law to make it easier for employers to offer
up to three years of early retirement for workers in arduous jobs. The particu-
lars of some issues in the agreement remain to be specified, but a tripartite
steering committee will work out the details. Importantly, this time, FNV held
a referendum shortly after they had signed the tripartite agreement and a large
majority accepted it (Anderson, 2019; Van der Graaf, 2019).

4.3 UNEMPLOYMENT INSURANCE

From the Introduction to the Great Recession

The first Dutch unemployment insurance (UI) legislation was passed in Parliament in 1949, but bipartite unemployment insurance funds in the Netherlands area date back to the period before World War II. These funds received state subsidies. After World War II, UI was administered in a tripartite structure separate from the rest of the administrative structures of the Ministry of Social Affairs (Nijhuis, 2013; Soentken and Weishaupt, 2014). Contrary to the situation in Denmark, the scheme is statutory and mandatory for all persons in employment with a private employer (Keune and Payton, 2016). Since the UI maximum benefit level is higher than in Denmark and the UI minimum level lower, the UI system is more earnings related and less egalitarian than the Danish UI system and, hence, more in line with the continental welfare state model.

The economic recessions of the 1970s and 1980s led to a high increase in the number of social benefit claimants. This challenge was met with a series of reforms from the 1980s onwards. In particular, it was the high number of disability claimants and misuse of the disability insurance that attracted attention and led to the expression 'the Dutch disease'. The reason for the misuse of the disability pension scheme was apparently that it was used in cases of redundancy. No costs were incurred for the employers and at the same time it was economically attractive for the employees, because the level was higher than UI (Visser and Hemerijck, 1997; Yerkes, 2011).

Although UI is a different type of social security from sickness benefit, the joint administration in the tripartite Social Insurance Council and the general dissatisfaction with social partner self-governance in the early 1990s meant that the social partners' role in connection to UI also came under attack. A parliamentary committee proposed in 1993 that government control of social security should be strengthened, and corporatist self-governance dismantled. This happened when the tripartite council was replaced with two organizations: a Supervisory Board of Social Insurance (CTSV) created in 1995 and the National Social Insurance Institute (LISV), which joined with it in 1997 to prepare the introduction of market mechanisms in social security. Whereas CTSV only included government-appointed independent members, LISV became a tripartite body that was assisted and supervised by 30 sector bipartite social insurance councils (Visser and Hemerijck, 1997). Hence, the corporatist disengagement was only partial in the first place.

Changes in the content of UI were also made in the 1990s. A reform in 1995 tightened the eligibility criteria for UI, in that the qualification requirement was increased from 12 to 26 weeks of employment within the last 39-week period and from three to four years within the last five-year period. Those only meeting the first requirement (or having exhausted the maximum benefit period) were given the right to a flat-rate UI for two years, while UI for those meeting both requirements remained earnings related. Moreover, eligibility was made dependent on willingness to accept job offers and to take part in activation measures (Schils, 2009; Visser and Hemerijck, 1997, pp. 147–8). The maximum UI period remained at five years.

Also related to UI (and to labour law) was the Flexibility and Security Act agreed in 1997 (also known as the Flexicurity Act) that came fully into force in 1999. It was based on a tripartite agreement (see Table 4.2), but preparatory work was done on it before that. In 1996, STAR published a report on flexibility and security. The report was a sort of package deal in which both the demands of the unions for the protection of the workers and the demands of the employers for more flexibility were integrated. Legislation concerning dismissals and employment contracts was amended on the basis of the report. The Flexibility and Security Act included such measures as the shortening of notice periods, easier access to unemployment benefits in the case of dismissal on economic grounds, and a procedure of 'no objection' if the employee accepted his or her dismissal and claimed unemployment benefit. The ban on the dismissal of sick workers was lifted if the sickness was declared after the dismissal request was received by the Regional Director of Public Employment Service (Wilthagen, 1998).

Another reform of the institutional set-up of UI took place in 2000, and the social partners' roles were further reduced as a result. The reform – whose overall aim was to further enhance the role of market mechanisms in UI – established two new organizations: the Centre for Work and Income (CWI), responsible for registration of the unemployed and with overall responsibility for activation policies, and the Administration of Unemployment Insurance (UWV), responsible for all matters related to unemployment benefits. The social partners did not acquire any seats or role in these organizations. However, a Council for Work and Income (RWI) with the participation of employers, trade unions and municipalities was established to advise the government on short-term issues in relation to both UI and ALMP, while SER remained the tripartite body involved in larger and longer-term initiatives (Schils, 2009).

As expected, the side-lining of the social partners was criticized, not least by the trade unions. Prior to the 2006 reform, in October 2004, the trade unions had organized a demonstration with 300 000 participants, with the aim of forcing the government to involve them and to follow a common SER recommendation for a new UI system, which was issued in April 2005. Subsequently, the government did largely follow the SER's recommendations, indicating that the criticism and protests were effective (Knegt, 2012).

The content of UI was also reformed in the years leading up to the Great Recession. In 2003, the flat-rate UI was abandoned and in 2006 the maximum benefit period was reduced from five to three years and two months at the same time as the earnings-related dimension of UI was weakened. The government's aims with these reforms were to improve the health of the public finances and to increase work incentives (ibid.).

Since the Great Recession

As in a number of other EU countries, an initial response to the crisis with regard to UI was to introduce or extend cover for short-time work arrangements. Hence, in 2008, a scheme was introduced. It was replaced in 2009 by another scheme that allowed companies facing a reduction in trade of 30 per cent or more to apply for working-time reductions for their employees. If accepted, the employees were able to receive a temporary UI, equivalent to the working-time reduction. The Minister of Social Affairs wanted the scheme to be terminated by January 2010, but STAR convinced him to prolong it to July 2011 (Keune and Payton, 2016; Knegt, 2012).

Apart from these short-time work arrangements, changes in the general UI were also under consideration. In June 2008, a government-appointed commission – the Bakker Commission chaired by the chairperson of the Dutch Postal Service company, TNT – formulated recommendations for a new UI system, including employer payment of UI for the first six months of unemployment and a shortening of the maximum benefit period from 38 to 18 months. However, there was not a great deal of support from the social partners or anywhere else for this proposal and the financial crisis – which appeared just a few months later – further reduced the possibility of 'selling' the proposal (Bandel, 2008; Knegt, 2012). The government declared in 2010 that they intended to keep the maximum benefit unchanged. The opposition in Parliament and the employers argued that mobility and labour market participation would be increased if the maximum benefit period was shortened. The trade unions were, unsurprisingly, on the side of the government and went further in asking for a restoration of the role of the social partners in UI formulation and administration.

Changes in the institutional set-up took place too. In 2009, CWI and UWV were merged into one single organization – UWV – responsible for both UI and ALMP. Furthermore, RWI was wound up in 2012 and, thus, the last channel for social partner participation specifically for UI had gone (Knegt, 2012). The only remaining channels for formal influence were through STAR and SER, which continued to place UI on the agenda.

CASE: THE SOCIAL ACCORD 2013 (MONDRIAAN PACT)

The Social Accord, signed in April 2013, was a broad social pact with elements of UI and ALMP as well as labour law. Although the pact included substantial initiatives with regard to all these three areas, the UI elements can be considered the core of the pact. Hence the inclusion as a case in this UI section.

The Social Accord is the last broad tripartite agreement in the Netherlands in the period studied. It was concluded within the first six months of the Rutte-II government, the so-called purple (Liberal-Social Democrat) government, which was in power from November 2012 until October 2017.

Setting the Agenda

In 2012, unemployment was still increasing in the Netherlands. The expectations of the government and the employers were that an improvement in the economy and a decline in unemployment would soon be under way. However, the budget deficit, at 3.9 per cent of GDP in 2012, was exceeding the EU's 3 per cent limits and the Netherlands was at risk of EU sanctions.

Therefore, in December 2012, unions, employers and the government discussed a new social agenda, including austerity measures and measures to stimulate the economy. The social partners knew that if they could not agree with the government, the government would start to negotiate austerity measures with the opposition parties instead. Hence, in this case, the negotiations also took place in the shadow of hierarchy. Moreover, the social partners were – although for different reasons – unsatisfied with the government's work programme and saw a social pact as a possible way to influence and amend it. Still, it took some time before the FNV chairperson got the FNV parliament's support for entering negotiations for a tripartite agreement. That approval was only given in early March 2013 (Kurstjens, 2015).

According to some of the interviewees, whereas the previous Liberal-Christian Democrat Rutte-I government had, as described above, rejected cuts in the maximum benefit period, the Rutte-II government had planned – as part of its austerity measures – to get the UI maximum down from three years to one year.

Decision-making Process

Although, as mentioned above, FNV's formal approval for entering into negotiations was only given in March 2013, the negotiations did in fact start a couple of months earlier. Interviewees reported that the decision-making process was not embedded either in STAR, or in SER, although some of the SER and STAR staff were involved in several of the issues.

According to the interviewees, the degree of openness at the beginning of the process varied substantially from the degree of openness at the end. The first phase of the process seems to have been relatively open compared to earlier pacts. Contributing to this was the intense media attention. However, the end of the process was described by the interviewees as being very closed, both towards the media and in terms of the number of persons involved. During the last two months, only four people were directly involved in the negotiations – the prime minister, the deputy prime minister, the FNV chairperson and the managing director of VNO-NCW (see also Hemerijck and van der Meer, 2016).[4]

The government got support from the employers' organizations with regard to the aim of reducing the unemployment benefit period, but it was, not surprisingly, difficult to get the trade unions on board. The 'bait' to get the unions' support turned out to be improvements for flexible workers and various ALMP-related measures, as well as changes in UI governance structures, which are detailed below.

The core of the agreement was a reduction in the publicly financed part of the UI period to a maximum of two years, with the third year to be financed by the social partners. This kind of supplementary UI, financed by the social partners, had been seen before in the Netherlands (Schils, 2009). For the trade unions, the incentive for accepting the financial contribution to UI was to regain some of the influence they had lost during the past decades. As a side-effect, FNV hoped that more employees would sign up as members as a result of their greater visibility due to their role in UI. FNV's willingness to go down the road of UI financing should also be seen in the light of an internal crisis they went through in 2011 regarding an occupational pension scheme (see above). The reason the employers in VNO-NCW decided to enter the negotiations and make concessions was partly because, as previously mentioned, they feared that even worse measures could result from a unilateral parliamentary initiative, but also, according to the interviewees, because it was in the interests of the employers to support the moderate leadership in FNV and make sure they got a deal that could be accepted by its constituency. If this succeeded, the employers thought they could avoid a more activist FNV leadership coming into power (see also Knegt and Verhulp, 2016 for a similar conclusion).

The social pact 'Social Agenda for the 21st Century' included a very large number of actions, but the main points of the social pact could be said to be as follows:

- the duration of public unemployment benefits will gradually be reduced from three to two years maximum, with the social partners to finance the third year of unemployment;
- the social partners will become responsible and involved in the executive boards of the unemployment benefit funds and ALMP. To promote cooperation between the social partners and municipalities and arrive at a well-functioning labour market, the social partners and the VNG have taken a number of measures, including setting up the Workroom, a multipartite consultative body with participation of the social partners and VNG;
- a strong commitment to avoid unemployment by introducing incentives for 'job-to-job' transitions. The Sector Plan Co-financing Scheme will invest a total of 1.2 billion euros (600 million euros from the Ministry of Economic and Social Affairs and 600 million euros from the social partners and regions) to support jobs in sectors and regions hard hit by the Great Recession;
- the law on dismissals will be revised, in order to put an end to the situation that employers may one-sidedly choose between different ways of terminating the employment contract;
- the legal position of flexible workers will be improved. The statutory rights of flexi-workers will be improved. The social partners wish to tackle both 'excessive flexibility' in labour relations and ensure a balanced application of dismissal laws;
- the (private) employers and the government will create 125 000 jobs, 25 000 of which will be created by government (Knegt and Verhulp, 2016; Stichting van de Arbeid, 2014).

With regard to the involvement of the social partners in UI and ALMP, the agreement restored part of the representation the social partners had previously (periodically) had in relation to ALMP and in UI. At the national level, the pact introduced the Workroom to take over the functions that the Council for Work and Income had had until it was liquidated in 2012. According to the interviewees, the liquidation occurred because of tense relations within the council and because the council was not able to come up with joint opinions. The Workroom has representation from the social partners and from VNG. One of several responsibilities of the Workroom is to find ways to deliver the creation of the promised 125 000 jobs. The jobs will be at least at the level of the statutory minimum wage. In cases where the employee is not able to earn the minimum wage, he or she will receive a wage subsidy corresponding to the difference between the minimum wage and the reduced work capacity (Nederlandse regering, 2014). According to one of the interviewees, the 125 000 jobs quickly became the main topic in the Workroom, because it was a means for them to take control over the ALMP policy area, which they still have little formal power over.

At the regional level, the agreement introduced 35 regional tripartite bodies to improve the labour exchange in the regional labour markets and ensure that job seekers who were not able to earn the statutory minimum wage were placed with employers. The municipalities would take the lead in the centres, but the employers' organizations, trade unions and UWV would participate in the management. Other actors, such as educational institutions and organizations for the disabled, could also be involved (Stichting van de Arbeid, 2015).

Evaluation, Implementation and Effects

With regard to the decision-making process, it was considered to be too closed by several of the interviewees. As one of the interviewees expressed it, 'too many people were unhappy afterwards'. VNG, which was excluded from the decision-making process, despite the fact that the agreement clearly covered their areas of responsibility, was especially frustrated. After the Social Accord, trust had to be rebuilt between VNG and the social partners and especially between VNG and the government.

The pacts were, as mentioned, very broad, and its various elements were only implemented gradually. In terms of the core elements of the UI and the social partner financing of the third year of UI, even towards the end of the interview period (November 2017–July 2018), there was still uncertainty about how the task should be addressed technically. However, four pilots had been run in four regions and the plan was to use the evaluation of these in forming the technical solution for the third year of UI.

Legal provision for flexi-workers was improved due to a new 'flexicurity' law agreed in June 2014. Under this law, hiring the same employee for more than two years on consecutive temporary contracts was no longer permitted. After two years of temporary contracts, or when a fourth contract was offered, the new contract had to be of a permanent nature. It was only possible to prevent a change from a temporary to a permanent contract if there was a mandatory period of at least six months (previously three months) between the two contracts. Moreover, the law introduced a transition allowance. All workers, including those with temporary employment contracts, got this transition allowance if they had been employed by the same employer for at least two years (Amsterdam Business, 2015; Bekker and Mailand, 2018).

Moreover, the law on dismissals was revised. Due to this revision, the employers could no longer choose via which 'route' (Public Employment

Service [PES] or court) the worker was made redundant. In court, employees often get severance pay, whereas PES hardly ever decides to grant severance payment. Dismissals on economic grounds were now automatically judged by PES, whereas redundancies on personal grounds would appear before court, which would make the system fairer. For workers with a temporary employment contract, insecurity was reduced by shortening the time frame within which open-ended employment had to be offered. Workers who were employed via payrolling[5] got better protection, getting the same level of employment protection as employees who had a direct employment relationship with their employer. Moreover, the long-term use of on-call contracts (zero hours) was limited (Bekker and Mailand, 2018).

A number of the other points in the agreement were followed up and implemented through the so-called Participation Act. These will be described in one of the cases in the following section on ALMP (Section 4.4).

It should also be mentioned that some of the main social partner organizations – after they changed their top-level management positions – have, to some extent, regretted the Mondriaan Pact. This is most clearly the case on the employers' side in relation to the Work and Security Act, which is based on the Mondriaan Pact. The reason given by the employers' organization for their attempts to change the newly implemented legislation was that smaller employers in particular faced difficulties due to the legislation (Stichting van de Arbeid, 2017). Negotiations on changes on a larger scale took place in 2017, but these ended without agreement in November 2017. Employers had suggested weaker job protection for employees on open-ended contracts, thus limiting the protection gap between employees on open-ended contracts and so-called 'flexi-workers', whereas the trade unions wanted to improve protection for the latter group, including the solo self-employed (self-employed without employees) and aimed at stopping the use of what they perceived as bogus self-employment (payrolling). In the end, no agreements could be reached (Zwinkles, 2017). Afterwards, some of the changes the employers wanted were decided unilaterally by the government.

4.4   ACTIVE LABOUR MARKET POLICY (ALMP)

Until the Great Recession

The Netherlands, despite severe cuts since the beginning of the 2010s, has a relatively high level of public expenditure on ALMP (0.72 per cent of GDP in 2016). Although far lower than in Denmark, it is, nonetheless, the sixth highest level in the EU (OECD, 2018). The development of Dutch ALMP has a number of similarities with that of Danish ALMP, including short periods of strong tripartite involvement in the 1990s, which was afterwards gradually weakened as the policy areas were partly marketized through extensive use of outsourcing of the activation effort and decentralized to the municipalities. However, the history of ALMP is shorter than in Denmark in that the first supply-oriented active measures were only seen in the late 1980s (Van Berkel, 2007).

During the years, SER has, as in many other areas, played a role in the development of the overall guidelines for activation policy (Visser and Hemerijck, 1997), and although the centre-left governments in power for most of the 1990s abolished the obligation to consult SER in the pre-legislative processes (Ebbinghaus, 2002), SER is still consulted and issues recommendations regarding activation policy. However, before the 1990s, the social partners had no formal influence on this policy area. It was not until 1991 that they gained any influence on the Public Employment Service (PES) via representation in the regional and central employment councils. But PES was met with strong criticism and an official evaluation report from 1993 (see also Section 4.3) concluded that stronger government regulation was necessary, partly because of slow decision making and action paralysis in the tripartite forums, and partly because the parties allegedly pursued their own self-interests rather than the general good. Against this background, the government decided that the state should, to a greater extent, be in the driver's seat in activation policy and the government began to recentralize activation policies and gradually phase out corporatist governance in the policy area (Mosley, Keller and Spackesser, 1998; Visser and Hemerijck, 1997).

Since then, reforms have continued both for the insured and the non-insured unemployed. Until recently, these reforms have further reduced the role of the social partners, but have generally replaced it with market governance rather than with unilateral (state) governance.

PES was privatized in 2002 and a new unified system was established that included both the insured and the non-insured unemployed and both activation and payment of unemployment benefits. Responsibility for the placement of the unemployed, including the judgement about ability to work, was passed to the 113 local centres of the Centre for Work and Income (CWI) following the reform of 2002. CWI was at the core of the new system. It represented a 'one-stop shop' for all unemployed people and for companies seeking employees. CWI had the general responsibility for activation policies, overseeing the centres and registering all the unemployed, whereas the Employee Insurance Agency (UWV) was responsible for all matters related to unemployment benefits. Moreover, those unemployed not ready for work were referred to the UWV if they were insured and to the municipalities if they were not. It was then, in these cases, UWV and the municipalities who were responsible for both payment of unemployment benefit and for the active measures for these groups, although the active measures were outsourced to a number of private job intermediaries and consulting firms that were paid according to the 'no cure, less pay' principle. The largest of these organizations was Kliq, the privatized former Public Employment Service (Andersen and Mailand, 2002; Van Berkel and van der Aa, 2004).

The social partners did not obtain any seats or role in CWI and UWV. However, a Council for Work and Income (RWI) with the participation of employers, trade unions and municipalities was established to advise the government on short-term issues, while SER remained the tripartite body with responsibility for larger and longer-term initiatives (Schils, 2009). On the regional and local levels, new bodies with social partner representation came into being. The so-called regional Work Squares were introduced in 2002. One of the main aims of establishing the 100 Work Squares (later reduced to 35) was to create closer cooperation with the national-level authorities (Spies and van de Vrie, 2014). According to some of the interviewees, proper organizations were not established in all 35 regions, and the Work Squares did not become the meeting points for unemployed people and employers they were planned to be. Moreover, where they did establish proper organizations, there was little cooperation. Contributing to these problems was the fact that no clear tasks were formulated for the Work Squares.

Although a development in the direction of marketization, as described above, has clearly been seen, some rolling back of marketization has also taken place. With the introduction of a new Social Assistance Act in 2004, the obligation of local CWIs to outsource activation was abolished. It was thereafter up to the local centres themselves to decide whether or not to outsource or provide the activation measures in-house (Van Berkel and de Graaf, 2011). Even more importantly, the Social Assistance Act of 2004 fully decentralized the responsibility of ALMP to the municipalities.

In addition, a number of reforms with a focus on specific target groups was introduced in the years leading up to the Great Recession. Among them was a new integration law for immigrants in 2007 that obliged immigrants from non-European countries without Dutch nationality to pass an exam on the Dutch language and basic Dutch cultural traits, to finish a vocational education, or to pass an exam for 'Dutch as a second language'. Failing to fulfil any of these demands would mean that it was not possible to stay for an indeterminate period in the Netherlands (Van der Aa and van Berkel, 2013).

All in all, the development shows a clear reduction in the role of the social partners from actual decision making to weaker involvement in the form of consultation, while both unilateral government management and especially market management has been strengthened, and policy has been decentralized to the municipalities. The extensive reduction in the role of the social partners is largely linked to the state's perception of a lack of implementation capacity by the parties.

From the Great Recession

The most important ALMP reforms, both in terms of the policy content and in terms of governance, took place in the early to mid-2000s, but a few significant reforms were also introduced during the Great Recession. The Act on Investing in Young People of 2009 coincided with the crisis but was formulated and developed in an earlier period when there were labour shortages in some sectors but high youth unemployment in general. The law obliged the municipalities to help young social assistance recipients up to the age of 26 to find employment or obtain a minimum qualification level. It was the first law since the full decentralization of ALMP in 2004 to limit the decision-making competences of the municipalities and VNG protested strongly. In 2012, a four-week 'waiting period' was introduced before the young social assistance recipients could receive active assistance from the municipalities and the social assistance payment (Spies and van de Vrie, 2014; Van der Aa and van Berkel, 2013).

Due to the continued high level of youth unemployment, the government launched a National Action Plan on Youth Unemployment in 2013. This was partly connected to the EU initiative known as the Youth Guarantee. From 2013 until 2015, the government, local government, social partners and educational institutions undertook several measures to ensure work or further education for young people. These measures included several actions at a regional level with social partner involvement and were partly linked to the Sectoral Plan initiative (see Section 4.5).

With regard to the governance structures, as mentioned above, CWI and UWV were, in 2009, merged into one single organization – UWV – responsible for both UI and ALMP. This new organization had no representation from the social partners. Furthermore, RWI was wound up in 2012 and, thus, the last channel for social partner participation specifically for ALMP had gone (Knegt, 2012). According to the interviewees, this happened partly as a result of problems with cooperation in the council, and partly because of the introduction of austerity programmes. The only channels left for formal national-level influence were STAR and SER, which continued to place ALMP on the agenda.

Furthermore, as part of the government austerity policies, a severe reduction in the budget for ALMP took place during the Great Recession. Between 2011 and 2015, the government introduced cuts in no less than 60 per cent of the ALMP budget allocated to the municipalities (Spies and van de Vrie, 2014).

However, without doubt, the most important post-2008 ALMP reform was the Participation Act, which was implemented in 2015 but was formed in connection with the negotiation of the Social Accord of 2013. The social partners were involved in the decision-making process of the act itself and, as part of what was agreed, their involvement was increased in the administrative structures. The Participation Act is described as a case below.

CASE: PARTICIPATION ACT 2014

Setting the Agenda

The Participation Act was connected to the Social Accord of 2013 in the sense that it implemented several parts of the pact, more specifically most of its ALMP-related parts. The most important of these were: (1) that the employers and the government would create 125 000 jobs; (2) that the social partners would take on the responsibility of becoming involved in the executive boards dealing with ALMP and other organizations related to the ALMP; (3) a strong commitment to avoid unemployment by creating incentives for 'work-to-work' transitions.

The overall aim of the act was to increase labour market participation. With regard to governance, the main change was that the municipalities were made responsible for all disabled people (people with occupational impairment). The young disabled, whose numbers were rising, were previously the responsibility of the UWV.

Decision-making Process

The decision-making process of the Social Accord was also relevant for the Participation Act, as the framework of the pact was decided here. The decision-making process provided the social partners with strong influence on all aspects of the pact. However, the interest organization of the municipalities, VNG, was not involved despite their strong interest in, and responsibility for, several aspects of the pact. As mentioned, this lack of involvement created some tension between VNG and the central government and a need for rebuilding of trust.

The Social Accord was signed in April 2013 and the Participation Act was adopted by the Dutch Parliament in December 2014, shortly before its implementation in January 2015. In the period in between, additional consultation of the social partners and VNG took place. However, the VNG interviewee described the consultation as being limited in the sense that the papers related to the act were not sent out in advance and could not be taken out of the meeting room. Another interviewee explained the cautious approach by the government due to the sensitivity of the act, especially in relation to the reductions in benefit levels and the lack of funding to the municipalities that would be responsible for the implementation of the act. Despite this, VNG did manage to impact the draft in terms of increasing the payment (compared to what the government had proposed) for each disabled person in a job in order to create work incentives. In addition, a trade union interviewee reported that the unions were able to change some minor issues in the act.

The Outcome and Implementation

The scope of the act in its final form is quite broad. The most important aspects of the act could be said to be the following:

- the act replaced three earlier acts, two of which were mentioned above: (1) the Social Assistance Act; (2) the Sheltered Employment Act; and (3) the Young Disabled Persons Acts (also known as the Wajong Act). In this way, the municipalities' responsibility was enlarged to encompass the disabled unemployed, including young disabled people;
- although not formally part of the act, contributing to the Social Accord's aim of creating 125 000 jobs was also one of its aims;
- the Participation Act formally allocated additional funds for active measures for the target groups[6];
- regional job centres were established.

The implementation of large parts of both the Mondriaan Pact and the Participation Act have been discussed in the Workroom. However, the interviewees' overall assessments of the first years of this new forum were unfavourable. Building consensus in the Workroom has not been an easy task, and the most critical of the interviewees describe its first year as one big fight. The issue of the payment for people with a reduced capacity to work in active measures, which was agreed as part of the Mondriaan Pact and confirmed in the Participation Act, was reopened in the Workroom. It was not possible to obtain consensus on this issue. In the end, the government decided, unilaterally, to make it possible to employ disabled people below the statutory minimum wage, although the trade unions and the VNG were opposed to this. Moreover, VNG often found themselves under pressure from the joint forces of the social partner organizations. Hence, VNG decided to leave the Workroom. Among the social partner interviewees, some saw this as a logical consequence of the VNG's lack of engagement. According to these interviewees, the municipalities were never really interested in the Workroom but were simply forced into it. They wanted to take decisions on ALMP unilaterally.

CASE: REFUGEE COMMITTEE 2015–

Setting the Agenda

Like several other EU countries, the Netherlands faced an increasing inflow of refugees in the middle of the 2010s. With 229 people applying for asylum for each 100 000 inhabitants, the Netherlands was, in the peak year of 2015, placed slightly above the EU average level for asylum seekers, and a few places below Denmark (Frandsen, 2016). As in Denmark, immigration had been a sensitive issue for more than a decade prior to 'the refugee crisis', and the wave of refugees and immigrants around 2015 did, according to the interviewees, lead to serious concerns. Apart from discussions on action to limit the number of refugees coming to the Netherlands, a number of initiatives also targeted the review of asylum status.

Among these initiatives was the set-up of a working committee on refugees in SER, initiated by SER itself. Among the main actors, it was widely perceived that – and this was supported by empirical studies – the Netherlands historically had not performed very well when it came to including refugees in the labour market, including the latest wave made up of ex-Yugoslavians arriving in the mid-1990s. Moreover, it appeared that many refugees stayed much longer in refugee centres than expected, and only after long periods of time were able to get their own housing and start looking for a job.

The tripartite working committee was far from exclusively focused on ALMP-related issues, but these issues formed part of the agenda. The working committee was established shortly after the set-up of a task force on refugees in the Ministry of Social Affairs and Employment, which SER also participated in, but which had no participation from the social partners. The task force – which still existed when the interviews on this issue were conducted in November 2017 – was all about improving knowledge sharing. It did not produce reports or recommendations, but it did have a number of working groups affiliated to it, which worked with more concrete initiatives. One outcome of the task force was a new common understanding among its participants that information about refugees was spread out on several platforms. Therefore, when SER decided to set up a working committee, one of the tasks of this group was to establish a website to bring all the information together.

Policy Formulation

The tripartite working committee was established in late 2015 and was initiated by SER itself. It was the first time SER had had a project on refugees specifically. The working committee was chaired by SER's president. It had four staff members from SER's secretariat, two so-called 'Crown members' (appointed researchers) and a number of social partner representatives.

According to the interviewees, the social partner representatives took rather predictable and traditional positions in the committee. Employers wanted to tailor measures to the needs of private employers, including protecting the existing private language suppliers (see below). Moreover, they wished to improve companies' access to employable refugees and tried to avoid specific promises on behalf of their members. The trade union representatives were keen to avoid unfair competition from these groups and were therefore careful about new measures targeted at the refugees. A specific example here was the trade unions' hesitance regarding the so-called 'intermediary contract', which gave refugees the opportunity to work for three months for social assistance before offering them a contract on minimum wage or above. In addition, the trade unions wanted to decrease the social assistance period and strengthen the guarantee that a real contract would be offered afterwards.

It was difficult to reach a consensus on recommendations regarding 'civic integration' (the general integration of the refugees in society), but nevertheless a generally formulated recommendation was included in the report (see below). It was also possible to create enough common ground to finalize a home page with specific initiatives and two reports, including recommendations.

Outcome and Implementation

After only three months, the first output from the committee in the form of the website was ready. The website included information for refugees, companies, Dutch citizens and interest groups. It provided information on rules and regulations, tools, best practice and a half-yearly update on the status of the refugees. The website was intended as an online starting point for employers and organizations focusing on the participation of refugees in Dutch society. Examples of the information provided on the website are answers to questions such as: 'What rules do employers who want to hire refugees have to comply with?' and 'Are refugees permitted to do volunteer work or follow an educational programme?' The website also included SER's contribution to the ministerial Refugee Work and Integration Task Force.[7]

Shortly after the website was put online, there followed a report with the title *New Ways for More Successful Labour Market Integration of Refugees* (SER, 2016) with recommendations to the government for refugee policies. The recommendations included calls for earlier support from the municipalities to the refugees in order to improve the state of affairs where refugees were being held in reception centres for long periods of time. Another of the working group's recommendations was to end the individualized responsibility for integration, which was introduced in 2007. This individualization implied, among other things, that the refugee was responsible for finding and financing his or her own Dutch-language courses in a very complex market with many uncertified suppliers. A third recommendation was not to treat language and integration as different paths, but to embed language teaching in workplaces as well as in the educational system. A fourth was to improve coordination at the regional level, because of the strong degree of decentralization/municipal autonomy in this area and the large number of other local actors in the area that led to the risk of duplication and a too fragmented integration policy. All in all, the recommendations were very general, and no new specific initiatives – at the workplace level or elsewhere – were suggested.

The recommendations were well received by the government. In terms of the effect of the recommendations, it can be argued that, although they were not the only driver, they were probably one of the reasons that the Dutch civic integration framework is going to be changed. From 2020, the municipalities will be responsible for organizing language courses for refugees with a budget of 4000 euros per refugee for the municipalities. The changes will, in general, be more in the nature of work practices than changes in legislation.

4.5   CONTINUING VOCATIONAL TRAINING

The Netherlands has, overall, a well-developed vocational education system, including an ample supply of continuing vocational training (CVT). This was confirmed by the extensive and detailed *OECD Skill Strategy Diagnostic Report* (OECD, 2017). With 18 per cent of employees participating in CVT within the last four weeks of 2017, the Netherlands ranks high among the EU countries, but below Denmark with 27 per cent (Eurostat, 2019). Another difference from the situation in Denmark and in several other EU countries is that public funding of CVT activities is limited (Smulders, Cox and Weisterhuis, 2016). According to interviewees, the publicly funded part of CVT stands at around 15 per cent. Hence, the market for CVT in the Netherlands is overwhelmingly private and therefore also not highly structured. This also means that it is difficult to provide an overview of the Dutch CVT sector. Moreover, initial vocational education and CVT is even more interwoven than in Denmark, in that the legislation is basically the same (see also Onstenk and Duvekot, 2017). This also means it is difficult to create a clear picture of the CVT system alone.

CVT and lifelong learning are issues dealt with in both SER and STAR. According to a government interviewee, there has been a trend, with regard to lifelong learning, where the social partners increasingly prefer to discuss the CVT in STAR and not in SER, in order to get better control of the discussions and because consensus building (as described in a later section) has been difficult in recent years. FNV was mentioned as the clearest example of an organization that preferred to discuss CVT in STAR.

The focus here will mainly be on CVT for the employed, whereas CVT for the unemployed will only be touched upon briefly.

From the Introduction to the Great Recession

CVT in the Netherlands has a long history, but publicly funded CVT did not – as in Denmark – experience a strong institutionalization and growth in the 1960s and 1970s. While privately funded CVT has been spreading, publicly funded CVT has been described as stagnating since the late 1990s. However, in the early 1990s, adult education became a government priority and a number of initiatives and increased funding could be identified (Onstenk and Duvekot, 2017).

The most recent CVT-related reform, which still provides its legal base, is the Vocational and Adult Education Act of 1996. Among other changes, this reform merged upper-secondary education and CVT into one system, placed apprenticeship education and school-based education under the same administrative structure, decentralized training policy and established the Regional Training Centres.

As the CVT system operates now, the government provides the general legal framework, laws and regulations at the national level. Despite the fact that CVT is now generally under the same legal base as vocational education and training (VET), a few 'CVT-only' legal initiatives have been taken. One of these was a tax reduction programme for companies using CVT, which existed for a number of years but was abolished around 2008 due to misuse. As a consequence of this, CVT activity levels declined, according to interviewees. These legal initiatives are often taken after the involvement of SER and STAR.

Although most focus in the Netherlands, as previously described, has been on the initial stages of education, the attention given to CVT and life-long learning has grown since the 2000s (Borhans et al., 2014; Onstenk and Duvekot, 2017). SER and STAR are among the bodies at the national level where involvement of the social partners in CVT issues takes place. In 2002, SER issued their first report on CVT in the form of the advisory report *The New Learning*, which, inter alia, asked for more demand-driven CVT, where publicly funded courses could be supplied on market conditions and where individual learning accounts (ILAs) were mentioned as a useful instrument (SER, 2002).

Apart from the ad hoc involvement of the social partners via SER and STAR, the social partners are involved on a more regular basis via the Corporation for Vocational Training (SBB). SBB promotes and accredits employers for VET and CVT in the form of workplace-based learning. SBB is also responsible for the development of qualifications (qualification dossiers) for both VET and CVT. There are four qualification levels of VET (MBO levels) and two paths, which are, de facto, both dual systems combining school-based and company-based learning. The school-based system includes 20–60 per cent practical training and the apprenticeship system at least 60 per cent practical training (Scholten, 2018).

SSB has a tripartite structure in the sense that the training institutions, the Regional Training Centres, have half the seats and the social partners the other half, divided equally between employers' and trade unions' representatives. However, the interviewees' perception is that the employers are much more interested, active and influential than the trade unions. Some interviewees felt that the trade unions in SBB mainly focused on the vocational aspect of the educational programmes, that is, if the education leads to jobs. Other interviewees reported weak trade union engagement with a lack of organizational capacity to develop strategies on CVT. While the perceived levels of engagement were found to be unequal, the interviewees found a great deal of common interest between employers and trade unions in terms of having good-quality educational programmes.

Until 2012, there were 18 sectoral Knowledge Centres whose main task was to improve and maintain the qualification system. The centres were governed by bipartite boards. These were replaced from 2012 to 2015 with SBB and 79 Regional Training Centres. The Regional Training Centres are vocational schools that supply both vocational education and CVT. Regarding CVT, one of their tasks is to assess the qualification levels of individuals and issue certification of their qualifications, if these qualifications are approved. With regard to governance, the social partners are not represented in the training centres. According to one interviewee, although the Regional Training Centres are responsible for both vocational education and CVT, they tend to focus on the former. This bias is reflected in the uptake of students that overwhelmingly are vocational education students.

Finally, it is important to mention that a large number of collective agreements, especially in the private craft-oriented sector, include training funds. There are between 140 and 200 branch/sector agreements – the precise number depends on the source. A survey from 2006 found 122 such funds existed at either the sector or company level, and that 10 000 employees were covered by the sectoral funds and 3000 by company funds (Schaapman, 2009). According to the interviewees, the contributions to the funds are not discussed at every bargaining round, and those collective agreements that include rights for training limit this right to two to four days annually.

From the Great Recession Onwards

There have not been a large number of CVT initiatives since the Great Recession, but there have been some, most of them taken after 2013. One initiative is the set-up of Offices for Learning and Working (*Leerwerloket*) which are one-stop shops where employed and unemployed people can receive information on CVT. These one-stop shops are administered by Regional Training Centres. Another initiative from the period is the Sectoral Plan Co-financing Scheme, which was agreed on a tripartite basis as part of the Mondriaan Pact. The initiative focuses on the unemployed and is related both to ALMP and to CVT. The financial resources allocated from the government were meant to be matched with funding of a similar level from the regions. The Sectoral Plan initiative involved SBB, its sector divisions and Regional Training Centres. Every SBB sector was asked – in cooperation with the Regional Training Centres – to draft action plans for the unemployed and employed people who were going to be made redundant. These plans had a strong focus on CVT and were often focused on retraining for sectors that still had high labour demand during the crisis years.

In 2017, SER issued an advisory report on lifelong learning, which also addressed CVT issues. The report included 46 recommendations under three headings: reinforcement of the infrastructure for post-initial skills development; support for the demand for post-initial skills development; and establishing an inviting and encouraging learning culture. Under the second heading, one of the recommendations was to introduce a 'skills development savings account to cover post-initial skills development'. This included, more specifically, the recommendation that every individual should have the opportunity to open a skills development savings account and that the balance in the account could be spent on any relevant career development activities. Moreover, it was recommended that the social partners use the account to encourage career development and make collective deposits into the account, and that public authorities directly encourage skills development among special target groups by making deposits into skills development accounts or by offering vouchers. Finally, the advisory report proposed a tax regime that would encourage training and provide vouchers that the social partners would finance from collective funds or collective agreements (SER, 2017).

In STAR, a similar issue was discussed in 2016, when the government revealed its intention to liquidate a tax-deduction programme for CVT and replace it with training vouchers, an approach that is similar to individual learning. The social partners in SER were against the liquidation of the programme, but felt that it would be better to hold off on detailed discussions until the SER advisory report was ready (Stichting van de Arbeid, 2017).

The recommendation on ILAs was taken up in a political initiative in 2018, which is analysed in the case below.

CASE: THE INDIVIDUAL LEARNING ACCOUNTS (ILA) 2018–

Setting the Agenda

During the Great Recession, the Netherlands experienced (along with several other countries with dual vocational education systems that required cooperation from individual employers) a reduction in the companies' willingness to take in interns/provide practical training places. A couple of years after the recession, around 2016, the companies started to experience a lack of qualified labour in a number of branches. One interviewee found that an unintended consequence of having the same institutions responsible for initial education and (publicly funded) further training was an undersupply of the latter. These two factors – together with an awareness that the life cycle of many jobs is decreasing, the ageing of the population and the coming to power of a new government – might explain why the government in mid-2018 proposed to introduce ILAs.

Decision-making Process

In March 2018, the government sent a letter to Parliament that called for improvements in the provision of lifelong learning in the Netherlands and for an ILA initiative. More specifically, the letter called for greater individual influence on own learning development, including the introduction of ILAs – which was already formulated as part of the cabinet agreement of October 2017. In addition to this main message, the letter called for more flexible learning opportunities. The ambition was that everybody should have an ILA. However, private learning accounts already existed, and the government's intention was not to replace those but add to them.

The letter was discussed in STAR before it was sent to Parliament. In order to get support from the social partners, the government representative had to change position on the social partners' role in developing and implementing the policy, but the disagreements between the government and the social partners on these issues were described as minor by the interviewees. Moreover, the employers' organizations and the trade unions disagreed with the government regarding financial issues. In addition to the involvement of the social partners, research and development funds, educational organizations and other stakeholders were also consulted.

A more developed version of the initiative was sent from the Ministry to the Parliament at the end of September 2018 in the form of a longer letter (Ministerie van Sociale Zaken en Werkgelegenheid, 2018). According to this letter, the overall aim in terms of the lifelong learning initiative (including the ILAs) was to promote a strong learning culture and to stimulate people's own management of their careers and lives. This would happen through the provision and communication of information about CVT, the establishment of learning accounts and the provision of a flexible range of educational opportunities (making it possible to combine training and work).

The letter included several references both to the SER's advisory report (2017) and the OECD *Skill Strategy Diagnostic Report* (2017) and quoted these in support of the need for a 'cultural change' to create the new learning culture. On the issue of individual learning accounts, it was emphasized that these could motivate people to keep developing their competences and contribute to inter-sector mobility. More technically, the letter asked for various features related to individual learning accounts, such as:

• digital overview for each individual, including overview of the training options relevant for the individual and possible financial sources;
• 'unused drawing rights' that represent publicly funded education for those who have not yet undertaken a bachelor's or master's degree;
• ILAs, both publicly funded (through the 'individual learning and development budgets') and private individual learning accounts;
• temporary ILAs for special groups, such as people over the age of 45.

The letter also addressed the question of how the accounts should be funded. The abolition of the tax credit scheme for training was one of the sources.

One of the issues mentioned in the letter that was intensively discussed during 2018 was who should be covered by the accounts. As stated above, the idea behind the initiative was not that all adults should have a publicly funded learning account, but that the new accounts should be supplemental to pre-existing private and social partner-funded account-like arrangements. Thus, the letter stated that 'given the limited public budget, the fact that many people already have access to other resources, and that the individual learning and development budget is only effective if it is of a reasonable size, the government wants to use the resources in a targeted manner' (Ministerie van Sociale Zaken en Werkgelegenheid, 2018, p. 13; own translation). However, neither the funding nor the target group issue was solved during the discussions. Another issue was how the accounts should work in practice, including whether tax deduction should be part of the initiative or not.

By the spring of 2019, the decision-making process had come to a standstill. The government had allocated money in the budget for the ILA, but not enough to implement the plans they had described in the October letter. Several interviewees pointed out that there was already, by July of 2018, a dilemma between the government's very ambitious plans and their lack of willingness to invest what was needed in order to fulfil these plans. The standstill was also linked to the stalemate surrounding another initiative, which was higher on the political agenda: a new reform of the Dutch pension system.

4.6   DISCUSSION

The findings in relation to the three research questions are discussed below.

To what extent are tripartite arrangements still used?
First, the frequency of tripartite agreements has not decreased since the Great Recession. The overview of tripartite agreements in Table 4.2 shows an increasing rather than a decreasing frequency. Leaving aside the Wassenaar Agreement and focusing on the 30-year period from 1989 to 2018, the first 19-year period (until the start of the recession)[8] had seven agreements and the last 11 years had four agreements, excluding the so-called ad hoc pacts. The four agreements in the 11-year period represent a maintenance of the status quo and not a decline in frequency compared to the earlier period.[9] Hence, measured in numbers of tripartite agreements, tripartite cooperation is not in crisis. Moreover, the rolling back of the role of the social partners in various consultative bodies, which started at the end of the 1990s and continued well into the 2000s, stopped in the present decade and their role was partly restored. However, in the period 2015–18, the social partners experienced difficulties in reaching consensus both on new social pacts and in more specific decision-making processes.

Second, the analysis hints at variation between the three policy areas with regard to the ability of the actors to reach consensus. Although not indicated in Table 4.2, nearly all the interviewees focusing on CVT were of the opinion that it was easier for consensus to be reached between the main actors on education and training issues than on most other labour market and welfare issues, including UI and ALMP. But, it was also generally agreed that CVT is an area of de facto lopsided engagement and influence between the social partners, with the employers being the most active and the most influential of the social partners. Unlike UI and ALMP, CVT – and lifelong learning more generally – has apparently not been very high on the political agenda in the Netherlands, but seems to have moved up the agenda recently.

Are the social partners still able to influence the regulation?
Third, in spite of their loss of members, which started 40 years ago and only stopped very recently, the social partners have nonetheless been able to impact

work and welfare policies in the post-2008 period. This is seen in high-profile initiatives, such as the Pension Pact 2011 (although it was afterwards rejected by FNV's two largest member organizations) and the whole 'dance' around the pension issue since 2008, where support from both employers and trade unions was necessary for the government in order to obtain its preferred increase in pension age. It is also seen in the Mondriaan Pact of 2013, which included important quid pro quos for the trade unions (and the employers' organizations) in order to obtain a reduction in the UI maximum period accepted – among these, a partial rebuilding of the national as well as regional/ local representation. The influence, although less strong, is also seen in some lower-profile initiatives such as the Participation Act and SER Refugee Committee.

Fourth, despite the sustained ability of the actors to reach tripartite agreements in the period from the Great Recession onwards, there are several signs that tripartism in the Netherlands is under pressure. As already mentioned, until the new pension agreement was signed in 2019, the period after 2015 revealed a lack of ability to reach tripartite consensus on work- and welfare-related issues. Furthermore, some of the main actors do not have warm feelings for some of the main tripartite agreements of the last decade that they signed themselves, including the Mondriaan Pact. The main problem here was not that the UI part of Mondriaan was renegotiated after bitter criticism from SME employees who desired a less bureaucratic approach to the third year of UI, but that a fair number of the interviewees (some of them publicly) fully or partly regretted the Mondriaan Pact and/or felt that the tripartite pacts during the last decades had given them too little and therefore would not be such a high priority for them in the near future. The malfunctioning of some of the new tripartite bodies is also a challenge. Moreover, SER has not, since 2006, been able to formulate the joint multi-annual strategies they used to formulate in the past (Van der Meer et al., 2019). Finally, related to this, but as part of the context of tripartite institutions, the fact that FNV, in an increasing number of cases, is not signing collective agreements, reveals a crisis in the collective bargaining system that might in time risk spilling over to tripartite regulation.

Fifth, in various ways, the analysis has touched upon the issue of new actors. As in Denmark, the social partners must increasingly share the decision-making arenas with other actors, such as the municipalities and their inter-organization, VNG, and voluntary organizations. There are at least two dimensions to this. First, the municipalities have gained in importance due to decentralization. This process took place mainly in the 2000s but has not been rolled back in the present decade. In the three areas selected for analysis, it is primarily with regard to ALMP that they have gained in importance. The interviewees' report on the relations within the old RWI consultative body and the new Workroom shows that the relations between the social partners and the municipalities are often more conflictual than consensual. The limits to the influence of the municipalities were also evident in their exclusion from the Mondriaan Pact – a process that further complicated relations with the social partners. Second, SER's activity and all 'pacting' practice have been expanded to include new issues as well as new actors. However, the social partners are still privileged actors to whom the government most often turns when formulating pacts. And there are no plans to allow for the representation of volunteer organizations in SER.

Which factors explain best the development?

Sixth, the four selected explanatory factors can be summarized as follows: like a number of earlier economic crises, the Great Recession has been a driver for tripartism, and the substantial reduction of trade union power has not prevented the social partners from still being able to influence work and welfare policies through tripartite agreements. Nevertheless, the trade unions' loss of organizational power in particular could in the long run lead to a slow death of Dutch tripartism and might already have impacted it qualitatively. There are no signs that the government ideology is important in determining their willingness to negotiate with the social partners, and the effect in terms of government strength seems to be weak. This short answer to the research question is elaborated below.

The Great Recession was a more important and direct driver for tripartite arrangements than in Denmark. For instance, the Crisis Pact addressed the crisis directly and one of the drivers behind the Mondriaan Pact was the large public deficit. The fact that the Great Recession seems to have been a driver more than a barrier to tripartism in the case of the Netherlands is also indicated by the observation that the frequency of tripartite agreements has not gone down but remained on the same level before and after 2008. The positive effect of economic crises is also illustrated in the earlier studies of Dutch corporatism. Visser and van der Meer (2011), for instance, show that six out of eight social pacts in the period 1982–90 were agreed in an economic crisis and find economic crises to be the most important driver of social pacts in the Netherlands. They find economic crisis to be an almost sufficient, though not necessary, condition for social pacts.

With regard to the strength of the social partners, the trade unions' loss of power is undeniable and substantial. The question then is whether this loss has impacted on the quantity and quality of tripartism in the Netherlands. Although the frequency of tripartite agreements, as previously described, has not been reduced, it seems nevertheless likely that the trade unions' loss of power is part of the explanation for some of the recent problems experienced in this area: for example, the Rutte-III government's hesitance to involve the social partners; the perception of FNV of not getting enough out of their participation in the pacts; the general perception of more troubled relationships in SER; and some employers' search for new employee voices. In relation to some of these developments, one of the most experienced observers of the polder model, Maarten Keune, sees a crisis in the model. However, in his study of the legitimacy of the model he finds that the trade unions' loss of power is not the only institutional challenge to the model. With regard to 'input legitimacy', the trade unions are challenged by declining membership but they still enjoy a high level of trust from the population, whereas the government's high formal legitimacy based on its Democrat mandate is not reflected in high levels of trust from the population. The employers' organizations display a relatively high organizational density, but struggle, according to Keune, with their ability to represent the interests of both large and small employers and have a weaker orientation towards the public interest than the trade unions. Moreover, although the 'output legitimacy' of the model is strong in terms of employment, growth and social peace, the model has fared less well when it comes to, for example, quality of work, productivity, quality, innovation and increasing the working hours of part-time jobs (Keune, 2016).

The effect of the government's ideology on the development of tripartism does not seem to be strong in the Netherlands. As in Denmark, multi-party minority government dominates, but unlike in Denmark, government coalitions between left and right are common. As Table 4.2 illustrates, left-right governments have been responsible for two tripartite agreements (excluding ad hoc agreements), whereas centre-left and centre-right governments have each signed three.

The effect from the strength of the government is trickier to analyse, as it is not always straightforward to determine whether a government should be classified as strong or weak. As the data collection, including the interviews, has not focused on this issue to any large extent, the attempt here will partly be based on other researchers' classifications (Avdagic, Rhodes and Visser, 2011; Van der Meer et al., 2019; Visser and van der Meer, 2010). As in the Danish country study, the strong–weak classification is primarily, but not only, based on whether the government represents a majority in Parliament and if the government is united or divided internally.

The two Christian Democrat-Liberal majority governments in power between 1982 and 1989 were strong and each signed one tripartite agreement (the first being the important Wassenaar Agreement). The following 1989–94 Christian Democrat-Social Democrat majority government was also strong, and, as in 1982, strong enough to threaten the social partners with unilateral initiatives. This government signed one tripartite agreement. Wim Kok's first Social Democrat-Liberal majority government (1994–98) was challenged in the sense that it could not agree internally on the course for labour market reform, but was nevertheless a strong government. It invited the social partners to tripartite negotiations, which resulted in a tripartite agreement (the well-known Flexicurity Agreement). The second Kok Social Democrat-Liberal majority government (1998–2002) was a strong government that did not sign any tripartite agreements. Also, the first and second Balkenende Christian Democrat-Liberal governments (2002–06) were weak, despite their majority status, which had to do with internal division and declining public support. These two governments together signed three tripartite agreements. The third Balkenende government (Christian Democrat-Liberal, 2006–07) was the first minority government for years and it was weak and short-lived and signed no tripartite agreements, whereas the fourth was a Christian Democrat-Social Democrat majority government that was in office from 2007 to 2010 and thus had to address the first impacts of the Great Recession. It postponed many decisions, but still signed two tripartite agreements (although FNV later withdrew from one of them, the Pension Agreement). Altogether it was a divided and weak government. The subsequent government was the Rutte Liberal-Christian Democrat minority government (2010–12). It only had one-third of the seats in Parliament and was a weak government. It did not sign any tripartite agreements and side-lined the trade unions in general. The second Rutte Liberal-Social Democrat government was a majority government but was seen as weak because their majority was small and because of ideological differences between the two parties. It nevertheless served for five years and the government (and its social partner-friendly Ministry of Labour) signed the large Mondriaan Pact as well as three 'unusual' smaller tripartite agreements. Finally, the incumbent third Rutte Liberal-Christian Democrat majority government, which is strong, has to date signed one tripartite agreement.[10]

This classification of government gives approximately 20 years with strong governments signing five tripartite agreements (0.25 agreements per year on average) and 15 years with weak governments signing seven agreements (0.47 agreement per year) – all in all, only weak support for the hypothesis of an effect from government strength, considering the uncertainty of the method.

NOTES

1. See the FNV website at https://www.fnv.nl/. Accessed 12 March 2019.
2. See the CNV website at https://www.cnv.nl. Accessed 20 March 2019.
3. See https://vng.nl/. Accessed 24 March 2019.
4. According to Van der Meer et al. (2019, p. 26) the four met in 12 meetings. To avoid media attention, many of the meetings took place in a military bunker.
5. A situation in which a company subcontracts, that is, employs another company to deal with the payment of its employees and responsibility for their official records, and so on.
6. However, one of the interviewees who took part in the decision-making process questions whether this was really the net outcome, or whether funds have just

been relabelled. According to this interviewee, the financial resources per person involved in ALMP schemes actually decreased.

7. See https://www.ser.nl/nl/thema/werkwijzer-vluchtelingen, accessed 5 April 2019; Stichting van de Arbeid (2017).

8. Because 'Doing Together What Is Possible' from October 2008 is a tripartite agreement in reaction to the crisis (Visser and van der Meer, 2010), it makes sense to include it in what elsewhere in the book is labelled the 'post-2008' period.

9. It is arguable whether the Pension Pact should be included in this calculation or not. On the one hand, all three parties were agreed upon it, but on the other hand FNV's two largest member organizations rejected it. However, even if this pact is excluded, the number of pacts per year is not notably higher before 2008 than after, and the number in both periods is 0.36 if the year 2019 is included.

10. Although not analysed in any depth because the most important part of its decision-making period took place after the period in focus this chapter, the Rutte-III government and the social partners' tripartite pension agreement in June 2019 is included here.

5. Austria: political challenges in the corporatist country par excellence

5.1 THE INSTITUTIONAL SET-UP OF LABOUR MARKET REGULATION

In Visser's classification of labour market models (Visser, 2008), Austria is placed in the same regime as the Netherlands, namely the Centre-West social partnership regime, which is characterized by features such as a coordinated market economy, balanced power relations between the social partners, a dualistic and status-oriented employment regime and an institutionalized role for social partners in welfare policies. However, the Austrian labour market model also includes a number of differences from the Netherlands, as will be apparent from this chapter.

The Historical Development of the Labour Market Model

Austria has often been seen as the corporatist country par excellence and the Austrian version of corporatism is sometimes labelled 'Austro-corporatism' (Bischof and Pelinka, 1996) or 'social partnership'. The terms 'social partners' (referring to the trade unions and employers' organizations) and 'social partnership' have German and Austrian origins and, to some extent, reflect Christian-Democratic philosophy. In the case of Austria, social partnership describes the attempt to replace the class antagonism of the inter-war years' civil war and the following collapse of democracy with class cooperation (Hyman, 2001).

A key feature of the Austrian model of corporatism is the presence of three so-called 'chambers', with compulsory membership for most employers, employees and farmers, respectively. Ignoring a few German *Länder*, these chambers are unique to Austria. The chambers exist alongside more traditional trade unions and employers' organizations. The chambers have been incorporated into public policymaking from the mid-nineteenth century (Tálos and Kittel, 1996). The compulsory membership of the employers' organizations means a high degree of centralization in industrial relations and very high coverage rates for the collective agreements (98 per cent in the private sector;

Glassner, 2019). The social partner organizations are presented in more detail below.

Another key feature of Austrian corporatism is a strong tradition of tripartism. With regard to the role tripartite cooperation plays across policy areas, a number of tripartite (and bipartite) bodies should be mentioned. The Parity Commission (with subcommittees) was founded in 1957 and was for some decades the core of the Austrian model of corporatism. The commission has four subcommittees, some of them tripartite and some bipartite. The Subcommittee for Prices was, initially, the core of the Parity Commission. The main task of the subcommittee was, in the early period, to set prices for consumer products like flour, bread and gas in a way that was socially equitable and, at the same time, would not violate the free market too much. When this task became outdated, the focus was transferred to questions regarding the competitiveness of various trades. The Subcommittee for Wages decided the timing of the collective bargaining rounds at national level. The Subcommittee for International Affairs is a newer subcommittee. It grew out of Austria's entry into the EU in 1995 – a process that included extensive tripartite cooperation. Its main task is to evaluate international developments and submit expertise and proposals. The bipartite Advisory Board for Economic and Social Affairs, founded in 1963, discusses and issues reports on a large number of economic, social and also environmental issues (Fichtner, 2002; Karlhofer, 1996).

According to the interviewees, as of today, the Parity Commission superstructure does not meet anymore, and its subcommittee has only a consultative (advisory) status. The only subcommittee that has played more than a marginal role in Austrian work and welfare policies in the 2010s is, accordingly, the Advisory Board, and even this subcommittee has been marginalized lately. The board's 89 publications since 1963 include both publications of fact-oriented reports without recommendations and more recommendation-oriented reports. The latest reports have been on the structure of wage costs (2017), digitalization (2017), competition law (2014), innovation (2013) and migration (2011). Since around 2000, it has nearly exclusively been the social partners who have initiated the activities, whereas, previously, the initiative sometimes came from the government. This was the case, for instance, in connection to Austria's accession to the EU and the Economic Monetary Union (EMU) in the mid-1990s. In addition to these permanent bodies, there have, for years, been peak-level annual thematic meetings held between the government and the social partners in the town of Bad Ischl, the so-called 'Bad Ischler Dialog'.

Apart from the permanent tripartite bodies, tripartism in Austria also implies that the social partners have traditionally been involved in concertation or consultation processes with regard to social, employment, welfare, industrial and economic policies. According to some scholars, this is more important for the social partnership model than the permanent bodies (Traxler and Pernicka,

2007). Moreover, the links between the social partner organizations and the political parties have been close. For instance, the Minister of Employment and Social Affairs has often had a background in the unions, and between 1970 and 2000 seven prime ministers and six secretaries of state had a background in the Advisory Council for Economic and Social Affairs (Karlhofer, 2007).

A third key feature of the Austrian labour market model is historically very low strike levels, reflecting a consensus culture in industrial relations, and this continued into the new millennium. Between 2005 and 2010, no strikes occurred in the overall economy in Austria, whereas 2011 saw the most extensive strike action in recent years – in the metalworking industry – with over 87 000 employees involved and more than 56 670 working days of strikes. Since then, there have been strikes and strike warnings in most years, reflecting slightly more conflictual collective bargaining rounds. Still, compared with other countries, Austria has an extremely low level of strike action: per 1000 workers, there were only two days lost per year in the period 2008–16 (European Trade Union Institute [ETUI], 2018; Glassner, 2019).

A fourth key feature is centralized social partner organizations and relatively centralized collective bargaining. This fourth feature will be addressed in the following section.

Who Are the Social Partners and How Representative Are They?

There are three main cross-industry *employer* organizations in Austria (see Table 5.1). The mandatory Austrian Chamber of Commerce (Wirtschaftskammer Österreich, WKO), the voluntary Chamber of Agriculture (Landwirtschaftskammer Österreichs, LKO) and the voluntary Federation of Austrian Industries (Industriellenvereinigung, IV), which organizes large enterprises mostly in the manufacturing industry. IV is not formally recognized as a social partner organization and does not take part in collective bargaining, but does takes part in several tripartite bodies. All companies and entrepreneurs holding a business licence must register with the WKO (and its corresponding subunits), which is organized along geographical subdivisions (provinces, known as *Länder*) and sectoral sections, which are further subdivided into sectoral subunits. The fact that all companies are legally bound to be members gives small and medium-sized enterprises (SMEs) – that in most other countries are less likely to be members of employers' organizations – a strong weight within WKO (Trampusch and Eichenberger, 2012). Companies holding more than one business licence must register with all corresponding WKO sectoral groups; this means that there are more members than companies due to the fact that many employers hold more than one business licence. Due to the compulsory membership of all of Austria's companies – with the exception of those in agriculture, the liberal professions and the non-trading public sector – of the WKO and its respective subunits, the density of WKO in terms of both companies and employees is 100 per cent. No information is available on the IV's membership density (Krenn et al., 2018), but according to an IV interviewee, IV represents 4500 companies. The large majority of manufacturing companies and private service companies linked to the manufacturing sector are members.

Table 5.1   *The Austrian social partner organizations and their organizational densities*

	Members	Organizational Density
Employers (private sector)*		
Chamber of Commerce (WKO)	528 000	100%
Chamber of Agriculture (LKO)	161 200	?
IV**	4 500	?
Employees		
Chamber of Labour	3 700 000	100%
ÖGB	1 200 000	27%

Sources: Adam (2019); * Krenn et al. (2018) (figures from 2016–17); ** information from IV interviewee.

On the *employee* side, regarding the Austrian trade unions, it is first notable that their organizational density has been reduced from 57 per cent at its peak in 1970 to 26 per cent in 2015 (Figure 5.1) – a development that has weakened the unions' organizational power[1] (Krenn et al., 2018; Rathgeb, 2018). Second, their close links with the Chamber of Labour is a strong organizational resource for the trade unions. Although the Chamber of Labour has been under attack from both the first and second People's Party-Freedom Party (ÖVP-FPÖ) governments (see below), they have so far managed to avoid severe cuts in their funding and changes in the rules of compulsory membership. Since the organizational resources of the Chamber of Labour, in terms of staff, are many times bigger than those of the Austrian Trade Union Federation (Österreichischer Gewerkschaftsbund, ÖGB; Table 5.1), the Chamber of Labour's resources are crucial for ÖGB's ability to have access to the high-quality preparation of their decision-making processes. Third, the fact that the Austrian trade union movement is a unitary movement makes it more integrated than union movements in most other European countries. ÖGB has sectoral member organizations, but these sector unions are not independent affiliates but rather subdivisions, and ÖGB exercises full control over the members' financial resources and is able to shift decision making to the inter-sectoral level (Rathgeb, 2018). Fourth, whereas the link between the Social Democratic/Socialist parties and the trade unions has been loosened substantially in several European countries, including Denmark and the Netherlands, the ties are strong in Austria. An analysis of the ties in the 1995–99 period found that 32 per cent of the Social Democratic Party of Austria's (Sozialdemokratische Partei Österreichs, SPÖ) members of parliament had direct or indirect ties to the trade unions (Heinish, 2000). The ties remain strong and include, for instance, the fact that the ÖGB still has the right to appoint members to SPÖ's committees and conferences and SPÖ still regularly appoints prominent union leaders as ministers of employment and social affairs (Rathgeb, 2018, p. 67).

In recent years, the Austrian trade unions have increasingly been confronted by the need to merge due to a combination of factors – in particular, a decline in membership and financial weakness, especially in the wake of the revelation of ÖGB's involvement in the financial debacle concerning its former bank. As a consequence of the bank crisis, ÖGB was forced to sell all its shares in the bank in 2006. Since then, the only source of revenue for ÖGB and its member unions has been the membership dues. With the latest restructuring and merging processes, ÖGB was significantly streamlined, compared with the late 1990s. Within a ten-year period, the number of trade unions affiliated to the ÖGB was reduced from 14 to seven unions, while no notable developments have occurred during the past few years (Krenn et al., 2018).

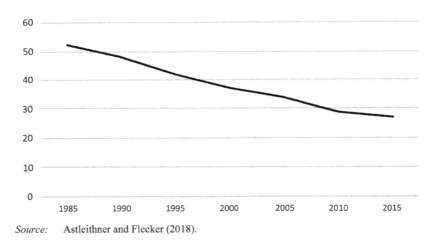

Source: Astleithner and Flecker (2018).

Figure 5.1   *Trade union density in Austria, in percentages*

Austria does not have large formal interest organizations for the subnational level, like the Danish and Dutch interest organizations for the municipalities.

The Landeshauptleutekonferenz (Conference of the State Governors) is only an informal institution. However, according to one interviewee, it is quite powerful. It consists of top-level representatives from the *Länder*. While the Austrian constitution gives the central government the priority in practically all fields of policymaking, the *Länder* have a say too or are at least responsible for important parts of the implementation. Without the support of the Landeshauptleutekonferenz and the use of binding agreements between the federal and *Länder* level, the federal government is often quite limited in their power to implement policies. The field of further education is an example, as the central state has practically no legal competences as the Constitution regards adult education as a matter for the regional states. Only by construing further education as a matter of labour market policy can the central state play an important role in the field of further education and continuing vocational training (CVT), as described below.

5.2 CORPORATIST ARRANGEMENTS IN A 30-YEAR PERSPECTIVE: AN OVERVIEW

For decades, an important context for tripartism in Austria has been the presence of so-called Grand Coalition majority governments, including the Social Democrats in SPÖ and the Christian Democrats in ÖVP. They were in office together from 1987 to 1999, and again from 2006 to 2017. However, also important are the shorter periods where ÖVP has formed a government with the right-wing Freedom Party, FPÖ, which, in various ways, has been eager to challenge the Austrian social partnership model. ÖVP and FPÖ formed a government from 2000 to 2006 and again from 2017 to 2019 (see Table 5.2 for a summary of the following history of tripartism in Austria covered in this section).

Several observers have described the social partnership model as a fairly stable model up until the end of the 1980s/beginning of the 1990s, both with regard to the permanent tri- and bipartite bodies mentioned above and in relation to processes not involving these bodies. Some of the most experienced scholars of Austro-corporatism have described the period's typical decision-making process in social, employment, industrial and economic policies as this: first, consultations between the ministry in focus, SPÖ, ÖVP and the social partners; second, review – one or more times – of draft legislation in the formal hearing processes; third, when consensus is reached, the Council of Ministers sends the draft to Parliament, where the social partners have an informal second opportunity to exert some influence because several MPs have ties to the trade unions. The corrections made at this stage in Parliament were often minor (Tálos and Kittel, 2002). Even though the authors found it difficult to make a clear distinction between concertation and consultation processes in the case of Austrian decision making, the system here could be said to lean towards concertation, considering the strong role of the social partners.

The social partners' roles were also strong in relation to some of the new challenges that Austria faced from the 1990s onwards. Hence, the social partners were deeply involved in the EU accession process. The social partner organizations played important roles in the decision-making processes up to the accession. After some hesitation from the trade unions, all social partner organizations ended up advising electors to vote 'yes' in the referendum in 1994. The social partners were also granted significant roles in policy implementation for the EU legislation and they secured formal status in Austria's representation in Brussels (Karlhofer, 1996; Müller, 2009). Although the social partners, in many cases, were still strong in the 1990s, during the decade there were more instances than previously when the Grand Coalition governments diverged from the social partnership path in a unilateral direction, without fundamentally challenging the social partnership model.

In relation to the efforts to meet the Maastricht convergence criteria, austerity policies were introduced in the mid-1990s. For the first time since World War II, an Austrian government formulated an economic policy package without the involvement of the social partners. This happened when one of the Grand Coalitions in 1994 presented a package of savings called the '52-point Programme'. This savings package formed the backbone of an austerity package in 1995. However, ÖGB protested loudly about both process and content and presented alternative ways to improve the public finances. The presence of a strong ÖGB faction within SPÖ made this criticism forceful. In the end, the government decided to renegotiate the austerity package and made concessions to the trade unions in order to have sufficiently strong support for the 1995 package. In 1996, after general elections, the new Grand Coalition government found that a new austerity package was needed and this time parts of the negotiations on the package were delegated to the social partners (Rathgeb, 2018, pp. 73–4). However, it later became clear that the social partners could no longer expect to be consulted early on every single important reform when the government, in 1997, announced far-reaching changes in the pension system without the prior consultation of the social partners. After consulting the social partners on the details only, the government let the legislation pass in Parliament despite strong opposition from the workers' organizations (Tálos and Kittel, 2002).

New challenges appeared when FPÖ gained as much representation at the general election in late 1999 as ÖVP, with whom they formed a government under an ÖVP prime minister in early 2000. Initially, the ÖVP-FPÖ government challenged the social partners in several ways, and a large number of reforms was introduced by the government unilaterally during its first year in power: a reduction in the family surcharges and in federal contributions to labour market policy; a reduction of the basic replacement rate of unemployment insurance (UI) from 57 to 55 per cent and an extension of the qualifying period from 26 to 28 weeks; and a freezing of benefit indexation and tightening of sanctions (Fink, 2006, p. 181). Other challenges were discussed, but never put into practice, such as reducing the budget of the chambers by 50 per cent.

According to the interviewees, this period of challenging the social partnership ended around 2004, with 2002–03 being a 'transition period' with a mixture of hostility and respect towards the social partnership model. In 2002, the government failed to agree internally on a reform of the severance payment system. FPÖ had a strong anti-neo-liberal strain, whereas it was precisely the neo-liberal part of ÖVP that was strengthened in that period. Part of the problem with the severance payment regulation at the time was that only the employment record from one employer was used in the calculation of the severance payment in case the employee changed employer. This was to the benefit of employees staying in the same enterprise but not to the benefit of the growing number of non-standard employees. Moreover, the potentially large sums that employers had to pay in one go in case of mass redundancies could pose liquidity problems particularly for SMEs (Rathgeb, 2018; Weishaupt and Privara, 2013).[2]

To the surprise of some, the government then delegated decision making for the reform to the social partners. According to one of the interviewees, the reasoning of the government was that – given their own lack of ability to reach consensus – they would not lose much with this strategy: either the social partners would agree, and have a small victory on something that was not a high priority for the government, or they would fail to agree and the failure would be theirs and not the government's. The bipartite process led to some level of consensus between the social partners and the bipartite process was then taken over by tripartite negotiations that ended in an agreement that made it obligatory for all employment relationships, regardless of their employment type, to accumulate portable savings for severance pay. In this way the regulation was homogenized across employment types to the benefit of non-standard employees (Rathgeb, 2018).

Later in 2003, the government was back on its anti-social partnership track when it formulated a pension reform unilaterally, even though the worker organizations opposed it and ÖGB organized one of its few mass demonstrations against the changes. The reform included an extension of the reference period for calculating the pension from 15 to 40 years and phased out access to early retirement pensions. The government proposal was, with a few modifications, adopted in Parliament. But the agreement included the opportunity of modifying the reform further, which happened after tripartite talks one year later. Some of the interviewees felt that the government, following the severance payment agreement, had simply learned the lesson that things are easier

Table 5.2   *Overview of tripartite agreements in Austria, 1989–2017*

Year	Name	Government	Areas
1989	Amendment of UI Reform	SPÖ-ÖVP	UI
1992	Gender Equality in Working Life Reform	SPÖ-ÖVP	Gender equality
1992	Youth Apprenticeship Mobility Law	SPÖ-ÖVP	Vocational education
1994	Public Employment Service Reform	SPÖ-ÖVP	Active labour market policy (ALMP)
1996	Austerity Package	SPÖ-ÖVP	Public budget, several areas
2000	Sickness Payment Harmonization	SPÖ-ÖVP	Sickness payment
2001	Health and Safety Reform	ÖVP-FPÖ	Work environment
2003	Severance Payment Reform	ÖVP-FPÖ	UI
2004	Modification of Pension Reform	ÖVP-FPÖ	Pensions
2007	Amendments of UI Reform	SPÖ-ÖVP	UI
2007	Youth Unemployment Reform	SPÖ-ÖVP	ALMP
2009	Labour Market Package 1	SPÖ-ÖVP	ALMP, UI
2009	Labour Market Package 2	SPÖ-ÖVP	ALMP, UI
2009–10	Tax Reform	SPÖ-ÖVP	Income tax
2010	Labour Market Package 3	SPÖ-ÖVP	ALMP, UI
2011	Act Against Wage and Social Dumping	SPÖ-ÖVP	Wages, labour migration
2011	Red-White-Red-Card	SPÖ-ÖVP	Labour migration
2013	Amendment to Educational Leave Scheme	SPÖ-ÖVP	CVT
2013	Skilled Workers Grant	SPÖ-ÖVP	CVT
2014	Tax Reform	SPÖ-ÖVP	Tax policy
2016–17	Aktion 20,000	SPÖ-ÖVP	ALMP

Sources: The analyses below; Rathgeb (2018); information from the interviewees.

with than without the social partners. However, the fact that the unilateral pension reform took place after this does not support this interpretation.[3]

After the pension reform, the ÖVP-FPÖ government did not challenge the social partnership model again, although relations in some contexts – for instance, in the Advisory Board for Economic and Social Questions – never got back to normal, according to some interviewees.

In 2006, a new Grand Coalition (SPÖ-ÖVP) came into office and announced its intention to involve the social partners in virtually all areas of economic, labour and social issues. WKO and ÖGB enjoyed good relations in this period. These good relations helped to stabilize the Grand Coalition, which had various plans for reform, and facilitated reforms of both youth unemployment in 2007 (see Section 5.4) and UI in the same year (see Section 5.3), as well as working time.

Since the Great Recession

Whether as a result of their effective response to the crisis or as a result of other factors, the impact of the crisis in Austria was not very strong. In 2009, there was only a modest increase in unemployment to 5.2 per cent from 4.1 per cent the previous year. However, in 2013, unemployment started to increase again and it peaked as late as in 2016 with 6 per cent. In 2018, it stood at 4.9 per cent (Eurostat, various years).

A new Grand Coalition under SPÖ leadership took office more or less simultaneously with the outbreak of the Great Recession. According to the interviewees, the government was quick to set up tripartite talks in order to meet the challenges, which resulted in three labour market packages between 2008 and 2010, in addition to an economic stimulus package. An overview report from early 2011 mentioned no fewer than 25 political initiatives of varying importance. Among the most important of these measures was an increase in the budget of active labour market policy (ALMP) by 24 per cent and – as in several other countries – changes to the short-time work arrangements' regulations. In the Austrian case, the arrangements were made more inclusive with regard to reductions in working time and target groups, in that temporary workers were included and benefits were extended both in relation to the time period and by including training (Federal Ministry of Labour, Social Affairs, Health and Consumer Protection, 2011). In addition to the public policy initiatives, the social partners came up with ALMP initiatives on their own. WKO, for instance, issued a publication with advice to their members on how to reduce wage costs without laying off employees (Gleißner, 2009).

In the years 2011–16 there were relatively few new reforms in the Austrian labour market (ETUI, 2018; see, though, the three policy area sections for some of these). Although only indirectly related to work and employment regulation, the tax reform of 2014 is worth mentioning, in that, through annual negative tax refunds, it increased real income for low-income groups. The social partners were consulted on the form of the 'concertation-like' path described above. On top of this, the workers' organizations ran the campaign 'More Money in the Wallet', which proposed a tax reform that – with some modifications – was adopted by the government (ibid.). This was yet another example of the strong influence of these organizations.

Around 2015, discussions on reducing working time were restarted by the trade unions, which teamed up with a large number of non-governmental organizations in their campaign. However, in the 2015 collective bargaining round, the trade unions demanded an extra holiday week and not a general working-time reduction (ibid.). However, the issue of working time continued to be on the agenda (see below).

The 'revival of social partnership' (Pernicka and Hefler, 2015) came to a halt in late 2017 when a new ÖVP-FPÖ government took office. As in 2000, the government announced a reduction in the influence of the trade unions. From the outset the government demonstrated that it would walk the talk.

One of the Grand Coalition's later initiatives in the work and welfare areas involved the delegation in 2016 of the negotiations on new working-time regulation to the social partners, which, inter alia, aimed to extend the maximum daily and weekly possible working time from their maximum of ten hours and 50 hours, respectively. The social partners made progress on creating consensus and, during the following tripartite negotiations, an agreement was so close that, according to interviewees, it was announced prematurely by the minister in a way and at a time that was unacceptable to the trade unions. After this, the negotiations stopped and no agreement was reached. At that point, the ÖVP-FPÖ government stated that the social partners had had their opportunity to make changes and failed – and that the government would, therefore, unilaterally decide on the changes in the working-time regulation. As a result, the maximum working times were extended to 12 hours per day and 60 hours per week in September 2018. ÖGB was very dissatisfied with both the process and the outcome and arranged one of their few mass protests in response, in which some 100 000 people participated – a lot for an Austrian demonstration.

Other steps that represented a challenge for the trade unions included, according to several government and trade union interviewees, a substantial shortening of the time for the hearing process for draft legislation – with the social partners at times being excluded from the process altogether. In some cases, the hearing process could be counted in hours rather than in days. This shortening of the hearing process, according to these interviewees, has been seen both in connection with the new working-time legislation and with several other initiatives. Moreover, the pre-legislative consultation and concertation processes of the Grand Coalition disappeared and was replaced with what might be called a 'post-legislation' hearing, in that the hearing took place only after draft legislation was already formulated.

As in their period in office from 2000 to 2006, the ÖVP-FPÖ government signalled their intention of reducing funding for the chambers. In line with the work programme of the government, the chambers were asked to be more efficient and economical and to target their work closer to the citizens. The government therefore invited the chambers to present reform programmes (on efficient structures and financial relief) by June of 2018. At the same time, the government stated that if the proposals did not appear to be broad enough or sufficiently targeted, the government would reserve the right to propose legislation to ensure the necessary reforms itself. Both the Chamber of Labour and the Chamber of Commerce were affected, although the Chamber of Commerce stated that they had already carried out improvements to their organization in a cost-efficient manner, whereas the Chamber of Agriculture, according to the interviewees, was, oddly, not mentioned directly in the debate. As a response to the request, the Chamber of Labour suggested in mid-2018 that, rather than reduce costs, they could instead offer more services for the same budget as they had planned, but the government did not follow up on their request. Had the cuts gone ahead, the interviewees agreed that they would have hit the Chamber of Labour much harder than the Chamber of Commerce, because, unlike the Chamber of Commerce, it would be difficult for them to raise alternative funding. Although some kind of organizational change in the chambers was not off the table – the chambers were asked by the government to come up with some kind of reform programme – no initiatives had been taken by the time the government had to resign in May 2019. Several of the interviewees had the impression that, after the confrontation with the trade unions in connection with the new working-time regulations, the government was hesitant to have further hard confrontations.

Another government challenge to trade union representation was passed in Parliament, not in the field of work and welfare regulation but rather in relation to the health insurance system, and focused on the governance structures for sickness and disability benefits. Its governance structures had always been bipartite (plus a ministerial representative to supervise it), but lopsided, in the sense that the trade unions had the majority of the seats, which was justified on the basis that the insured parties were the employees not the employers. The ÖVP-FPÖ government changed this structure in 2018 into bipartite parity, a move that was met by protests from the trade unions, whereas WKO accepted the change. In addition to these challenges, the ÖVP-FPÖ government introduced a number of other new policies and abandoned some old ones to the general regret of the trade unions. Some of these are presented in the next three sections.

In addition to the changes driven by the government, some interviewees from the workers' organizations reported that the employers' organizations had also contributed to the weakening of the social partnership model. The long-serving (2008–18) president, Christoph Leitl, of WKO had a close relationship with the equally long-serving (2008–18) president of ÖGB, Erich Foglar. Recently, both these ÖGB and WKO leaders were replaced and, according to some of the workers organizations' interviewees, the new WKO president, Harald Mahrer – who is also an MEP for ÖVP and second president of the National Council – was more concerned with his close relations to the Austrian prime minister, Sebastian Kurz, than with the new ÖGB president, Wolfgang Katzian, and was in general much less open towards ÖGB than the previous president of WKO. One interviewee, on the other hand, questioned the importance of the changes in top management positions and pointed to the fact that these changes took place more or less simultaneously with the, arguably, more important change in government.

5.3   UNEMPLOYMENT INSURANCE

From the Introduction Until the Great Recession

The institutionalization of unemployment insurance (UI) in Austria goes back to 1920, when legislation established a national UI scheme, including a large number of local UI offices governed by social partner bodies. The local UI offices were responsible for job placement too (Soentken and Weishaupt, 2014). The Austrian Bismarckian welfare state tradition influenced the construction of the UI system in Austria, which was based on the male breadwinner model and implied strong roles for the social partners and advantages for full-time employees and disadvantages for atypical employees of various kinds (Rathgeb, 2018).

The compulsory UI is mainly financed by employers and employees. At present, up to 6 per cent of the wage bill is paid by the employer (3 per cent) and employee (0–3 per cent depending on wage level) for this purpose. Recent reforms mean that marginal part-timers with very low income, civil servants and most self-employed people are exempted from paying contributions (Allinger, 2012; Austrian Presidency of the Council of the European Union, 2018).

In 1987, the general maximum replacement rate was reduced from 66 to 64 per cent, and for single persons to 55 per cent. Amendment of unemployment insurance law (1989) included the upward homogenization of net replacement rates that benefited low-wage earners and eased access to unemployment benefit for young people below the age of 25 by cutting the qualifying period from 52 to 20 years. The general maximum replacement rate was reduced further in the early 2000s to 61 per cent and again to 60 per cent in the late 2000s (Rathgeb, 2018, p. 70).

The roles of the social partners have, since 1994, been secured in the tripartite board of the Public Employment Service (PES; see Section 5.4 for a description of PES and its tasks). Moreover, the social partners were, to various extents, involved in these reforms, but they also have additional schemes themselves. However, very few sector agreements offer additional unemployment insurance, though several unions unilaterally offer their members supplementary benefits (Wöss, Reiff and Gruber, 2016).

From the Great Recession

As stated above, one of the responses to the crisis in Austria was to make the existing short-time work arrangements more inclusive with regard to reductions in working time and target groups, by including temporary workers. Moreover, the benefit was extended both in relation to the time period and what it could be used for, in that training was included as an eligible activity (Federal Ministry of Labour, Social Affairs, Health and Consumer Protection, 2011).

Currently, UI accounts for 55 per cent of previous net income and 60 per cent if the benefit does not exceed 883 euros per month (2016 figure). When the UI is exhausted, it is possible to receive a benefit in between UI and social assistance called 'Notstandshilfe' (Unemployment Assistance, UA). This amounts to 92–95 per cent of UI, but until 2017 the level was reduced if a partner within the household also had income. UA is de facto without time limit. Social assistance is the last tier (Wöss et al., 2016).

The UA scheme has been included in the reform plans of the latest ÖVP-FPÖ government. This is analysed in the case below.

CASE: PLANS TO ABANDON OR REDUCE THE UNEMPLOYMENT ASSISTANCE SCHEME, 2017–19

This case is different from most of the others in the book, in that it did not reach Parliament before it was halted – at least temporarily – because the ÖVP-FPÖ government had to resign in May 2019. However, a number of interviewees indicated that the government had decided, even before that, to at least postpone the reform in order not to have too many fights with the trade unions and the opposition and also to prevent alienating a part of their own electorate (the FPÖ affiliates). The high level of stability in the UI area in the present decade is the reason that reform of the UA was selected as a case in spite of its 'unfinished' nature.

Setting the Agenda

According to the interviewees, the employers in WKO have for a long time wanted to abandon the UA scheme, which could be said to be somewhere in between a standard UI and a social assistance scheme. In WKO's opinion, the existence of a UA scheme – at the rate of 92–95 per cent of UI to be received for a de facto unlimited period – is reducing the job search activities among the unemployed and hence the employment level. In 2015, the employers' organization, IV, suggested making changes to adopt some elements comparable to the German 'Hartz-IV' welfare benefits and UI reform, which got rid of its

UA-type scheme. Interestingly, for the focus of this book, the president of IV declared that 'social partnership in its current form is dead' around the time the proposal was presented. The trade unions sharply rejected the IV proposal (Krenn, 2015).

In the past, the UA scheme was partly means tested, in that the income of the partner of the unemployed person could lead to a reduction in the unemployment assistance benefit level. This means testing was abandoned in 2017 under the Grand Coalition, but by an 'alternative' majority secured by the Social Democrats and FPÖ with backing from the trade unions and opposition from FPÖ and the employers.

The plan of the ÖVP-FPÖ government – which is based on and briefly described in the government agreement from late 2017 – added to changes made in the social assistance system in 2018 by the newly elected government. These changes included reductions in the benefit level for disabled people and for migrants. The changes for migrants both included the lowering of total benefit level for families with many children, and the lowering of benefit for all others, in that, following the changes to the legislation, the refugees had to pay for the previously free German-language courses.

Decision Making

The interviewees did not fully agree about whether the government would have abandoned the UA scheme totally or if they would just have limited the duration of it.

The government did conduct a study of how the new UI/UA system would work when implemented, but the social partners were not involved in the study and it had not yet been developed into a concrete proposal when the government resigned in May 2019. Apart from abandoning or limiting the UA, the government's plan was to make the system more digressive, that is, with higher levels at the beginning of the unemployment spell and also more dependent on the individuals' insurance contribution.

Although UI and UA are among the areas of responsibility of the Public Employment Service (PES), new policy initiatives are rarely discussed in PES. This was also the case with the attempt to abandon/limit the UA scheme. However, the respective positions of the social partners were, unsurprisingly, that the employers' organizations were in favour and the trade unions were against. According to some of the interviewees, WKO's interest in getting rid of UA was to lower the 3 + 3 per cent employer/employee contribution and thereby lower the wage costs. According to a Chamber of Labour interviewee, the trade unions joined forces with a number of civil society organizations to counteract the government plans. In their argumentation, the trade unions and civil society organizations tried to target the sizeable share of the FPÖ electorate that could be expected to have their benefits reduced due to the reform. At the time of writing it remains to be seen what future the initiative will have.

5.4   ACTIVE LABOUR MARKET POLICY

Spending on active labour market policy (ALMP) in Austria has, ever since the mid-1990s and until very recently, shown a slow, but steady, increase. In 1994, spending was 0.36 per cent of GDP, which by 2017 had increased to 0.75 per cent (Eurostat, 2019). In 2018, however, the budget decreased for the first time in decades as a result of cuts introduced by the newly elected ÖVP-FPÖ government but, according to some interviewees, the reduction is the result of the winding up of a single programme – Aktion 20,000 (see below). Compared to Denmark and the Netherlands, tripartite cooperation has been more stable in Austria, as will be described below.

Until the Great Recession

Austria established its first Public Employment Service (PES) in 1920. PES was governed by social partner committees and the social partners have had strong advisory or decision-making competences in one form or another ever since. In the 1980s, when unemployment was rising, the employers – who had traditionally been less engaged and influential in PES questions than the unions – strongly criticized PES for being slow and inefficient. Therefore, the employers felt that the state should no longer be the main responsible actor for ALMP. ÖVP also argued for reforms, in their case from a market perspective. As a response, the SPÖ-ÖVP government was forced to reform PES (Soentken and Weishaupt, 2014).

The present structure of PES goes back to the 1994 reform that gave it a semi-autonomous status with regard to the Ministry of Labour and Social Affairs and granted the social partners greater decision-making competences. This reform was decided more or less simultaneously with reforms in Denmark and the Netherlands that strengthened tripartite structures. But, unlike the other two countries, the formal tripartite structures were not subsequently weakened in Austria.

Since the 1994 reform, PES has been governed by a tripartite board, where the government, the trade unions and the employers have one-third of the seats each. There are also tripartite boards in the nine provincial (*Länder*) PES offices and the 101 regional (local) offices. The main competences of PES can briefly be said to be: implementing ALMP measures; verifying claims for and paying UI; implementing other labour market policies, such as the admission of third-country nationals to the labour market; and providing vocational training options to young people through placement in suitable apprenticeships

(Federal Ministry of Labour, Social Affairs, Health and Consumer Protection, 2017).

A core task for PES is the setting of guidelines for ALMP. General guidelines, or guideline indicators, are formulated by the Minister of Labour and Social Affairs. After receiving these, the PES board (known as AMS) transforms them into specific guidelines, which PES then quantifies. In 2017, there were eight quantitative targets (AMS, 2017). Hence, it is a three-step process. If the PES board cannot agree on a guideline – which requires two-thirds of the votes + 1 – the guideline goes back to the Ministry of Labour and Social Affairs. This happens rarely. In addition to discussing the guidelines, PES also discusses the ALMP budget and is responsible for allocating and prioritizing resources for different activities.

Decisions in PES are nearly always taken unanimously. However, this should not be understood as meaning that all disagreements are then solved. One illustration of this is a relatively recent guideline on refugees. This guideline aimed at directing refugees into short-term jobs in agriculture. The fact that the social partners voted for this does not imply that they agreed. According to interviewees, the trade union representatives were outspoken in their resistance and the employer representatives were – despite being less outspoken – also against it. But the social partners know that if the government gives high priority to a certain goal the social partners will have to accept it. PES might have formal independence from the Ministry of Labour and Social Affairs but the example indicates that this independence works in 'the shadow of the state'.

During the ÖVP-FPÖ government's first period in office from 2000 to 2006, as part of plans to further liberalize the use of placement agencies, PES came under pressure from the government and risked being turned into a private company without tripartite boards. However, the social partners stood shoulder to shoulder and defended the existing PES. It turned out to be an effective strategy and the government plans did not make it very far (Soentken and Weishaupt, 2014).

Since the Great Recession

When the Grand Coalition came back into office in 2006, ALMP partly moved away from the work-first approach towards a more human capital-focused approach. However, according to the interviewees, this development did not imply substantial new initiatives, but merely a change of administrative practices. In fact, there were not a great deal of new initiatives in relation to ALMP between the Great Recession and the change of government in 2017.

Some of the few new initiatives taken were a direct response to the Great Recession. These included, inter alia, three youth initiatives: the Youth

Employment Package 2008 (focusing on providing disadvantaged youth and drop-outs with apprenticeship training); the action programme, Future for Youth 2009 (subsidized jobs and other measures for hard-to-employ young people); and the Youth Foundation Just Now 2011 (providing counselling and qualifications to unemployed youth as a bridge to an ordinary job). Other initiatives were focused on other target groups, such as the unemployed 50+ or entrepreneurs, but none could be considered major ALMP reforms (Federal Ministry of Labour, Social Affairs, Health and Consumer Protection, 2011).

Moreover, as in Denmark and the Netherlands, the inflow of refugees and immigrants caused concern and led to new initiatives as well as changes in existing initiatives in ALMP and in other policy areas. With 10.3 asylum seekers per 1000 inhabitants in the peak year of 2015 – three times as many as in Denmark and four times as many as in the Netherlands – Austria ranked third in the EU (Frandsen, 2016). Previous studies showed that Austrian asylum seekers had less chance of finding jobs than other migrant groups. According to legislation, the asylum seekers, after a three-month waiting period, were only allowed to work or be apprentices in a few branches. And it could take several more months, or even years, until asylum was granted or rejected.

The social partners asked, in a position paper from April 2016, for faster and broader openings into the workplace for asylum seekers. The issue was further discussed in the media and at the annual Bad Ischler Dialog tripartite meeting, whose theme that year was migration and integration. A chairperson of an integration expert board suggested so-called 'one-euro jobs'[4] as a way ahead for integrating refugees, but this was rejected by both PES and the trade unions. WKO suggested bonus payments to companies and refugees when refugees were employed, but this suggestion was met with scepticism from the trade unions. The government welcomed the social partners' position paper and introduced a new bill that included faster recognition of qualifications, expansion of information centres for refugees and more flexible procedures for those without formal evidence of their qualifications (Allinger, 2016).

Further changes have taken place since the change of government in late 2017. Some of them had to do with a shift in the government's perspective from integrating refugees in the labour market towards preventing them from arriving and placing greater demands on those who come. With regard to the 'standard' ALMP administered by PES, the previously mentioned goal about refugees was added. Other changes regarding refugees have included reductions in the budget for language courses and for vocational training for refugees, making a certain level of German-language skills a precondition for obtaining the means-tested social assistance, and introducing a ceiling, meaning that, in practice, families with many children will receive a lower total benefit. ÖGB protested against most of these new measures, whereas WKO welcomed them.

As in some other policy areas, and similar to their first period in office, the ÖVP-FPÖ government had, according to some of the interviewees, considered reducing the influence of the social partners in PES, but these considerations were never transformed into concrete plans. In PES, discussions on the budget have intensified. The slow, but steady increase in the budget mentioned above has become increasingly controversial in times of decreasing unemployment. However, labour market shortage is also an ALMP challenge and the defenders of the status quo of continued increases have so far avoided reductions.

At the time the Austrian interviews were conducted (May 2019), a new approach to active measures was on the table. The so-called Algorithm Initiative – or personalized implementation initiative – seeks to use PES's statistics to predict what will happen with the employment record of individual unemployed people in the near future. By doing this, the algorithm is supposed to tailor-make active measures for the individual. In a way, the initiative is taking the commonly used group-based approach down to the level of the individual. The initiative – which has similarities to initiatives from several other EU countries – was taken by PES itself and it has gained support from all three actors in PES's tripartite board. However, critical voices have been raised – especially from the trade union side – since it is foreseen that activities will move from the human capital-oriented activation programmes to more work-first-focused individual counselling. Moreover, the trade unions and others have been worried about the use of detailed personal data. Although considered important by the actors, the initiative is about changing the balance of active measures and has still to be approved by Parliament. Finally, according to one of the university interviewees, the real aim of the initiative is to save money by setting up barriers for the access of hard-to-employ unemployed people to more expensive active measures.

CASE: AKTION 20,000, 2016–17

Preparing the Initiative

As in many other EU countries, people over the age of 50 are over-represented in the unemployment statistics in Austria. SPÖ mentioned in one of their party programmes early in the 2010s that a special ALMP action for this group should take place, and titled it Aktion 20,000 (Allinger, 2018).

Decision-making Process and Outcome

Therefore, the SPÖ-ÖVP government proposed an initiative with the aim of reducing long-term unemployment for older people – which stood at approximately 50 000 – by 50 per cent. The initiative was discussed in the PES tripartite board in late 2016–early 2017. According to the interviewees, the social partners took their typical stands for ALMP initiatives: ÖGB was very much in favour of the programme and felt that the public as well as the voluntary sector should be involved, whereas WKO was more sceptical and felt that the large budget could have been better used for wage-subsidy measures in the private sector. Although the social partners were involved and did manage to make their mark on the initiative, one of the interviewees closest to the process described the social partners as less influential than was normally the case in PES decision-making processes, simply because the budget for the initiative was a government budget and not a PES budget.

Regarding the outcome, in its final version the initiative was targeted towards people who had been out of work for over a year. The aim was to create 20 000 new full-time jobs either in the public sector at the federal, regional, provincial or municipal level, or in social enterprises and the voluntary sector.

The subsidized jobs could be established within a wide spectrum of professions and qualification levels (e.g., administrative jobs in schools and assistance and companionship of older persons in need of care), and should be paid at the level of the respective collective agreements (the 'rate for the job'). The jobs were to be subsidized for a maximum duration of two years with up to 100 per cent of the wage costs. PES was to coordinate the initiative as a whole, including the recruitment process of eligible persons. In total, 778 million euros were to be made available for this measure (Allinger, 2018), which, according to the interviewees, made it one of the single largest ALMP programmes seen in Austria.

Implementation and Effects

In July 2017, Aktion 20,000 was implemented, first as a pilot project in model regions and then, from January 2018, nationwide. However, the ÖVP-FPÖ government stopped the programme in early 2018, partly because they were worried that it helped people into 'artificial' jobs that that – the business cycle considered – would be better transformed into ordinary jobs, and partly because they wanted to reduce the budget for employment and social policies in order to reduce the overall tax burden. Hence, only applications made before January 2018 were processed. At that time, some 1500 jobs had been created with the pilot projects, with 1000 more open positions announced, and long-term unemployment had been decreasing in the model regions. An evaluation of the programme implementation took place, but there was never any evaluation of its effects because of the programme's termination.

5.5   CONTINUING VOCATIONAL TRAINING

As in the two other countries analysed in this book, the Austrian continuing vocational training (CVT) system should be seen in connection with the initial vocational education system. In Austria this is characterized by a strong role for companies and the state. The initial education system is typically attended by 15–18/19-year-olds combining two school-based and two apprenticeship-based types of programmes with nearly equal proportions of pupils in the school-based and apprenticeship-based tracks. In Austria, the CVT system is not just a 'second best' alternative but enjoys high social esteem. This combination of equally strong school-based and apprenticeship-based tracks is also found in the Netherlands, but not in Denmark, where the school-based track is a secondary option (Pernicka and Hefler, 2015).

The CVT system is not considered, to the same extent as the initial vocational education system, to be a success nationally (ibid.) and the CVT system has not attracted the same level of attention. Still, CVT is extensively used in Austria. According to the European Continuing Vocational Training Survey from 2010, the number of companies actively involved in CVT was 87 per cent, which is well above the EU-28 average of 66 per cent. The share of employees who attended CVT courses was 33 per cent in 2010 (Tritscher-Archan, 2016). A European Centre for the Development of Vocational Training (Cedefop) classification of scale, scope and quality of CVT placed Austria (and the Netherlands) in the second highest category, whereas Denmark was placed in the highest (Cedefop, 2015).

The focus here will mainly be on CVT for the employed, whereas CVT for the unemployed will only be analysed where it is difficult to separate this from CVT for the employed.

Until the Great Recession

An important particularity of CVT in Austria is that the only way to get a training programme funded by public sources – with a few exceptions – is to declare it as part of ALMP. Therefore, a few CVT programmes targeting employed persons are found under the umbrella of PES. One of these is the Educational Lift Scheme (Facharbeiter-Intensivausbildung, FIA), which enables adults to acquire formal vocational qualifications by means of an adult-friendly short-cut qualification course. PES does not pay for the courses itself but provides a wage replacement payment of 78 per cent of up to 20 hours per week. Funding for the courses themselves can be provided by a number of training institutions/funds. The courses should lead to the same qualifications as those in the formal apprenticeship system. The Educational Lift Scheme was introduced as a legal option in 1987. The use of the scheme had, according to one well-informed interviewee, been increasing since, and peaked with nearly 5000 users in 2015 – since when it has experienced a drop due to overspending of the budget.

Roughly a quarter of all training taking place in Austria is financed by PES and PES is the only channel through which to get CVT financed by public sources. According to an interviewee, one consequence of this has been that CVT initiatives are often declared as ALMP. It is also notable that UI legislation makes it possible to receive an equivalent to unemployment benefit (the so-called Beihilfe zur Deckung des Lebensunterhalts) during training if a person has been employed for a certain period.

While there are several bi- and tripartite CVT bodies in Denmark and the Netherlands, there are almost none in Austria. There is a Conference for Adult Education (KEBÖ), which has a number of the large training institutions as members, both those affiliated to the social partners and those that are not. This organization communicates with the government about CVT-related issues, but mostly not about the vocational part of it. However, although the social partners are indirectly represented through the Institute for Economic Promotion (WIFI) and the Austrian Trade Union Federation Vocational Training Institute (BFI) (see below), it can hardly count as either a tripartite, or a bipartite, organization and the forum was not considered to be important by any of the interviewees with knowledge of it.

However, this does not imply that the social partners are not carrying out important roles in the provision of CVT. First, since PES, as described above, also plays a role in CVT for those in employment, PES is (also) de facto a CVT tripartite body. Second, the two largest providers of CVT are run by the Chamber of Labour and the Chamber of Commerce, but separately. Both training providers were established in the aftermath of World War II at a time when the government did not finance any CVT activities. They provide not only CVT, but also some upper-secondary vocational education. The training providers have close links with the social partners who have substantial representation on their boards. The Institute for Economic Promotion (WIFI) is the educational institute of the Chamber of Commerce. WIFI provides education within almost all areas of the private sector. Their courses, which are offered to self-employed people as well as to employees, range from management and business management to personal development, languages and sector-specific subjects. The BFI is the training institute for the Chamber of Labour. They offer courses in personal development and management, IT training, office and business administration and languages, as well as courses for social and healthcare professionals, unemployed people and people facing the threat of unemployment. In addition to these two very large providers, the Institute of Agrarian Education and Training (LFI) should be mentioned. This is the education and training company for the Chamber of Agriculture, and it offers CVT mainly in branches of agriculture and forestry (Tritscher-Archan, 2016).

Third, the social partners are involved in CVT through collective agreements. In 2000, it was found that only around 2–3 per cent of collective agreements had 'specific arrangements' on CVT, whereas 6–8 per cent of collective agreements in 2019 were estimated, by a well-informed interviewee, to include some kind of CVT regulation – for instance, the right to a certain number of hours of training. However, it is still not very common to have CVT funds linked to collective agreements. A study from 2012 found only one such fund (Trampusch and Eichenberger, 2012). According to interviewees, this fund – which is targeted at temporary agency workers – is still the only CVT fund in Austria. The fact that collective bargaining only plays a limited role regarding CVT could be, according to one interviewee, because the social partners' strong role in PES makes it tempting for them to externalize the cost to the PES system.

Other sources of publicly provided CVT include the Austrian *Länder*. All nine *Länder* run individual learning accounts, and every state has its own model. These accounts can be used for CVT in several training institutions, including WIFI or BFI. Moreover, so-called territorial employment pacts were established in all nine *Länder* in 1997 and some still exist, although the impression of the interviewees is that they are not as active as before. These pacts are regional partnerships aiming to better link employment policy with other policies at regional and local level and they have often been established as a means of attracting funding from the European Social Fund. The pacts have often used existing organizational infrastructure as a framework for the regional authorities, such as the regional PES, the social partners and other parties, to agree upon and implement joint programmes for promoting employment. Most of the territorial employment pacts have provided training and retraining programmes for unemployed people and vulnerable employee groups, such as young, unskilled, migrant and female employees (with child care obligations) as well as older employees threatened with unemployment.

Shortly before the crisis, in 2007, the yearly Bad Ischler Dialog tripartite meeting focused on the topic of lifelong learning. The report to the meeting (Sozialpartner Austria, 2007) described the social partners' goals for lifelong learning in Austria. It pointed to weak spots in the Austrian school system, such as low PISA[5] scores in initial education and the low number of graduates in the technical and science areas. The report called for action in these areas and for a national lifelong learning strategy. However, the changes called for were mostly concerned with initial education and vocational education, while it had less to say about CVT. One of the few CVT goals mentioned was to improve part-time education opportunities in higher education. According to one of the interviewees, the document later strongly influenced Austria's 2020 Strategy for Lifelong Learning, which was published in 2011, and was effective in guiding policy for some years.

In 2008, prior to the crisis, the Grand Coalition had been reforming the Educational Leave Scheme (Bildungskarenz) with the result that participation after five years had increased from less than 2000 to 9000 people. The key element of the reform was to change it from a lower lump sum allowance to the equivalent of unemployment benefit. According to one interviewee, various arrangements of territorial 'pacts' between firms, trade unions and PES made good use of the scheme, adding to an already strongly increasing uptake. The Educational Leave Scheme has since been marketized by PES as a way of easing the pain of redundancy and bridging short-term difficulties.

Since the Great Recession

The Austrian social partners were still pushing for a lifelong learning strategy shortly after the outbreak of the Great Recession. WKO and IV identified a series of limitations in Austria's system of CVT and therefore asked for multiple actions, including: the introduction of an inter-agency task force mandated by the government in order to develop a national lifelong learning strategy; the setting up of a comprehensive data bank concerning all lifelong learning measures and their funding, as well as the funding of comprehensive research in the area of lifelong learning; the continuous evaluation of all publicly financed lifelong learning and CVT measures for their effectiveness; and the creation of transparency in the CVT market, by establishing a certi-fication system awarding quality seals. The worker organizations supported most of these positions. In addition, they asked for the introduction of an encompassing law on further training, devised to grant low-skilled employees equal opportunities in terms of access to further training schemes. Such a law should also provide for the eligibility of each employee to catch up on all publicly acknowledged educational attainments to complete upper-secondary qualifications, free of charge. Moreover, they asked for the introduction of a nationwide, uniform individual learning account for all employees to provide individual retraining entitlements with regard to those vocational training measures that are neither part of a statutory training programme nor covered by in-service training schemes (Adam, 2009).

An important scheme from the post-2008 period was the Educational Part-time Work Scheme, which was introduced in 2013 and was aimed at employees who wanted to reduce their working time and gain additional quali-fications. People who had been with the same employer for at least six months were eligible, though the employer's consent was needed. Normal working hours would be reduced by between 25 and 50 per cent. The person taking the leave had to work a minimum of ten hours a week and had to qualify as a minimally employed worker. At the time of its introduction, the maximum benefit was 456 euros per month to be paid for a minimum of four months and a maximum of two years. The social partners on both sides welcomed the scheme, which they saw as an adequate improvement in the opportunities for adults to improve their qualifications. However, IV emphasized, at the same time, that they would have liked to have seen a reduction in the minimum length of the courses eligible for the scheme to two months (Allinger, 2013).

Like the two other areas analysed, the shift from the Grand Coalition to the ÖVP-FPÖ government in 2017 implied important changes in the CVT area. The new government showed less interest in financing CVT, especially for refugees and immigrants (see above). The budget for various forms of CVT was reduced. Since BFI is more dependent on government funding than WIFI, BFI has been harder hit by these changes. Although the general perception of the interviewees was that the CVT area was easier to reach consensus on than other work- and welfare-related areas, the impression of the workers' organizations was that the ÖVP-FPÖ government was less keen than the previous government to talk to them about CVT.

CASE: SKILLED WORKERS GRANT 2013

Setting the Agenda

The Skilled Workers Grant (Fachkräftestipendium) initiative was introduced in 2013 and has been extended until 2020. The initiative was developed in the Chamber of Labour and later adopted by the government. The initiative was presented as a package together with the Educational Leave Scheme in 2013, although they are separate initiatives.

According to some interviewees, the initiative actually started in the mid-2000s, when the Chamber of Labour obtained reports from their training centres of a lack of opportunities and support for adults to train for skilled positions as nurses and other occupations. The Chamber of Labour had at that time close connections to the Minister of Education (who had a trade union background) and was looking for ways to improve adult education. Hence, a window of opportunity to 'sell' the draft plan of a grant for skilled workers was open and the Chamber of Labour and the trade unions exploited it.

Decision-making Process

The decision-making process was difficult. As the real initiators of the initiative, the trade unions gave it a high priority and had a close ally in the Social Democratic Minister of Labour and Social Affairs. The employers' organizations, however, were, both during and after the decision-making process, sceptical about the initiative. The interviewees pointed to several aspects of the employer's scepticism and did not feel it was the right way to address labour shortages. Among their criticisms was, first, that employers did not find the use of UI resources (that burden employers as well as employees) to be adequate. If an initiative like this was going to be introduced at all, the employers' position was that it should be funded from the state budget. Second, the employers were sceptical because the approved list of qualifications did not sufficiently extend to cover occupations in the manufacturing industry. Third, they aimed for shorter and more intensive educational courses than the other two actors had in mind. The trade unions and the Chamber of Labour were, not surprisingly, in favour of the initiative.

The Outcome and Evaluation

In its final form, the basis of the Skilled Workers Grant was that, for a defined list of qualifications/programmes, support from the PES could be received both for fees of the courses/programmes and for a wage replacement payment. The list is adjusted on a yearly basis after consultation with the social partners.

At the time the person receives the grant, he or she has to be unemployed or on leave – the former is most often the case, since the person is, so to speak, educating him- or herself out of the previous job and the employer, therefore, in many cases lacks the incentive to accept an application for leave. If a person is unemployed, the grant will be financed by the UI budget. If the person is employed when applying, it will be financed from the ALMP budget, which according to one interviewee, de facto limits the use of the grant for people in employment. The minimum period is three months, the maximum period three years, and the training has to be at least 20 hours a week.

When it was first introduced, the workers' organizations praised the initiative, while the employers remained sceptical. However, once it was finalized, the employers, to some extent, accepted the scheme in their official statements. WKO announced that they were happy the subsidies were only available in sectors with labour shortages (Allinger, 2013).

According to most of the workers' organizations and the government interviewees, the Skilled Workers Grant has been a relative success. Since 2013, more than 10 000 people have received the grant. The employers' organizations have continued to be critical and asked for shorter minimum hours and shorter maximum periods as well as changes in the eligible occupations. Moreover, they pointed to a negative employment effect of the scheme in the official 2014 evaluation of it (AMS, 2015). The worries about the employment effect were shared by a number of other interviewees, who feared that the relatively generous scheme could lead to reduced employment in the short run, because some employees were quitting their job in order to be able to sign up to the grant.

5.6 DISCUSSION

The findings will be discussed below in the context of the three research questions.

To what extent are tripartite arrangements still used?
First, as in Denmark and the Netherlands, the frequency of tripartite agreements has not decreased since the Great Recession. Tripartite cooperation in Austria was used extensively in the period from the Great Recession until 2017. However, the frequency was also high in the years leading up to the crisis as the general analysis and the three sector analyses indicate. Looking at the whole of the 30-year period, tripartite cooperation was frequent and intense in the late 1980s and the 1990s, whereas it ran into difficulties for a short period in the beginning of the 2000s – and again from 2017. However, although tripartite cooperation was still widely used, it is notable that, apart from the period right after the crisis – where a number of smaller adjustments and initiatives were introduced – both the general level and the three policy areas show stability and only a few initiatives from 2009 and until the change of government in 2017.

Second, in terms of the content of the agreements, there has been more tripartite activity in relation to UI and ALMP than in relation to CVT. This is both a reflection of the relatively low profile of the CVT area and of a lack of permanent bi- and tripartite bodies in this policy area. Indications that CVT is more of a consensus area than UI and ALMP – found in the Netherlands and to some extent in Denmark – were also found in Austria.

Are the social partners still able to influence the regulation?
Third, in spite of the relative lack of large-scale reforms since the Great Recession and the challenge of the social partnership model during the short life of the ÖVP-FPÖ government, the social partners have (still) been able to influence work and welfare policies through tripartite agreements post-2008. Cases illustrating this include the Aktion 20,000 and the Skilled Workers Grant initiatives, where the worker organizations were acting as key policymakers with equal importance to the government, and by the attempt to change the

unemployment assistance scheme, in which the employers' organizations (at least in the agenda-setting phase) were very important. The sustained role of tripartism is also illustrated by the continued strong position of PES's tripartite board. Whereas PES to some extent has been de-corporatized in both Denmark and in the Netherlands, PES's decision-making competences are unchanged in Austria and its tripartite board still has strong influence, especially on ALMP, but, to some extent, also on UI and CVT issues.

Fourth, although tripartism is still playing a role, that role is being challenged. Most obvious is the challenge from the political system. For two periods in this century an ÖVP-FPÖ government has challenged the role of the social partners, and although their second time in office was short and far from all the intended changes were implemented, most interviewees felt that the challenges were more serious this time. The shortening or exclusion from 'real' hearing and consultation processes, the changes of representation in permanent bodies, the planned cuts on the chambers and the perception (by the workers' organizations) of the strong bias in favour of the employers in the changes in work and employment regulation, have shaken the system. Another challenge is the abolition, erosion or hollowing out of a number of bi-and tripartite organizations. For instance, few of the subcommittees under the Parity Commission are meeting any longer, and those that do have experienced both a reduction in the frequency of meetings and a reduction in influence. Moreover, among the workers' organizations there is a perception that the days when the social partners could join forces against the government – something that had previously been the case in the UI and ALMP areas – are now over, partly as a result of changes in the top-level management of the social partner organizations and of the close links between ÖVP and WKO. Finally, another challenge to Austrian corporatism is the more than 50 per cent reduction in trade union membership since the 1970s. It seems that the trade unions, until relatively recently, have relied on the Chamber of Labour's institutional power (deriving from the obligatory membership of the chambers), their own political power (from the near constant Grand Coalitions under Social Democratic leadership) and their resultant strong organizational power – and not, to a sufficient extent, nursed their own organizational powers. However, recently, slightly more conflictual relations during collective bargaining rounds and slightly greater willingness among the trade unions to organize mass demonstrations and strikes have offered ways of addressing this loss of organizational powers, that is, ways to engage and recruit new members. It remains to be seen if increasing membership in 2016 – that might arise from this change in trade union strategy – will be the beginning of a new development. Noteworthy in terms of trade union strategy is also the example of trade union cooperation with voluntary organizations, as seen, for instance, in the case of the government attempt to abandon or change the unemployment assistance scheme. Still, this does not change the general picture of the challenges: with repeated political plans to diminish the Chamber of Labour's organizational resources and with only a quarter of the workforce represented by the trade unions, the social partnership model and its legitimacy might be in danger.

Fifth, with regard to challenges from new actors, in Austria there is a strong interest organization for the subnational public authorities with whom the social partners have to share the national decision-making arena, although this organization is more informal than comparable organizations found in Denmark and the Netherlands. Moreover, there is strong cooperation between the *Länder*. Of the three areas, the roles and competences are likely greatest in relation to ALMP and CVT.

Which factors explain best the development?

Sixth, the factors that best explain the development in corporatist arrangements in the Austrian case – with its long relatively stable periods and (so far) shorter unstable periods – are political ideology and the weakness of the government, while indications of the effects from the reduced power of the workers' organizations and from the Great Recession are weaker. Political ideology has clearly been a factor given the role that FPÖ has played in recent decades. Less obvious but also potentially important (though not analysed in any depth in the present study) are the different factions in ÖVP and the changing power balance between them. The shifting power balance between the social partnership-oriented faction of the party and the more neo-liberal faction (see also Rathgeb, 2018) might help to explain why the party has sometimes (most often) taken a social partnership path and sometimes (less often) diverged from this path.

There seems to be an effect from weak governments as well. Here, I must consult secondary literature in that my own interviews and text studies did not systematically cover this explanatory factor. Philip Rathgeb's (previously mentioned) study of partisan politics and trade union inclusion (Rathgeb, 2018) argues convincingly that the numerous Austrian Grand Coalitions were, since at least the 1990s, repeatedly plagued by internal disagreements that rendered many of them weak, although they were majority governments. A long sequence of cases illustrates the role this weakness played in the governments' decisions to include the trade unions, and the role that the trade unions subsequently played in stabilizing these SPÖ-FPÖ governments. The only example of a strong government Rathgeb mentions is the ÖVP-FPÖ government (2002–06), that came into power after an election where ÖVP alone got 42 per cent of the votes and the government shortly thereafter unilaterally introduced a pension reform. However, the argument is undermined by Rathgeb's claim that there have been very few strong governments in Austria. Moreover, not long after the pension reform, the same strong ÖVP-FPÖ government drew back – as described above – from challenging the social partnerships – which also somewhat undermines the argument. Furthermore, it is not entirely clear from his study that the social partnership tradition, including the strong and sustained ties between the workers' organizations, was not sufficient reason for the governments' decisions to involve them. Finally, Rathgeb focuses nearly exclusively on the trade unions, whereas the focus in the present study is on tripartism and therefore also includes the employers' organizations.

Regarding the explanatory factor of the economic crisis, there are some indications that the Great Recession impacted positively on the actors' willingness and ability to enter into tripartite cooperation, because of the higher than average frequency of tripartite agreements right after the outbreak of the crisis. However, as stated above, the frequency of tripartite cooperation was also high in the years leading up to the crisis. On the face of it, it was as much the change of government in 2006 as it was the Great Recession that reinvigorated the social partnership model.

With regard to the power resources of the social partners, the trade unions' organizational resources have clearly been diminished as a result of trade unions' declining membership, whereas the Chamber of Labour's resources, though under attack, have so far been defended. The trade unions seem, to some extent, to have relied on the organizational resources of the chamber as well as their own political resources grounded in the domination of Social Democratic-led Grand Coalitions, and their own institutional resources deriving from a near total coverage of the collective agreements, which is a side-effect of the companies' compulsory membership of the Chamber of Commerce. However, whereas the power resources deriving from the collective bargaining are not under pressure, the last two decades have shown that the trade unions' political resources are, because Social Democratic government leadership, or even government participation, can no longer be taken for granted.

The employers' organizations' resources have not been reduced or challenged to the same extent. Their political resources have perhaps even been strengthened in the past two decades as a result of ÖVP's unbroken government participation and their leadership in two periods. The question is how this lopsided loss of power has impacted the quantity and content of tripartist arrangements. So far, the government-related explanatory factors seem to be stronger, in that it is the political ideology and strategies of the government that, more than anything else, determine whether the social partners are involved. However, it is still possible that the reduced member base of the trade unions has contributed to the ÖVP-FPÖ governments' willingness to challenge the unions.

As in the Danish and to some extent the Dutch cases, the Austrian findings indicate that it is not only the employers' organizations and the trade unions' separate power resources that count, but also their ability to establish consensus across the class divide. Cases such as the social partners' previous successful opposition to the restructuring of PES show that the social partners are able to block government initiatives as well as to define new initiatives.

NOTES

1. Register-based figures from 2016 show, for the first year since 1970, a small increase in membership, but still a decline in density (Krenn et al., 2018).
2. This explanation was questioned by one of the interviewees. According to them, all enterprises had to set aside reserves for the potential severance payments on a yearly basis; in case of economic default, severance payments were paid by a collective fund alongside unpaid wages.
3. Rathgeb (2018), who sees ÖVP more than FPÖ behind the anti-social partnership approach, has proposed that the election in 2002 that reduced FPÖ to a clear junior partner in the government made it possible for ÖVP to pursue its goals without fearing the blocking of these by FPÖ. In Section 5.6, the role of government strength is discussed.
4. That is, jobs that pay just one euro per hour.
5. PISA is the Organisation for Economic Co-operation and Development's Programme for International Student Assessment. PISA measures 15-year-olds' ability to use their reading, mathematics and science knowledge and skills to meet real-life challenges.

6. Comparison and conclusions

In this chapter, the findings from the three countries and three policy areas will be compared (see Table 6.1 for a summary) and the research questions will be answered. Moreover, a number of theoretical and methodological perspectives will be discussed. The three research questions are partly overlapping, and therefore the answers will be partly overlapping too.

6.1 ANSWERING THE RESEARCH QUESTIONS

The overall aim of the book – as described in Chapter 1 – has been to analyse the social partners' roles in work and welfare regulation since this has been a less researched area in recent years and because the issue is important, not only for illuminating who governs, but also because the mode of regulation has consequences for efficiency and equality in labour markets and in society as a whole.

The first research question asked, 'To what extent are tripartite arrangements still used in work- and welfare-related policy areas?' The sections discussing each of the three countries concluded that tripartite agreements are still used in all three countries following the Great Recession. Hence, Hypothesis 1: 'Tripartite arrangements are still frequently used in work and welfare policies in the three selected countries' is supported. This comes as no surprise as the three countries were selected as exceptions to the general trend not to involve the social partners. What is more interesting is that the frequency of tripartite agreements has been sustained or even increased in all three countries, when comparing the post-2008 period with the 30-year period before. All three country chapters, though, also show several failed attempts to strike tripartite agreements in the relatively short post-2008 period.

Regarding the content of the agreements, in the Netherlands and Austria, active labour market policy (ALMP) and unemployment insurance (UI) were more frequent areas of tripartite agreements than continuing vocational training (CVT), reflecting the lower status of CVT and, in Austria, there was also a lack of tripartite fora in this area. In Denmark, ALMP and CVT were more frequently in focus for tripartite agreements than UI, reflecting a higher status accorded to CVT than in the other countries. The low frequency of UI tripartite agreements in Denmark might partly be explained by the fact that trade union influence in this area, to some extent, is secured through the 'Ghent system', at least when it comes to the administration and implementation of UI.

There is another content-related difference between the Netherlands and Austria on the one side and Denmark on the other. Due to the so-called 'voluntarist' tradition in Denmark, pay and working conditions are almost exclusively matters for collective agreements and have therefore – with a few important exceptions – been excluded from tripartite negotiations and unilateral state actions. Therefore, there are very few tripartite agreements that include these issues in Denmark, whereas pay and – especially – working conditions (including the employment contract) have frequently been addressed in tripartite negotiations in both the Netherlands and Austria.

The second research question was worded 'Are the social partners still able to influence the regulation of societal challenges through tripartite arrangements following the Great Recession?' The answer here is yes in the case of all three countries, and both for trade unions and employers' organizations. In other words, the social partners are not just taking part in tripartite negotiations for procedural reasons – although these have also played a role in several cases – and they are not just rubber-stamping government policies. Hence, Hypothesis 2: 'The social partners in the three countries will still be able to exercise decisive influence on work and welfare policies through tripartite arrangements from the Great Recession onwards' is supported.

However, two of the three countries show signs that tripartism is under substantial pressure – signs that have become stronger in the second half of the 2010s. In the Netherlands, social partner organizations on both sides have regretted important parts of the biggest tripartite agreement of the decade and, for a period, experienced difficulties in striking new ones. Moreover, the organizational power and legitimacy of the trade unions are under so much pressure that employers' organizations openly admit they are searching for alternative voices, and the largest trade union in some cases has not signed collective agreements.

In Austria, the compulsory membership of the chambers represents an important institutional power resource for the social partners, which impacts on the organizations as well as on collective bargaining. These resources seem, to some extent, to have compensated for the loss of the trade unions' organizational power, but the Chamber of Labour has been under pressure and it can be a risky strategy for the trade unions in the long run to rely on the chambers' organizational resources. The political resources of the employers' organizations have increased and the trade unions' decreased due to the employers' close links with the ÖVP government leadership, the anti-social partnership policies of their government partner, FPÖ, and lack of signs that the Social Democrats in SPÖ will regain their former strength in the near future. On top of this, the trade unions are experiencing a less cooperative attitude from the

Table 6.1 Short summaries of findings from the three country chapters

	DK	NL	AT
Use of tripartism since the Great Recession (RQ1)	Overall increase (limited)	Overall stable/increase (limited)	Overall stable
Variation between areas	More ALMP and CVT; after Great Recession no difference between three areas	More ALMP and UI because CVT not high priority, but easier to reach agreement in CVT	More ALMP and UI because CVT not high priority there are few tripartite bodies
SP ability to influence decision making (RQ2)	Yes, but TU veto power is gone on some core issues	Yes, but SP partly regret the core pact 2015. Cooperation challenged 2015–18	Yes, but government–SP relations and SP internal relations in crisis recently
Crisis impacts (RQ3)	No effect on content, possible weak temporary influence on frequency	Some positive effect on frequency and on content	Some positive effect on frequency and on content
SP strength (RQ3)	TU lost some power > reduced veto points	TU lost much power > impact on tripartism	WO lost some power > impact on tripartism
Government strength (RQ3)	Weak government a bit more likely to encourage tripartism than strong	Weak government a bit more likely/not more likely than strong	Weak government more likely for tripartism than strong
Government ideology (RQ3)	Right-wing government a bit more likely for tripartism than left-wing	Right-wing government and left-wing government equally likely for tripartism	Right-wing government much less likely for tripartism than left-right
Sharing decision making with new actors (since 00s)	Increasingly sharing with academic experts and (in ALMP) NGOs. Municipalities more important in ALMP	Increasingly sharing (in ALMP) with NGOs. Municipalities more important in ALMP	Not much change
The context: the collective bargaining system	No crisis, but more conflictual relations in the public sector	Crisis due to, e.g., non-signing of agreements and reduced coverage	No crisis, but more conflictual relations

Note: TU = trade unions; WO = worker organization (Chamber of Labour + trade unions); RQ = research question; SP = social partner; NGO = non-governmental organization.

employers in work- and welfare-related policies. Collective bargaining, which has only been touched upon in this book, is not in a state of crisis in Austria as it is in the Netherlands, but relations have become more conflictual.

Hence, although corporatism is not dead either in Netherlands or in Austria, it is in trouble. In the Netherlands, the core of the trouble is the organizational development; in Austria the core is the political development. Compared to corporatism in these two countries, though also fluctuating, tripartism in Denmark seems in less trouble. The trade unions' organizational resources have been reduced less than in the two other countries and although trade unions have occasionally been challenged by governments, these challenges have mostly been of a temporary nature.

The third research question asked 'Which factors best explain the development in the quantity and quality of corporatist arrangements?' With regard to the explanatory factor of the economic crisis, the answer can more or less be extracted from the answer to the first research question. In Austria and especially in the Netherlands, the Great Recession has been an issue for tripartite negotiations, whereas it was not directly addressed in tripartite agreements in Denmark, despite being the country hardest hit by the recession in terms of the relative unemployment growth. None of the countries saw a reduction in the frequency of tripartite agreements in the period as a whole. In Denmark, there was an approximately three-year period just after the outbreak of the recession in late 2008 without tripartite agreements, but this period is not especially long in a Danish context, and the period included a failed attempt to agree on a social pact. This indicates overall that economic crisis is a driver for tripartism – as often hailed in the corporatist studies before the Great Recession – rather than a barrier to it. Hence, the economic crisis part of Hypothesis 3: 'Tripartite arrangements will be facilitated by strong social partners and weak government as well as left or centre-left governments, whereas the Great Recession is expected to have functioned as a barrier to tripartite arrangements' is not supported. The effect of the economic crisis on corporatism is therefore more in line with the corporatist studies of the last century than in line with the post-2008 studies.

The second explanatory factor focused on government strength. As mentioned, in all three countries the social partners have been able to influence work and welfare policies through tripartite agreements in spite of weakened workers' organizations. Reductions in the organizational power resources of the workers' organizations have taken place in all three countries, but most so in the Netherlands and least so in Denmark. Austria could be placed somewhere in the middle in that the institutional and organizational power resources of the Chamber of Labour as mentioned above, to some degree, compensate for the lack of the trade unions' resources. However, the Austrian workers' organizations have also had to fight with weakened political resources due to the appearance, since the year 2000, of alternatives to the Social Democrat-led Grand Coalitions in the form of governments hostile to the trade unions. Although the weakening of the trade unions, as described above, has not prevented tripartite agreements, it might have impacted on the frequency of the agreements and also impacted them qualitatively, especially in the Netherlands. The employers' organizations' power resources have not been reduced to nearly the same extent as the trade unions' in any of the countries, and some of the employer organizations' power resources might even have increased, as, for instance, in the case of their political resources in Denmark, due to the greater openness of the Social Democrats towards employers. In sum, the findings are ambivalent regarding the part of Hypothesis 3 focusing on social partner strength. On the one hand, the trade unions' weakened power resources have not led to reduced tripartite frequency. On the other hand, this weakening of resources has contributed to the difficulties that corporatism is increasingly facing. And the results do indicate that a certain level of social partner power might be a necessary, although not sufficient, condition for corporatism.

The findings with regard to the third explanatory factor, the role of government ideology, varies across the three countries. It is undeniable that political ideology plays a role in Austria where the numerous Social Democratic-Conservative governments have, with few exceptions, included the social partners in tripartite agreements when relevant, whereas the less numerous Conservative-populist governments have, with few exceptions, excluded them. Interestingly, it is the same Conservative Party that participates in the pro- and anti-social partner governments, illustrating the existence of different factions in the party. In Denmark there are indications that government ideology might play a role, but here it is right-wing governments that appear to more frequently sign tripartite agreements than centre-left, although the picture is far from being as clear as it is in Austria. One reason that the Liberal or Conservative-led governments in Denmark have been shown to be a bit more likely to strike tripartite agreements, could be that the Danish trade unions are more eager to participate in tripartite agreements than the employers' organizations and this means that the trade unions are likely to strike agreements with both Social Democratic and Liberal-Conservative governments, while the employers are more selective and prefer only to strike agreements with Liberal-Conservative governments. In the Netherlands, none of the sides show greater tripartite frequency than the others. Overall, the part of Hypothesis 3 on stronger centre-left tripartite intensity is not supported – but nor do the empirical analyses support a hypothesis that the right is more willing or able to strike tripartite agreements either.

The fourth and final explanatory factor is the strength of the government. Here the analyses about the Netherlands and Austria rely on other researchers'

classifications more than my own fieldwork. The hypothesis that weak governments more often than strong governments involve the social partners found
most support in Austria, relatively weak support in the Netherlands and the
weakest support in Denmark. In none of the countries were there indications of
a reverse relationship. However, the limited reliability of the classifications of
the government strength and the mix of my own and other researchers' classifications, implies that the findings on this explanatory factor should not be seen
as anything other than a rough estimate. Overall, only weak support for this
part of Hypothesis 3 was found. An interesting observation in this connection
is that the social partners are not the only type of main actor that are getting
weaker. Across the three countries there is a tendency for governments to get
weaker too. What effect it has on tripartism that not only the social partners,
but also governments, seem to be getting weaker, has not been analysed in the
present study, but is a perspective to be addressed in future research.

Summing up, attempting to generalize across the three countries there was
some impact from economic crisis, and limited impact from social partner
strength, government ideology and government strength – overall, not very
impressive support for the hypotheses. This could possibly indicate that,
although the four explanatory factors are relevant, their explanatory power in
these cases is limited. The question is whether any of the other several explanatory factors presented in Chapter 2 could have better explained the development. This is doubtful. Another possibility is that, even though the four factors
discussed have some explanatory power, the importance of context-specific
choices in each individual decision-making process – including a large number
of contextual factors – weakens the explanatory power of each explanatory
factor. The context-specific choices of the government, put simply, are about
estimating costs and benefits from including the social partners as opposed
to not including them. Here a long sequence of factors related to the specific
political situation are of importance, including the likelihood that the social
partners can agree with the government and among themselves. In addition
to the context-specific choices of the government, the social partners have
similar context-specific choices to make. This is probably part of the reason
that the explanatory factors do not show greater explanatory power than they
do, although the context-specific factors surrounding these choices of the government and the social partners are not independent of the four selected factors
and other explanatory factors.

6.2   OTHER FINDINGS

The analyses of the three countries have also revealed findings other than those
addressed in the research questions. Some of them are included here because
they relate to the issues addressed in the research questions without address-

ing them directly. These other findings relate to actors, context and effects, respectively. One of them is that the social partners, to a greater extent than previously, have to share the decision-making arenas with actors other than just governments. In this way, tripartite decision-making arenas have become more often 'tripartite+' or, if preferred, multipartite. This development has been very evident in the development of Dutch social pacts in recent years. Moreover, although it is arguable to what extent this actor is separate from the government, the interest organizations of the municipalities in Denmark and the Netherlands have gained in importance due to decentralization, especially in the ALMP area. In the same policy area, voluntary organizations representing special target groups entered the decision-making arenas in the 2000s. Another type of actor that the social partners must increasingly share the decision-making arena with is academic experts that increasingly take part in pre-legislative bodies, when these are established, and not only in ALMP. However, this development is mainly seen in Denmark. In Austria, none of these developments seem to have taken place to any notable extent. Academic experts have taken part in some tripartite bodies, but that is not a new development and ALMP has not been decentralized further during the last two decades. However, in Austria there is also a strong interest organization for the subnational public authorities and the *Länder* have for long been important actors in Austrian ALMP. Moreover, there is a strong informal coordination across the *Länder* with regard to ALMP.

Another finding that is indirectly relevant to the research questions is the state of the collective bargaining system in the three countries. Although being a different type of work and welfare regulation from tripartite regulation, collective bargaining in all three countries partly overlaps with tripartite negotiations when it comes to its content. Even in Denmark, where pay and working conditions are mostly excluded from the tripartite arena, a large number of other issues such as CVT, maternity/paternity leave, pensions, unemployment benefits, and disability and sickness benefits have been addressed both in the collective bargaining arena and the tripartite arena. Therefore, issues bargained on in one arena could have a very direct impact on bargaining on the same issue in the other arena. Moreover, the collective bargaining system is one of the sources of the social partners' power resources. For these reasons, the collective bargaining system is of importance for tripartism. Another connection between the two types of regulation is that the relations between the actors in one arena can influence the relations between the actors in the other.

In all three countries, relations between the bargaining parties have to some extent became more tense in recent years. This development is severe in the Netherlands, where the largest trade union has abstained in recent years from signing a number of collective agreements, and where the collective bargaining coverage is declining. In Austria, collective bargaining has, as described, traditionally been consensual and industrial conflicts are rare. In recent years, however, there has been a tendency towards more conflictual bargaining rounds, including in the pattern-setting manufacturing industries. In Denmark, collective bargaining rounds have also been more tense in the 2010s, but only in the large public sector, which employs close to one-third of all employees. It even got to the point of a more than three-week-long industrial conflict in the public sector in 2013 (Mailand, 2016b) – and in 2018, the whole of the public sector was very close to descending into yet another conflict, but an arbitration process prevented it at the last minute (Hansen and Mailand, 2019). The connection between collective bargaining and tripartite bargaining means that tensions in the collective bargaining systems could also be a challenge to tripartism. Whereas a well-functioning collective bargaining system can be imagined without well-functioning tripartism, well-functioning tripartism cannot in the long run be sustained if the collective bargaining system is very strained or even eroding. One of the explanations for this is that the state is not (apart from parts of the public sector) a main actor in the collective bargaining system, whereas the social partners are main actors both in collective bargaining and tripartite negotiations.

Third, the three country studies have addressed the question about the effect of the tripartite agreements. The effects of the three models on key socio-economic parameters was not the main focus in the present project and have therefore not been analysed systematically, although they are important and can be questioned (see, for instance, for the Dutch case, the study of Keune, 2016). However, the analyses of selected cases – 13 in all, summarized in Table 6.2 – included where possible assessments of the agreements' effects. The question of the effects of the tripartite agreements are of great importance, because the legitimacy of the agreements would be severely challenged if the agreements had no effects. However, some effects are easier to assess than others. Some effects follow automatically from the initiative, others do not and these effects could often also have other drivers than tripartite arrangements. These are therefore more difficult to evaluate. Most of the effects pointed to are related to the content of the specific policy areas, whereas others are process related. Moreover, some of the cases are so new that the effects are not yet evident or have at least not been evaluated, and two of the initiatives had not even been developed into full proposals at the time of writing. Finally, some cases span several issues and even policy areas, whereas others are much narrower.

With these limitations in mind, the effects of the 13 cases show a wide variety, some process related (regarding effects on the attention to a policy issue or policy area, relations between the social partners and establishing of new tripartite bodies), some related to the direct effect of content (such as increased income security) and some being more indirect and possibly with

Table 6.2   *Summary of the effects of the cases from the national chapters*

	UI	ALMP	CVT
DK	*UI Reform 2015:* Improved employment security for most groups, especially for non-standard employees. Political attention to the UI area reduced *UI Self-employed Reform 2017:* Simplification and harmonization, but apart from that to early evaluate	*Employment Policy Reform 2015:* Secured training as activation tool, reduced overall ALMP activity, strengthened tripartism regionally. Less attention to activation policies *Tripartite Agreement Refugees 2016:* Refugees met as labour market ready, new tool for integration *Tripartite Agreement Labour Supply 2016:* Employers penalized for not offering practical training places. Early evaluation positive on effect on practical training places	*Tripartite Agreement CVT 2017:* Early evaluation shows small increase in the use of core public funded CVT
NL	*Mondriaan Pact 2014:* Third year of SP paid UI not properly implemented. SP representation strengthened in UI and ALMP. Use of flexible contract increased contrary to intention	*Participation Act 2015:* Progress towards 125 000 as planned. New ALMP tripartite bodies generally not well functioning *Social and Economic Council Working Group Refugees 2015–:* Possible impact on overall Dutch immigration policy and better information on refugee regulation	*Individual Learning Accounts 2018–:* Decision-making process had not come to an end in spring 2019
AT	*Abandoned Employment Assistance Scheme 2017–19:*[a] The plans had not yet been transformed to proposal when government had to resign May 2019	*Aktion 20,000 2016–17:* Creation of 1500 jobs and declining unemployment in model regions	*Skilled Workers Grant 2013:*[b] 10 000+ people have had their qualifications increased, but worries about negative employment effects

Notes:
a. Only light consultation of workers' organizations in this case, and they were against the initiative.
b. Social partners consulted on this case, but the employers were against it.

additional drivers other than the tripartite arrangements (such as the impact on unemployment in an area or on a target group or on types of employment contracts).

6.3   THEORETICAL AND METHODOLOGICAL IMPLICATIONS

This section will first present a simple typology of corporatism based on the findings from the three countries. A number of theoretical and methodological implications will be described after the presentation of the typology.

A Simple Typology Related to Formality and Actor Support

There are several ways in which corporatism has been categorized in the academic literature. Some of these have been presented in the theoretical section above. Of these, Katzenstein's typology from his book *Small States in World Markets* (Katzenstein, 1985) is of special interest, because, like the present study, it focuses on small states and includes Denmark, the Netherlands and Austria. Katzenstein found that in Austria, Norway and Denmark there was 'social corporatism', which was dominated by strong social democratic parties and trade unions, whereas liberal corporatism, characterized by weaker and more divided unions, but stronger employers, was found in Switzerland, the Netherlands and Belgium. Katzenstein stated that Sweden combined elements from both types of corporatism.

Whereas Katzenstein focuses on the openness and flexibility of the economies, when he separates the small open export-oriented states from the closed large protectionist states, and on power to separate social corporatism from liberal corporatism, the alternative model set out below focuses on two dimensions that the empirical work with the three countries has illuminated. This alternative is not better and does not point to more important factors that Katzenstein's typology or any of the other corporatist typologies presented in Section 2.1 in Chapter 2, but it points to important factors that have not been addressed in the aforementioned typologies: first, whether there are sizeable formal institutions to support the tripartite activities or if the tripartite activities are purely informal; second, whether the social partners are supported by compulsory membership and compulsory financial sources or not.

In the Netherlands, the Social and Economic Council (SER) and the Labour Foundation (STAR) are, as described, two formal bodies that – although not tripartite in a strict sense – play important roles for tripartite cooperation. SER is a sizeable organization, whereas STAR is small, although still important. In addition to these, a number of tripartite bodies exist within the various policy areas, including the three analysed in this book. As the Dutch chapter showed, several of these have been restructured and their roles and influence have changed over time. With regard to the social partners, membership is voluntary and the organizational density of workers' organizations rather low, and the state does not pay or support membership financially.

In Austria, there are no general tripartite (or tripartite-like) bodies left that play important roles in policy formulation for work and welfare policies. The policy area-specific bodies have the main importance in policy implementation, although the national-level tripartite Public Employment Service (PES) board could be said to have some policy formulation competences. Hence, tripartism is overwhelmingly informal in present-day Austria. The social partners are supported by compulsory membership and compulsory financial sources, which is why organizational density of the Chamber of Labour and the Chamber of Commerce is near 100 per cent, whereas the non-compulsory membership of the trade unions is low.

In Denmark, there are no general tripartite bodies of importance for tripartite policy formulation. A number of tripartite bodies exist within work and welfare policy areas, but mostly with relevance for policy implementation. Membership of the trade unions is voluntary, and not supported by the state apart from the fact that the membership fee is tax deductible.

Hence, the three countries show three different combinations of having formal/informal tripartite institutions and having supported/unsupported social partners: the Netherlands shows the formal/unsupported combination, Austria the informal/supported combination and Denmark the informal/unsupported combination. What is interesting about these combinations is that corporatism is less troubled in the country that has neither large formal organizations to support tripartism, nor legal support for the actors.

A Common (Liberal) Destination or Continued Diversity?

With regard to the theoretical implication for the dichotomy – or the continuum if preferred – between approaches pointing to a common (neo-liberal) destination for all labour market and welfare states, although they move along different routes, and approaches that emphasize sustained diversity, this book does not clearly support one more than the other. On the one hand, the challenges to tripartism shown in the Dutch and the Austrian – and to a lesser extent the Danish – cases, could be seen as some form of institutional change in the form of either drift (deliberate neglect of institutional maintenance in spite of external change resulting in slippage in institutional practice on the ground) or exhaustion (gradual breakdown/withering away of institutions over time; Streeck and Thelen, 2005). The challenges referred to here are primarily the workers' organizations' loss of power in Austria and especially in the Netherlands (and the challenges for tripartism that lead from it) and the political challenge to tripartism in Austria. Because the three countries (as explained in the methodological section in Chapter 2) could be seen as critical cases in the sense that 'if tripartism is weakened here, it is likely that it will be weakened everywhere', the conclusion that tripartism faces important challenges in two of the three 'critical case' countries and some challenges in the third, supports, to some degree, those positions arguing that other types of regulation than the neo-liberal are in trouble, although my analysis has not directly shown what direction regulation takes.

On the other hand, the book has shown how the social partners, in a number of cases in all three countries, have been able to use tripartite arrangements to influence work and welfare policies, both with regard to the content of the policy and policy process (such as re-establishing tripartite bodies). And although there are examples of drift and exhaustion of tripartite institutions, there are also numerous cases of both ad hoc and permanent tripartite institutions that have not decayed and perform the same tasks as they have done for decades. Moreover, the book includes cases of institutional change that are neither drift nor exhaustion, but closer to what in Thelen and Streeck's typology is labelled as coversion (when institutions are used towards purposes beyond their original intent). For instance, when old tripartite institutions are used to face challenges in relation to new target groups.

The Benefits of Including Policy Processes and Single-issue Tripartite Agreements

As stated in Chapter 1, one of the features distinguishing this book from most studies of tripartism in recent years is a focus not only on policy content, but also on the decision-making processes. However, other corporatist studies have included decision-making processes or process-related questions of other kinds. The distinction between what Hassel (2009) describes as policy interests, which could more or less be understood as the actors' interest in policy content or substance, and power interest, which could be understood more or less as policy processes, is useful and, as especially a number of the Danish cases illustrate, the distinction is directly empirically relevant. The importance of power interest can, for instance, contribute to an understanding of why the Danish trade unions signed a tripartite agreement on refugees, which with regard to its policy content was hardly in line with the unions' policy interests. Power interests might also be able to explain why trade unions participated in the social pacts of the 1990s and the 2000s around Europe that, in some cases, it seemed they had little interest in. In the European countries where decentralization of collective bargaining has transferred competences from the confederation level to the sector federation, it has given the confederations incentives to secure their legitimacy and *raison d'être* through other relations, such as tripartite relations (e.g., Andersen and Mailand, 2002). This might also have enhanced the importance of power interests.

Another feature distinguishing this book from most studies of tripartism in recent years is the inclusion of single-issue agreements in addition to the, most often, multi-issue 'social pacts' that have attracted most attention. As the empirical analyses have shown, to get an encompassing picture of the role of tripartism in the corporatist countries it is necessary to include these lower-profile tripartite agreements.

Appendix: list of interviews[1]

Table A.1   *Denmark*

Interviews, December 2015–September 2016 (face-to-face)
DK-interviewee 1, Ministry of Employment (two interviews, in start and end of period)
DK-interviewee 2, Confederation of Danish Industry (DI)
DK-interviewee 3, Confederation of Danish Trade Unions (LO)
DK-interviewee 4, Confederation of Professionals in Denmark (FTF)
DK-interviewee 5, Danish Confederation of Professional Associations (Akademikerne)
DK-interviewee 6, Danish Metalworkers' Union
Interview January–February 2018 (face-to-face)
DK-interviewee 7, former Ministry of Employment/Danish Confederation of Employers (DA)
DK-interviewee 8, former Ministry of Employment
DK-interviewee 9, former Ministry of Employment
DK-interviewee 10, Danish Agency for Labour Market and Recruitment
DK-interviewee 11, Ministry of Children and Education
DK-interviewee 12, Danish Confederation of Employers (DA)
DK-interviewee 13, Danish Confederation of Employers (DA)
DK-interviewee 2, Confederation of Danish Industry (DI)
DK-interviewee 3, Confederation of Danish Trade Unions (LO)
DK-interviewee 14, Confederation of Danish Trade Unions (LO)
DK-interviewee 4, Confederation of Professionals in Denmark (FTF)
DK-interviewees 15 and 16, Danish Metalworkers' Union
DK-interviewees 17 and 18, Local Government DK
Ongoing shorter telephone conversations on three rounds of tripartite agreements, January 2016–October 2017
DK-interviewee 12 and 19, Danish Confederation of Employers (DA)
DK-interviewee 3, Confederation of Danish Trade Unions (LO)
DK-interviewee 4, Confederation of Professionals in Denmark (FTF)
DK-interviewee 5, Danish Confederation of Professional Associations (Akademikerne)

Table A.2   *The Netherlands*

Interviews, November 2017 (face-to-face)
NL-interviewee 1, Ministry of Social Affairs and Employment
NL-interviewee 2, Social and Economic Council (SER)
NL-interviewee 3, Association of Netherlands Municipalities (VNG)
NL-interviewee 4, AWVN (a Dutch employer organization)
NL-interviewee 5, Netherlands Trade Union Confederation (FNV)
NL-interviewee 6, Amsterdam Institute for Advance Labour Studies (AIAS), University of Amsterdam
Interviews, July 2018 (face-to-face)
NL-interviewee 7, Ministry of Social Affairs and Employment
NL-interviewee 8, Ministry of Education, Culture and Science
NL-interviewee 9, Ministry of Education, Culture and Science
NL-interviewee 10, Social and Economic Council (SER)
NL-interviewee 11, Confederation of Netherlands Industry and Employers (VNO-NCW)
NL-interviewee 12, Netherlands Trade Union Confederation (FNV)
NL-interviewee 13, Netherlands Trade Union Confederation (FNV)
NL-interviewees 14 and 15, National Federation of Christian Trade Unions (CNV)
NL-interviewee 16, Amsterdam Institute for Advance Labour Studies (AIAS), University of Amsterdam
NL-interviewee 17, Amsterdam Institute for Advance Labour Studies (AIAS), University of Amsterdam
Interviews, March 2019 (telephone)
NL-interviewee 18, Corporation for Vocational Training (SBB)/University of Tilburg

Table A.3   *Austria*

Interviews, April–May 2019
AT-interviewee 1, Danube University Krems (telephone)
AT-interviewee 2 and 3, University of Linz (telephone)
AT-interviewee 4, Georg-August University of Göttingen (telephone)
AT-interviewee 5, Ministry of Social Affairs and Employment (telephone)
AT-interviewee 6, Ministry of Social Affairs and Employment (face-to-face)
AT-interviewee 7, Public Employment Service Austria (AMS) (face-to-face)
AT-interviewees 8 and 9, Austrian Federal Economic Chamber (WKO) (face-to-face)
AT-interviewee 10, Federation of Austrian Industry (IV) (face-to-face)
AT-interviewee 11, Chamber of Labour (AK Wien) (telephone)
AT-interviewees 12 and 13, Chamber of Labour (AK Wien) (face-to-face)
AT-interviewee 14, Chamber of Labour (AK Wien) (face-to-face)
AT-interviewee 15, Chamber of Labour (AK Wien) (face-to-face)

NOTE

1. In order to comply with General Data Protection Regulation legislation, names and positions of the interviewees are not included in the tables.

References

Adam, G. (2009). Austria: collective bargaining and continuous vocational training. Dublin: Eurofound. Accessed 16 March 2019 at https://www.eurofound.europa.eu/publications/report/2009/austria-collective-bargaining-and-continuous-vocational-training.

Adam, G. (2019). Living and working in Austria. Dublin: Eurofound. Accessed 6 June 2019 at https://www.eurofound.europa.eu/it/country/austria.

AK-Samvirke (2013). 30.700 har mistet deres dagpengeret i de første ti måneder af 2013: status og prognose. Copenhagen: AK-Samvirke.

Allinger, B. (2012). Austria: social partners' involvement in unemployment benefit regimes. Dublin: Eurofound. Accessed 5 January 2019 at https://www.eurofound.europa.eu/publications/report/2012/austria-social-partners-involvement-in-unemployment-benefit-regimes.

Allinger, B. (2013). New training to plug skills gaps. Dublin: Eurofound. Accessed 6 April 2019 at https://www.eurofound.europa.eu/publications/article/2013/new-training-to-plug-skills-gaps.

Allinger, B. (2016). Austria: labour market integration and competences of refugees. Dublin: Eurofound. Accessed 5 March 2019 at https://www.eurofound.europa.eu/publications/article/2016/austria-labour-market-integration-and-competences-of-refugees.

Allinger, B. (2018). Austria: latest working life development – Q1 2018. Dublin: Eurofound. Accessed 9 February 2019 at https://www.eurofound.europa.eu/publications/article/2018/austria-latest-working-life-developments-q1-2018.

AMS (2015). *AMS Evaluierung Fachkräftestipendium 2015*. Vienna: Marketmind.

AMS (2017). *2017 at a Glance: Public Employment Service Austria (AMS)*. Vienna: AMS.

Amsterdam Business (2015). Changes in Dutch labour law 2015. Amsterdam: Amsterdam Business.

Andersen, S. K. and J. Arnholtz (forthcoming). Organisationsgraden og den danske model. Et notat udarbejdet af FAOS og AE. FAOS, Department of Sociology, University of Copenhagen.

Andersen, S. K. and N. W. Hansen (2018). Forskere: 13. april bliver en skæbnedag for dansk fagbevægelse. *Kronik i Altinget*, 22 February.

Andersen, S. K. and M. Mailand (2002). *The Role of Employers and Trade Unions in Multipartite Social Partnerships*. Copenhagen: Copenhagen Centre.

Anderson, K. (2019). New Dutch agreement in principle on a major reform of the pension system. *ESPN Flash Report 2019/41*.

Arbejdsgruppen om selvstændige i dagpengesystemet (2017). Et nyt dagpengesystem for fremtidens arbejdsmarked.

Arbejdsmarkedskommissionen (2009). *Velfærd kræver arbejde*. Copenhagen: Arbejdsmarkedskommissionen.

Arbejdsministeriet, Undervisningsministeriet and Finansministeriet (1999). *Mål og midler i offentligt finansieret voksen- og efteruddannelse.* Copenhagen: Finansministeriet.

Armingeon, K. and L. Baccaro (2012). The sorrows of young euro: the sovereign debt crisis of Ireland and Southern Europe. In B. Nancy and J. Pontusson (eds), *Coping with Crisis: Government Reactions to the Great Recession.* New York: Russell Sage Foundation.

Astleithner, F. and J. Flecker (2018). From the golden age to the gilded cage? Austrian trade unions, social partnership and the crisis. In S. Lehndorff, H. Dribbusch and T. Schulten (eds), *Rough Waters: European Trade Unions in A Time of Crisis.* Brussels: European Trade Union Institute.

Austrian Presidency of the Council of the European Union (2018). *Social Protection in Austria: Benefits, Expenditure and Financing 2018.* Vienna: BMAGSK.

Avdagic, S. (2006). One path or several? Understanding the varied development of tripartism in New European capitalisms. *MPIfG Discussion Paper 06/5.* Cologne: Max Planck Institute for the Study of Societies.

Avdagic, S., M. Rhodes and J. Visser (2011). *Social Pacts in Europe: Emergence, Evolution and Institutionalization.* New York: Oxford University Press.

Baccaro, L. (2003). What is dead and what is alive in the theory of corporatism? *British Journal of Industrial Relations*, 41(4), 683–706.

Baccaro, L. and C. Howell (2011). A common neoliberal trajectory: the transformation of industrial relations in advanced capitalism. *Politics and Society*, 39(4), 521–63.

Baccaro, L. and C. Howell (2017). *Trajectories of Neoliberal Transformation: European Industrial Relations Since the 1970s.* Cambridge, UK: Cambridge University Press.

Bachrach, P. and M. S. Baratz (1970). The two faces of power. *American Political Science Review*, 56(4), 947–52.

Bandel, C. (2008). 'Fiscalise' Dutch first pillar – Commission Bakker. *IPE News*, 16 June.

Bay, J. (2019). DA: Lysten til efteruddannelse skal øges. *Altinget.dk*, March 19.

Bekker, S. and M. Mailand (2018). The European flexicurity concept and the Dutch and Danish flexicurity models: how have they managed the Great Recession? *Social Policy and Administration*, 53(1), 142–55.

Beskæftigelsesministeriet (2016a). Kommissorium for arbejdsgruppe for selvstændige i dagpengesystemet. Copenhagen: Beskæftigelsesministeriet.

Beskæftigelsesministeriet (2016b). Kommissorium til trepartsdrøftelser om arbejds-markedsintegration. Copenhagen: Beskæftigelsesministeriet.

Binderkrantz, A. S. and P. M. Christiansen (2015). Decades of change? Interest group representation in Danish public committees in 1975 and 2010. *Journal of European Public Policy*, 22, 1022–39.

Binderkrantz, A. S., P. M. Christiansen and H. H. Pedersen (2014). *Organisationer i politik.* Copenhagen: Hans Reitzels Forlag.

Birkman, A. R. (2017). Faglige organisationer: trepartsaftale lader akademikerne i stikken. *Mandag Morgen*, 26 November.

Bischof, G. and A. Pelinka (1996). *Austro-Corporatism: Past, Present, Future.* New Brunswick, NJ: Transaction Publishers.

Borhans, L. D., D. Fouarge, A. De Grip and J. van Thor (2014). *Werken en leren in Nederland.* Maastricht: Research Centre for Education and the Labour market (ROA).

Brandl, B. and F. Traxler (2005). Industrial relations, social pacts and welfare expenditures: a crossnational comparison. Paper presented at the ESA Conference, Torun, 9–12 September, 2005.

Bredgaard, T., H. Jørgensen, P. K. Madsen and S. Rasmussen (2017). *Dansk Arbejdsmarkedspolitik.* Copenhagen: Jurist- og Økonomforbundets Forlag.

Bredgaard, T. and F. Larsen (2009). *Regionale og lokale beskæftigelsesråd: i spændingsfeltet mellem stat og kommune.* Aalborg: Aalborg Universitetsforlag.

Brüniche-Olsen, P. (1996). *Arbejdsmarkedspolitik.* Copenhagen: Handelshøjskolens Forlag.

Campbell, J. L. and O. K. Pedersen (2007). Institutional competitiveness in the global economy: Denmark, the United States and the varieties of capitalism. *Regulation and Governance,* 1(3), 230–46.

Carstensen, M. B. and C. L. Ibsen (2015). Barriers to and triggers of policy innovation and knowledge transfer in Denmark. *STYLE Working Papers, No. WP4.1/DK.*

Carstensen, M. B. and C. L. Ibsen (2019). Three dimensions of institutional contention: efficiency, equality and governance in Danish vocational education and training reform. *Socio-Economic Review.* https://doi.org/10.1093/ser/mwz012.

Carstensen, M. B. and V. A. Schmidt (2016). Power through, over and in ideas: conceptualizing ideational power in discursive institutionalism. *Journal of European Public Policy,* 23(3), 318–37.

Cedefop (2015). *CVET in Europe. The Way Ahead.* CEDEFOP reference series. Luxembourg: Publication Office of the European Union.

Christensen, J. G., P. E. Mouritzen and A. S. Nørgaard (2009). *De store kommissioner: vise mænd, smagsdommere eller nyttige idioter.* Odense: Syddansk Universitetsforlag.

Christiansen, P. M. and M. Klitgaard (2008). *Den utænkelige reform: en analyse af strukturreformens tilblivelse.* Odense: Syddansk Universitetsforlag.

Christiansen, P. M. and A. S. Nørgaard (2003), *Faste forhold – flygtige forbindelser – stat og interesseorganisationer i Danmark i det 20. århundrede.* Aarhus: Aarhus Universitetsforlag.

Christiansen, P. M., A. S. Nørgaard and N. C. Sidenius (2004). *Hvem Skriver Lovene? Interesseorganisationer og politiske beslutningsprocesser.* Aarhus: Aarhus Universitetsforlag.

Compston, H. (2002). Policy concertation in Western Europe: a configurational approach. In S. Berger and H. Compston (eds), *Policy Concertation and Social Partnerships in Western Europe: Lessons for the Twenty-first Century.* New York/ Oxford: Berghahn Books.

Crouch, C. (1994). *Industrial Relations and European State Traditions.* Oxford: Oxford University Press.

Culpepper, P. D. and A. Regan (2014). Why don't governments need trade unions anymore? The death of social pacts in Ireland and Italy. *Socio-Economic Review,* 12(4), 723–45.

Dagpengekommissionen (2015). *Dagpengekommissionens hovedanbefalinger.* Copenhagen: Dagpengekommissionen.

Dahl, R. A. (1958). A critique of the ruling elite model. *American Political Science Review,* 52(2), 463–9.

Dansk Arbejdsgiverforening (DA) (2014). *Arbejdsmarkedsrapport 2014.* Copenhagen: DA.

Danske A-kasser (2017). Salamimetoden. Notat. 8 February. Copenhagen: Danske A-kasser.

de Beer, P. (2016). Afbrokkelende legitimiteit van het poldermodel. In M. Keune (ed.), *Nog steeds een mirakel? De legitimiteit van het poldermodel in de eenentwintigste eeuw*. Amsterdam: Amsterdam University Press.

Dølvik, J. E., P. Marginson, K. Alsos, J. Arnholtz, G. Meardi, T. Müller and S. Trygstad (2018). Collective wage regulation in Northern Europe under strain: multiple drivers of change and differing responses. *European Journal of Industrial Relations*, 24(4), 321–39.

Due, J. and J. S. Madsen (2001). Fagbevægelsens struktur i det 20. århundrede. *LO-dokumentation No. 1/2001*. Copenhagen: LO.

Due, J. and J. S. Madsen (2003). *Fra magtkamp til konsensus: arbejdsmarkedspensionerne og den danske model*. Copenhagen: Jurist- og Økonomforbundets Forlag.

Due, J. and J. S. Madsen (2006). *Fra storkonflikt til barselsfond: overenskomstforhandlingerne 1998, 2000 og 2004*. Copenhagen: Jurist- og Økonomforbundets Forlag.

Due, J. and J. S. Madsen (2007). Det danske Gent-systems storhed – og fald? In J. H. Pedersen and A. Haagelund (eds), *Arbejdsløshedsforsikringsloven 1907–2007*. Copenhagen: Arbejdsdirektoratet.

Due, J. and J. S. Madsen (2008). OK 2007 og OK 2008 – Perspektiver og konsekvenser. Augustudvalget 100 år. Konference den 3. september 2008. *FAOS forskningsnotat No. 89*. FAOS, Department of Sociology, University of Copenhagen.

Due, J. and J. S. Madsen (2012). Når trepartssamarbejde skaber reformer: historien om trepartssamarbejde i Danmark i lyset af 25-året for Fælleserklæringen af 1987. Copenhagen: FAOS, Department of Sociology, University of Copenhagen.

Due, J. and J. S. Madsen (2014). Case – det kuldsejlede trepartsforløb. Upubliceret notat. FAOS, Department of Sociology, University of Copenhagen.

Due, J., J. S. Madsen and C. S. Jensen (1993). *Den danske model: en historisk sociologisk analyse af det danske aftalesystem*. Copenhagen: Jurist- and Økonomforbundets Forlag.

Ebbinghaus, B. (2002). Varieties of social governance: comparing the social partners' involvement in pension and employment policies. Cologne: Max Planck Institute for the Study of Societies.

Ebbinghaus, B. and A. Hassel (1999). The role of tripartite concertation in the reform of the welfare state. *Transfer – European Review of Labour and Research*, 5(1–2), 64–81.

Ebbinghaus, B. and A. Hassel (2000). Striking deals: concertation in the reform of continental European welfare states. *Journal of European Public Policy*, 7, 44–62.

Ekspertgruppen for voksen-, efter- og videreuddannelse (2017). *Nye kompetencer hele livet: fremtidens voksen-, efter- og videreuddannelse*. Copenhagen: Ekspertgruppen for voksen-, efter- og videreuddannelse.

Ekspertgruppen om udredning af den aktive beskæftigelsesindsats (2015). *Nye veje mod job – for borgere i udkanten af arbejdsmarkedet*. Copenhagen: Ekspertgruppen om udredning af den aktive beskæftigelsesindsats.

Esping-Andersen, G. (1990). *The Three Worlds of Welfare Capitalism*. Cambridge, UK: Polity Press.

European Trade Union Institute (ETUI) (2018). Strikes – map of Europe: Austria. Accessed 30 August 2019 at https://www.etui.org/Services/Strikes-Map-of-Europe/Austria.

Eurostat (2019a). Unemployment by sex and age – annual data.

Eurostar (2019b). Vocational education and training statistics.

Fajertag, G. and P. Pochet (1997). A new era for social pacts in Europe. In G. Fajertag and P. Pochet (eds), *Social Pacts in Europe*. Brussels: ETUI.

Federal Ministry of Labour, Social Affairs, Health and Consumer Protection (BMAGSK) (2011). *Basic Information Report – Labour Market Policy – Reporting Year 2010/2011.* Vienna: BMAGSK.

Federal Ministry of Labour, Social Affairs, Health and Consumer Protection (BMAGSK) (2017). *Basic Information Report – Labour Market Policy – Reporting Year 2016.2017.* Vienna: BMAGSK.

Fichtner, P. S. (2002). Historical dictionary of Austria. *Austrian History Yearbook*, 33, 253–4.

Fink, M. (2006). Zwischen 'Beschäftigungsrekord' und 'Rekordarbeitslosigkeit': Arbeitsmarkt und Arbeitsmarktpolitik unter Schwarz-Blau/Orange. In E. Tálos (ed.), *Schwarz-Blau: Eine Bilanz des 'Neu-Regierens'.* Vienna: LIT-Verlag.

Flyvbjerg, B. (1991). *Rationalitet og magt. Bind I: Det konkretes videnskab.* Copenhagen: Akademisk Forlag.

Frandsen, K. (2016). Danmark fastholder 9. plads som mest søgte asylland. *Altinget. dk*, 14 July.

Freyssinet, J. (2010). Tripartite responses to the economic crisis in the principal Western European countries. *Social Dialogue Working Paper No. 12.* Geneva: International Labour Organization.

Fris, S. E. (2017). Trepartsudvalg får ny formand efter protest-afsked. *Altinget.dk*, 20 January.

Glassner, V. (2019). Collective bargaining in Europe – Austria: from gradual change to an unknown future. PowerPoint presentation to the 11th Annual TURI Conference, Vienna, 20 May.

Gleißner, R. (2009). *Personalmaßnahmen in der Krise: Betriebe sichern, Arbeitsplätze erhalten: Kurzarbeit NEU, Arbeitszeit, Vertragsgestaltung, Förderungen, Muster.* Vienna: Austrian Chamber of Commerce.

Guardiancich, I. and O. Molina (2017) (eds). *Talking Through the Crisis: Social Dialogue and Industrial Relations Trends in Selected EU Countries.* Geneva: International Labour Organization.

Hall, P. A. and D. Soskice (2001). *Varieties of Capitalism: The Institutional Foundations of Comparative Advantage.* Oxford: Oxford University Press.

Ham, C. and M. Hill (1993). *The Policy Process in the Modern Capitalist State.* New York: Harvester Wheatsheaf.

Hamann, K. and J. Kelly (2003). The domestic sources of differences in labour market policies. *British Journal of Industrial Relations*, 41(4), 639–63.

Hancké, B., M. Rhodes and M. Thatcher (2007). Introduction. In B. M. Hancké, B. M. Rhodes and M. Thatcher (eds), *Beyond Varieties of Capitalism – Conflict, Contradictions, and Complementarities in the European Economy.* Oxford: Oxford University Press.

Hansen, N. W. and M. Mailand (2019). Overenskomstfornyelsen 2018 – musketered, magtbalancer og modelforandringer. *Forskningsrapport No. 166.* FAOS, Department of Sociology, University of Copenhagen.

Hansen, N. W. and Å. A. Seip (2018). Government employers in Sweden, Denmark and Norway: the use of power to control wage and employment conditions. *European Journal of Industrial Relations*, 24(1), 73–89.

Hassel, A. (2003). The politics of social pacts. *British Journal of Industrial Relations*, 41(4), 707–26.

Hassel, A. (2009). Policies and politics in social pacts in Europe. *European Journal of Industrial Relations*, 15(1), 7–26.

Hay, C. (2005). Two can play at that game. . .or can they? Varieties of capitalism, varieties of institutionalism. In D. Coates (ed.), *Varieties of Capitalism, Varieties of Approaches*. Basingstoke: Palgrave Macmillan.

Heinish, R. (2000). Coping with economic integration: corporatist strategies in Germany and Austria in the 1990s. *West European Politics*, 23(3), 67–96.

Hemerijck, A., B. Unger and J. Visser (2000). How small countries negotiate change: twenty-five years of policy adjustment in Austria, the Netherlands, and Belgium. In F. W. Scharpf and V. A. Schmidt (eds), *Welfare and Work in the Open Economy, Volume II: Diverse Responses to Common Challenges in Twelve Countries*. Oxford: Oxford University Press.

Hemerijck, A. and M. van der Meer (2016). Nieuw Nederlands polderen – Van brede sociale akkoorden naar 'ad hoc' hervormings coalities. In M. Keune (ed.), *Nog steeds een mirakel? De legitimiteit van het poldermodel in de eenentwintigste eeuw*. Amsterdam: Amsterdam University Press.

Howell, C. (2003). Varieties of capitalism: and then there was one? *Comparative Politics*, 36(1), 103–24.

Hyman, R. (2001). Some problems of partnership and dilemmas of dialogue. In C. Kjærgaard and S.-Å. Westphalen (eds), *From Collective Bargaining to Social Partnerships: New Roles of the Social Partners in Europe*. Copenhagen: The Copenhagen Centre.

Hyman, R. and R. Gumbrell-McCormick (2013). *Trade Unions in Western Europe*. Oxford: Oxford University Press.

Ibsen, C. L. (2015). Three approaches to coordinated bargaining: a case for power-based explanations. *European Journal of Industrial Relations*, 21(1), 39–56.

Ibsen, C. L. (2016). Making sense of employer collectivism: the case of Danish wage bargaining under recession. *Journal of Industrial Relations*, 58(5), 669–87.

Ibsen, C. L., J. Due and J. S. Madsen (2015). Fald i organisationsgraden igen. FAOS, Department of Sociology, University of Copenhagen.

Ibsen, F. (1985). *Organisationerne og arbejdsmarkedet*. København: Samfundsfagsnyt.

Iversen, T. and D. Soskice (2009). Distribution and redistribution: the shadow of the nineteenth century. *World Politics*, 61(3), 438–86.

Jensen, O. N. (1990). Dansk beskæftigelsespolitik siden krisens gennemslag – en samordnet beskæftigelsespolitik? Thesis. Aarhus: Aarhus Universitet.

Jørgensen, C. and T. Bühring (2019). Living and working in Denmark. Dublin: Eurofound. Accessed 9 December 2019 at https://www.eurofound.europa.eu/country/denmark.

Jørgensen, H. (1986), *Arbejdsmarkedsnævn i arbejdsmarkedspolitikken*. Aalborg: AUC.

Jørgensen, H. (2015). *Arbejdsmarkedsregulering*. Copenhagen: Jurist- og Økonomforbundets Forlag.

Jørgensen, H. and F. Larsen (2003). Aktivgørelse af aktivering kommer ikke af sig selv – betydningen af institutionelt design for udviklingen af ledighedsindsatser. In L. Petersen and P. K. Madsen (eds), *Drivkræfter bag arbejdsmarkedspolitikken*. Copenhagen: SFI.

Jørgensen, H. and F. Larsen (2013). Fagbevægelsens institutionelle magttab og korporatismens krise. *Økonomi og Politik*, 86(1), 58–70.

Jørgensen, H., M. Lassen, M. Staun, M. P. Klindt, V. H. Petersen and P. Buchholt (2017). Et udfordret AMU system – mod revitalisering og fornyelse. Aalborg: Aalborg University.

Karlhofer, F. (1996). The present and future state of social partnership. In G. Bischof and A. Pelinka (eds), *Austro-Corporatism: Past, Present, Future*. New Brunswick, NJ: Transaction Publishers.

Karlhofer, F. (2007). Filling the gap? Korporatismus und neue Akteure in der Politikgestaltung. *Österreichische Zeitschrift für Politikwissenschaft*, 36(4), 389–403.

Katzenstein, P. J. (1985). *Small States in World Markets: Industrial Policy in Europe*. Ithaca, NY: Cornell University Press.

Kelly, J. (2011). Theories of collective action and union power. In G. Gall, A. Wilkinson and R. Hurd (eds), *The International Handbook of Labour Unions: Responses to Neo-Liberalism*. Cheltenham, UK and Northampton, MA, USA: Edward Elgar Publishing.

Keune, M. (2016). Inleiding: de legitimiteit van het poldermodel in de eenentwintigste eeuw. In M. Keune (ed.), *Nog steeds een mirakel? De legitimiteit van het polder-model in de eenentwintigste eeuw*. Amsterdam: Amsterdam University Press.

Keune, M. (2018). Opportunity or threat? How trade union power and preferences shape occupational pensions. *Social Policy and Administration*, 52(4), 463–76.

Keune, M. and N. Payton (2016). Unemployment and pension protection in Europe: the changing role of social partners. *OSE Paper Series No. 28*. Brussels: Observatorie Social Européen.

Klitgaard, M. B. and A. S. Nørgaard (2010). Afmagtens mekanismer: den danske fagbevægelse og arbejdsmarkedspolitikken siden 1960'erne. *Politica*, 42(1), 5–26.

Knegt, R. (2012). The Netherlands: social partners' involvement in unemployment benefit regimes. Dublin: Eurofound. Accessed 9 February 2019 at https://www.eurofound.europa.eu/publications/report/2012/the-netherlands-social-partners-involvement-in-unemployment-benefit-regimes.

Knegt, R. and E. Verhulp (2016). *Country Report: Netherlands*. Dialogue for Advancing Social Europe – DIADSE. Amsterdam: AIAS-HSI, University of Amsterdam.

Korpi, W. (1985). Power resources approach vs. action and conflict: on causal and intentional explanations in the study of power. *Sociological Theory*, 3(2), 31–45.

Korpi, W. (2006). Power resources and employer-centered approaches in explanations of welfare states and varieties of capitalism: protagonists, consenters and antago-nists. *World Politics*, 58(2), 167–206.

Krenn, M. (2015). Austria: employers propose big changes in unemployment assistance based on the German model. Accessed 3 March 2019 at https://www.eurofound.europa.eu/publications/article/2015/austria-employers-propose-big-changes-in-unemployment-assistance-based-on-the-german-model.

Krenn, M., C. Hermann, G. Adam and B. Allinger (2018). Working life Austria. Dublin: Eurofound.

Kurstjens, N. M. J. (2015). The Dutch 'polder model': social pacts – an analysis of the key to success. Master's thesis. Nijmegen School of Management.

Larsen, F. and M. Mailand (2007). Danish activation policy: the role of the norma-tive foundation, the institutional set-up and other drivers. In A. Serrano and L. Magnusson (eds), *Reshaping Welfare States and Activation Regimes in Europe*. Brussels: P.I.E. Lang.

Lehmbruch, G. (1979). Liberal corporatism and party government. In P. C. Schmitter and G. Lehmbruch (eds), *Trends Towards Corporate Intermediation*. London: SAGE.

Lindsay, C. and M. Mailand (2010). Delivering employability in a vanguard 'active' welfare state: the case of Greater Copenhagen in Denmark. *Environment and Planning C: Government and Policy*, 27(6), 1040–54.

LO and DA (2013). *Aftale mellem Dansk Arbejdsgiverforening (DA) og Landsorganisationen i Danmark (LO): Udspil om reform af erhvervsuddannelserne.* Copenhagen: LO and DA.

Lødemel, I. and H. Trickey (2000). *An Offer You Can't Refuse: Workfare in International Perspective.* Bristol: Policy Press.

Lukes, S. (1974). *Power: A Radical View.* London: Macmillan.

Madsen, J. S., J. Due and S. K. Andersen (2016). Employment relations in Denmark. In G. J. Bamber, R. D. Lansbury and N. Wailes (eds), *International and Comparative Employment Relations: Globalisation, Regulation and Change.* London: SAGE.

Mailand, M. (1999). Den danske Model lokalt og regionalt – konsensus og samarbejde i arbejdsmarkedspolitiske netværk. PhD thesis. FAOS, Department of Sociology, University of Copenhagen.

Mailand, M. (2005). The involvement of social partners in active labour market policy – do the patterns fit expectations from regime theories? In T. Bredgaard and F. Larsen (eds), *Employment Policy from Different Angles.* Copenhagen: Djøf Publishing.

Mailand, M. (2008). *Regulering af arbejde og velfærd: mod nye arbejdsdelinger mellem staten og arbejdsmarkedets parter.* Copenhagen: Jurist- og Økonom-forbundets Forlag.

Mailand, M. (2010). Arbejdsmarkedets parter og de beskæftigelsespolitiske reformer: indflydelsen i beslutningsprocessens forskellige faser. *Samfundsøkonomen*, 35(5), 16–22.

Mailand, M. (2011). Trepartssamarbejdet gennem tiderne – hvordan, hvornår og hvilke udfordringer. FAOS, Department of Sociology, University of Copenhagen.

Mailand, M. (2014). Austerity measures and municipalities – the case of Denmark. *Transfer – European Review of Labour and Research*, 20(3), 417–30.

Mailand, M. (2015). Dagpengereformer og flexicurity i forandring. *FAOS forsk-ningsnotat No. 146.* FAOS, Department of Sociology, University of Copenhagen.

Mailand, M. (2016a). Danske trepartsforhandlinger og europæiske samfundsmæssige pagter: en asynkron historie. In T. P. Larsen and A. Ilsøe (eds), *Den danske model set udefra: Komparative perspektiver på dansk arbejdsmarkedsforskning.* Copenhagen: Jurist- og Økonomforbundets Forlag.

Mailand, M. (2016b). Proactive employers and teachers' working time regulation: public sector industrial conflicts in Denmark and Norway. *Economic and Industrial Democracy.* https://doi.org/10.1177/0143831X16657414.

Mailand, M. (2019). Trepart under og efter krisen. *FAOS rapport no. 172.* FAOS, Department of Sociology, University of Copenhagen.

Mailand, M. and J. Due (2003). Partsstyring i arbejdsmarkedspolitikken – perspektiver og alternativer. In L. Petersen and P. K. Madsen (eds), *Drivkræfter bag arbejds-markedspolitikken.* Copenhagen: SFI.

Mailand, M., J. Due and J. S. Madsen (2008). Efteruddannelse. In M. Mailand, *Regulering af arbejde og velfærd: mod nye arbejdsdelinger mellem staten og arbe-jdsmarkedets parter.* Copenhagen: Jurist- og Økonom-forbundets Forlag.

Marginson, P. (2016). Governing work and employment relations in an international-ized economy. *ILR Review*, 69(5), 1033–55.

Martin, C. J. and D. Swank (2012). *The Political Construction of Business Interests: Coordination, Growth, and Equality.* Cambridge, UK: Cambridge University Press.

Ministerie van Sociale Zaken en Werkgelegenheid (2018). Bijlage 1: overzicht over-heidsmaatregelen met raakviak LLO. The Hague: Ministerie van Sociale Zaken en Werkgelegenheid.

Molina, O. and M. Rhodes (2002). Corporatism: the past, present, and future of a concept. *Annual Review of Political Science*, 5(1), 305–31.

Molina, O. and M. Rhodes (2007). The political economy of adjustment in mixed market economies: a study of Spain and Italy. In B. Hancké, M. Rhodes and M. Thatcher (eds), *Beyond Varieties of Capitalism: Conflict, Contradictions, and Complementarities in the European Economy*. Oxford: Oxford University Press.

Mosley, H., T. Keller and S. Spackesser (1998). The role of social partners in the design and implementation of active measures. *Employment and Training Papers No. 27*. Geneva: International Labour Organization.

Müller, M. (2009). Taking stock of the Austrian accession to the EU – with regard to the arguments of its referendum campaign in 1994. Master's thesis. Université de Genève.

Navrbjerg, S. and C. L. Ibsen (2017). Arbejdsgiver-organisationer i Danmark: fra passiv tradition til aktiv tilpasning. *FAOS forskningsnotat No. 160*. FAOS, Department of Sociology, University of Copenhagen.

Nederlandse regering (Government of the Netherlands) (2014). *National Social Report: April 2014*. The Hague: Nederlandse regering.

Nielsen, S. P. (1993). *Erhvervsuddannelsessystemet i Danmark*. Berlin: det Europæiske Center for Udvikling af Erhvervsuddannelse.

Nijhuis, D. O. (2013). *Labour Divided in the Postwar European Welfare State: The Netherlands and the United Kingdom*. New York: Cambridge University Press.

Nørgaard, A. S. (2007). Parterne og A-kassesystemet – de forbundne spils politiske logik. In J. H. Pedersen and A. Haagelund (eds), *Arbejdsløshedsforsikringsloven 1907–2007*. Copenhagen: Arbejdsdirektoratet.

Onstenk, J. and R. Duvekot (2017). Vocational and professional education and lifelong learning. In E. de Bruijn, S. Billett and J. Onstenk (eds), *Enhancing Teaching and Learning in the Dutch Vocational Education System: Reforms Enacted*. Cham: Springer.

Organisation for Economic Co-operation and Development (OECD) (2017). *OECD Skills Strategy Diagnostic Report: Netherlands*. Paris: OECD Publishing.

Organisation for Economic Co-operation and Development (OECD) (2018). *Employment Outlook*. Paris: OECD Publishing.

Papadakis, K. and Y. Ghellab (2014). *The Governance of Policy Reforms in Southern Europe and Ireland: Social Dialogue Actors and Institutions in Times of Crisis*. Geneva: International Labour Organization.

Pedersen, J. H. (2007). Et rids af udviklingen i det danske arbejdsløshedsforsikringssys-tem fra 1907 til 2007: belyst ved centrale lovinitiativer og beslutninger. In J. H. Pedersen and A. Haagelund (eds), *Arbejdsløshedsforsikringsloven 1907–2007*. Copenhagen: Arbejdsdirektoratet.

Pedersen, O. K. (2006). Denmark: an ongoing experiment. In J. L. Campbell, J. A. Hall and O. K. Pedersen (eds), *National Identity and the Varieties of Capitalism: The Danish Experience*. Copenhagen: Djøf Publishing.

Pernicka, S. and G. Hefler (2015). Austrian corporatism – erosion or resilience? *Austrian Journal of Political Science*, 44(3), 39–56.

Prak, M. and J. L. van Zanden (2013). *Nederland en het Poldermodel*. Amsterdam: Uitgeverij Bert Bakker.

Rathgeb, P. (2018). *Strong Governments, Precarious Workers: Labor Market Policy in the Era of Liberalization*. Ithaca, NY: ILR Press.

Refslund, B. and J. Lind (2019). Enduring institutionalised wage concertation in a changing corporatist context: the case of Denmark. Paper for the project 'Crisis Corporatism or Corporatism in Crisis? Social Consultation and Social Pacts in Europe'.

Regeringen (2015). *Sammen om fremtiden*. June 2015.

Regeringen et al. (2012). *Aftale mellem regeringen (Socialdemokraterne, Socialistisk Folkeparti og Radikale Venstre) og Venstre, Liberal Alliance og Det Konservative Folkeparti. Aftale om en reform af førtidspension og fleksjob.*

Regeringen et al. (2013a). *Aftale mellem Regeringen (Socialdemokraterne, Radikale Venstre og Socialistisk Folkeparti) og Venstre, Dansk Folkeparti, Det Konservative Folkeparti og Liberal Alliance. Aftale om en reform af kontanthjælpssystemet – flere i uddannelse og job.*

Regeringen et al. (2013b). *Forlig om en reform af sygedagpengesystemet – Økonomisk sikkerhed for sygemeldte samt en tidligere og bedre indsats.*

Regeringen et al. (2014). *Forlig mellem Regeringen (Socialdemokraterne og Det Radikale Venstre) og Venstre, Dansk Folkeparti og Det Konservative Folkeparti. Forlig om reform af beskæftigelsesindsatsen*, 18 June.

Regeringen et al. (2015). *Aftale mellem regeringen (Venstre), Socialdemokraterne og Dansk Folkeparti om et tryggere dagpengesystem.*

Regeringen et al. (2017). *Regeringen (Venstre, Det konservative Folkeparti og Liberal Alliance), Socialdemokratiet og Dansk Folkeparti. Aftale om et nyt dagpengesystem for fremtidens arbejdsmarked.*

Regeringen og arbejdsmarkedets parter (2016a). *Trepartsforhandlinger 2016: Trepartsaftale om arbejdsmarkedsintegration.*

Regeringen og arbejdsmarkedets parter (2016b). *Trepartsforhandlinger 2016 II: Trepartsaftale om tilstrækkelig og kvalificeret arbejdskraft i hele Danmark og praktikpladser.*

Regeringen og arbejdsmarkedets parter (2017). *Trepartsforhandlinger 2017 III: Trepartsaftale om styrket og mere fleksibel voksen-, efter- og videreuddannelse.*

Rhodes, M. (1998). Globalization, labour markets and welfare states: a future of 'competitive corporatism'? In L. Neumann and K. Schaper (eds), *The Future of European Welfare: A New Social Contract?* Bonn: Die Sozialordnung der Bundesrepublik.

Rosdahl, A. (2003). Lediges understøttelsesperiode. In L. Petersen and P. K. Madsen (eds), *Drivkræfter bag arbejdsmarkedspolitikken*. Copenhagen: SFI.

Rosdahl, A. and H. Weise (2000). When all must be active – workfare in Denmark. In I. Lødemel and H. Trickey (eds), *An Offer You Can't Refuse: Workfare in International Perspective*. Bristol: Policy Press.

Schaapman, M. (2009). *The Netherlands: collective bargaining and continuous vocational training*. Dublin: Eurofound.

Scharpf, F. W. (1993). Coordination in hierarchies and networks. In F. W. Scharpf (ed.), *Games in Hierarchies and Networks: Analytical and Empirical Approaches to the Study of Governance Institutions*. Frankfurt am Main: Campus Verlag.

Schils, T. (2009). The Netherlands. In P. de Beer and T. Schils (eds), *The Labour Triangle: Employment Protection, Unemployment Compensation and Activation in Europe*. Cheltenham, UK and Northampton, MA, USA: Edward Elgar Publishing.

Schmidt, V. (2002). *The Futures of European Capitalism*. Oxford: Oxford University Press.

Schmidt, W., A. Müller, I. Ramos-Vielba, A. Thörnquist and C. Thörnqvist (2018). Austerity and public sector trade union power: before and after the crisis. *European Journal of Industrial Relations*, 25(1). https://doi.org/10.1177%2F0959680118771120.

Schmitter, P. C. (1979). Still the century of corporatism. In P. C. Schmitter and G. Lehmbruch (eds), *Trends Towards Corporatist Intermediation*. London: SAGE.

Schmitter, P. C. (1982). Reflections on where the theory of neo-corporatism has gone and where the praxis of neo-corporatism may be going. In G. Lehmbruch and P. C. Schmitter (eds), *Patterns of Corporatist Policy-Making*. London: SAGE.

Scholten, H. (2018). Vocational education in the Netherlands. PowerPoint presentation. July 2018. The Hague: Ministry of Education Culture and Science.

Smulders, H., A. Cox and A. Weisterhuis (2016). *Vocational Education and Training in Europe: Netherlands*. Cedefop ReferNet VET in Europe Reports. Thessaloniki: Cedefop.

Sociaal-Economische Raad (SER) (2002). *The New Learning: Advisory Report on Lifelong Learning in the Knowledge-based Economy*. The Hague: SER.

Sociaal-Economische Raad (SER) (2016). *New Ways for More Successful Labour Market Integration of Refugees*. The Hague: SER.

Sociaal-Economische Raad (SER) (2017). *Learning and Development During Career: Summary and Recommendations*. The Hague: SER.

Soentken, M. and T. Weishaupt (2014). When social partners unite – explaining continuity and change in Austrian and Dutch labour market governance. *Social Policy and Administration*, 49(5), 593–611.

Sozialpartner Austria (2007). *Chance Bildung: Konzepte der österreichischen Sozialpartner zum lebensbegleitenden Lernen als Beitrag zur Lissabon-Strategie. Beirat für Wirtschafts- und Sozialfragen. Bad Ischl, October, 2007*. Vienna: Sozialpartner Austria.

Spies, H. and N. van de Vrie (2014). From legitimacy to effectiveness: developments in activation in the Netherlands. In I. Lødemel and A. Moreira (eds), *Activation or Workfare? Governance and the Neo-Liberal Convergence*. Oxford: University Press.

Stichting van de Arbeid (STAR) (2010). Labour Foundation – in brief. The Hague: STAR.

Stichting van de Arbeid (STAR) (2014). Contribution of the Dutch social partners to the National Reform Programme within the context of the EU 2020 Strategy. The Hague: STAR.

Stichting van de Arbeid (STAR) (2015). Appendix 1: implementation of Social Accord. November 2015. The Hague: STAR.

Stichting van de Arbeid (STAR) (2017). Contribution of the Dutch social partners to the National Reform Programme within the context of the EU 2020 Strategy March 2016–February 2017. The Hague: STAR.

Streeck, W. and K. Thelen (2005). *Beyond Continuity: Institutional Change in Advanced Political Economies*. Oxford: Oxford University Press.

Tálos, E. and B. Kittel (1996). Roots of Austro-corporatism: institutional preconditions and cooperation before and after 1945. In G. Bischof and A. Pelinka (eds), *Austro-Corporatism: Past, Present, Future*. New Brunswick, NJ: Transaction Publishers.

Tálos, E. and B. Kittel (2002). Austria in the 1990s: the routine of social partnership in question? In S. Berger and H. Compston (eds), *Policy Concertation and Social*

Partnership in Western Europe: Lessons for the Twenty-first Century. Oxford: Berghahn Books.

Thelen, K. (2014). *Varieties of Liberalization and the New Politics of Social Solidarity.* New York: Cambridge University Press.

Torfing, J. (2004). *Det stille sporskifte i velfærdsstaten: en diskursteoretisk beslutningsprocesanalyse.* Aarhus: Magtudredningen.

Trampusch, C. (2005). Solidarity in times of welfare retrenchment: the development of collectively negotiated benefits in Denmark, France, Germany and the Netherlands. Paper presented at the ECPR General Conference, Corvinus University of Budapest, 8–10 September.

Trampusch, C. (2006). Industrial relations and welfare states: the different dynamics of retrenchment in Germany and the Netherlands. *Journal of European Social Policy* 16(2), 121–33.

Trampusch, C. and P. Eichenberger (2012). Skills and industrial relations in coordinated market economies – continuing vocational training in Denmark, the Netherlands, Austria and Switzerland. *British Journal of Industrial Relations*, 50(4), 644–66.

Traxler, F. (2004). The metamorphoses of corporatism: from classical to lean patterns. *European Journal of Policy Research*, 43, 571–98.

Traxler, F. and S. Pernicka (2007). The state of the unions: Austria. *Journal of Labor Research*, 18(2), 207–32.

Tritscher-Archan, S. (2016). *Vocational Education and Training in Europe: Austria.* Vienna: ReferNet Austria.

Udlændinge-ogIntegrationsministeriet(2018).EvalueringafIntegrationsgrunduddannelsen (IGU). Copenhagen: Rambøll.

van Berkel, R. (2007). Activation in the Netherlands: the gradual introduction of a paradigm shift. In A. S. Pascual and L. Magnusson (eds), *Reshaping Welfare States and Activation Regimes in Europe.* Brussels: P.I.E. Lang.

van Berkel, R. and W. de Graaf (2011). The liberal governance of a non-liberal welfare state? The case of the Netherlands. In R. van Berkel, W. de Graaf and T. Sirovátka (eds), *The Governance of Active Welfare States in Europe.* Basingstoke: Palgrave Macmillan.

van Berkel, R. and P. van der Aa (2004). Towards active welfare states in Europe: the case of marketization of reintegration and activation services in the Netherlands. Unpublished paper.

van der Aa, P. and R. van Berkel (2013). Identifying policy innovations increasing labour market resilience and inclusion of vulnerable groups: national report – Netherlands. *Inspires Working Paper Series 2013 No. 1.*

van der Graaf, A. (2019). Netherlands: latest developments in working life Q2 2019. Dublin: Eurofound. Accessed 5 December 2019 at https://www.eurofound.europa .eu/publications/article/2019/netherlands-latest-developments-in-working-life-q2 -2019

van der Meer, M. and A. Hemerijck (2019). Pragmatic reconversion: long-term reform policy in the multi-party 'consensus' economy of the Netherlands during the Rutte II administration. Paper for the project 'Crisis Corporatism or Corporatism in Crisis? Social Consultation and Social Pacts in Europe'.

van der Meer, M., A. Hemerijck and J. Karremans (2019). Rebalancing fragmented interest intermediation through constructive political opposition: crisis management, political exchange and social concertation in the Netherlands (2008–19). Unpublished paper.

van Gyes, G. and T. Schulten (2015). *Wage Bargaining Under the New European Economic Governance: Alternative Strategies for Inclusive Growth*. Brussels: ETUI.

van het Kaar, R. (2019). Living and working in the Netherlands. Dublin: Eurofound. Accessed 9 December 2019 at https://www.eurofound.europa.eu/country/netherlands.

Visser, J. (2008). *Industrial Relations in Europe 2008*. Luxembourg: Office for Official Publications of the European Communities.

Visser, J. (2013). The institutional characteristics of trade unions, wage setting, state intervention and social pacts. ICTWSS Database, Version 4.0. Amsterdam: Amsterdam institute for Advanced Labour Studies.

Visser, J. and A. Hemerijck (1997). *'A Dutch Miracle': Job Growth, Welfare Reform and Corporatism in the Netherlands*. Amsterdam: Amsterdam University Press.

Visser, J. and M. van der Meer (2010). Doing together what is possible: social pacts and negotiated reform in the Netherlands. In P. Pochet, M. Keune and D. Natali (eds), *After the Euro and Enlargement: Social Pacts in the EU*. Brussels: OSE and ETUI.

Visser, J. and M. van der Meer (2011). The Netherlands: social pacts in a concertation economy. In S. Avdagic, M. Rhodes and J. Visser (eds), *Social Pacts in Europe: Emergence, Evolution and Institutionalization*. New York: Oxford University Press.

Weishaupt, T. and A. Privara (2013). The Austrian flexicurity model: a source of inspiration for other European Union member states? *The New Economy*, 6(1), 99–108.

Welz, C. and A. Broughton (2014). Impact of the crisis on industrial relations in Europe. In K. Papadakis and Y. Ghellab (eds), *The Governance of Policy Reforms in Southern Europe and Ireland: Social Dialogue Actors and Institutions in Times of Crisis*. Geneva: International Labour Organization.

Wilthagen, T. (1998). Flexicurity: a new paradigm for labour market reform? *WZB Discussion Paper No. 98-202*. Berlin: WZB Berlin Social Science Center.

Winter, S. (2003). Kanalrundfart eller zapning? Om kanaler og arenaer i den aktive arbejdsmarkedspolitik. In L. Petersen and P. K. Madsen (eds), *Drivkræfter bag arbejdsmarkedspolitikken*. Copenhagen: SFI.

Wöss, J., C. Reiff and A. Gruber (2016). Unemployment and pensions protection in Europe: the changing role of social partners. *OSE Paper Series No. 24*.

Wright, E. O. (2000). Working-class power, capitalist-class interests, and class compromise. *American Journal of Sociology*, 105(4), 957–1002.

Yerkes, M. A. (2011). *Transforming the Dutch Welfare State: Social Risk and Corporatist Reform*. Bristol: Policy Press.

Zwinkles, W. (2017). *Netherlands: Developments in Working Life 2017. EuWORK Annual Review 2017*. Dublin: Eurofound.

Index